Advance Praise for

She's Out of Control

by Kristin Billerbeck

"If you've prayed *Please God, give me books that are fun, romantic, feminine, and intelligent,* then meet Kristin Billerbeck, the answer to your prayers. *She's Out of Control* is a speed walk into the colorful mind of a modern yet spiritually striving woman, Ashley Stockingdale, who is quirky, love-hungry, and yet ever well dressed—resorting to eBay only when necessary. If you haven't sampled the new chick lit to hit the Christian book market, meet its queen—Billerbeck is top drawer!"

—PATRICIA HICKMAN,
award-winning author of *Fallen Angels* and *Nazareth's Song*

"It's *I Am Woman* meets *Diamonds Are a Girl's Best Friend* in this quirky, hilarious account of life on the single side."

—LINDA WINDSOR,
award-winning author of *Along Came Jones*

"Kristin Billerbeck's perceptive and humorous look at the struggles of Christian singles packs more punch than a double espresso."

—SHARON DUNN,
author of *Romance Rustlers* and *Thunderbird Thieves*

"I laughed out loud at the further antics of Ashley Wilkes Stockingdale. No one can write chick lit like Kristin Billerbeck. *She's Out of Control* builds on Billerbeck's superb in-character voice and establishes her firmly at the pinnacle of the genre. What *this* girl wants is the control to keep them coming."

—COLLEEN COBLE,
author of *Without a Trace*, a 2004 RITA finalist

"Here's a writer who definitely gets chick lit! *She's Out of Control* is smart and witty and downright funny. Her characters are realistic without taking themselves too seriously. A delicious read for bed, bath, or beach. Can't wait for the next one!"

—MELODY CARLSON,
award winning author of *Finding Alice, Armando's Treasure, Diary of a Teenage Girl,* and *Crystal Lies*

"Bravo! *She's Out of Control* made me want to take my phone off the hook, lock the doors, pull the blinds and read straight through to the end. Ashley Wilkes Stockingdale is unabashedly real, lovably quirky, and laugh-out-loud funny. Kristin Billerbeck is THE new voice in Christian fiction!"

—DENISE HUNTER,
author of *Mending Places*

"I'm not sure how she does it, but Billerbeck has the amazing ability to make me laugh out loud while inspiring me to consider my deepest motivations. All that, and I now have a whole new wardrobe of cute clothes! Her books just keep getting better."

—HANNAH ALEXANDER,
author of *Hideaway* and *Safe Haven*

"Wild. Delightful. Laugh-out-loud funny. From the moment Ashley Wilkes Stockingdale opens her mouth, I was hooked. I can't find enough words to praise Kristin Billerbeck's newest novel, *She's Out Of Control.* This story of faith, love, and control is an absolute must read. I didn't want it to end."

—GAIL GAYMER MARTIN,
author of *The Christmas Kite*

"Kristin Billerbeck provides a fun ride and a read that grabs you in the spiritual gut when you least expect it."

—JANET CHESTER BLY,
author of *Hope Lives*

". . . deep truth embedded in milk chocolate."

—TRACEY BATEMAN,
author of *Finding Audrey*

she's out of
control

a novel

by kristin billerbeck

WestBow
P R E S S

A Division of Thomas Nelson Publishers
Since 1798

visit us at www.westbowpress.com

Published in Nashville, Tennessee, by WestBow Press, a division of Thomas Nelson, Inc.

Publisher's note: This novel is a work of fiction. Names, characters, places, and incidents are either products of the author's imagination or used fictitiously. All characters are fictional, and any similarity to people living or dead is purely coincidental.

Library of Congress Cataloging in Publication Data

Billerbeck, Kristin.
    She's out of control / Kristin Billerbeck.
      p. cm.
    ISBN 0-8499-4459-7 (pbk.)
    I. Title
    PS3602.I44S54 2004
    813'.54—dc22   2004005496

Printed in the United States of America

05 06 07 08 RRD 6

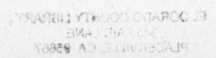

This book is dedicated to the fabulous women in my life who inspired me and reined me in when I needed it:

My mother, Kay Compani. (Poor thing, she never saw me coming.) All the sweet parts of my characters? That's my mom's influence.

My grandmother Jo Bechtel, my biggest cheerleader, who has since been forgiven for soap in the mouth. She tried to make me domestic, but then she couldn't know that take-out would someday get healthy in Silicon Valley.

My nana, Marie Compani, who indulged my pink side and gave me a different take on life. Tottering around in your high heels and trying on your jewelry was prophetic.

Colleen Coble, who mothers me every day and tries to knock some sense into my hard head.

And to my mothers who have gone ahead:

My Aunt Mary Bechtel, who was a chick to the end. From the Raggedy Ann dress you made me, to indulging Elle in her first swimsuit and matching cover-up. Your generosity will never be forgotten and your legacy lives on in us.

My mother-in-law, Ellen Billerbeck, who made writing possible with her sacrificial love for my family. I had so many questions yet. The way you handled utter chaos with ease will always be what I strive for.

My spiritual mom, Mary Lyons, the quintessential Proverbs 31 woman. Your influence on me and your love for your husband will forever inspire me to be a better wife.

How do I?

By ASHLEY WILKES STOCKINGDALE

How do I avoid commitment: Let me count the ways.
I love thee to the depth except when buying jewelry is involved.
I love thee in the daylight,
as long as my place of residence is not invaded by night.
(Nor any semblance of your grooming materials.)
I love thee freely, except when the guys are watching.
I love thee with all the passion of an engineer.
With my old girlfriends, I avoided the moment of Truth,
But with you, dear Ashley, I may not escape my fate.
And if God so choose, may I go to the Altar with strength—as Isaac did.

I swear this is how some men view marriage, like they're being laid out on the wood of the great Altar, ready to be sacrificed, and just praying the ram will arrive in time. I, Ashley Wilkes Stockingdale, have been dating Seth Greenwood for nine months. And while God can form a new human being in that same time frame, getting an adult male to the jewelry store is an entirely different kettle of fish.

I have a theory on commitment, and being a patent attorney, I'm considering getting the lock on it. I've always wanted to write a book where I state the incredibly obvious and people flock to the bookstore as though I am some psychological genius. Kind of like *Men are From Mars, Women are from Venus.* Here's my first attempt:

Steps Towards Getting a Male to Commit.

First, you must conquer "Whiplash." Whiplash is when your boyfriend thinks every woman in the vicinity might be potentially better for him. This involves several quick neck sprains while he looks until he eventually come to the conclusion that no, there's a reason he picked you. Allow about six months for this stage.

Then you enter the "Accommodation" phase. This is where Boyfriend discovers that, yes, you are the best one for him at the moment, but maybe God is calling him to a life of foreign mission work instead. He probably can't take you along on his great and deeply sacrificial ministry, so he accommodates you with the theory that some big life change will happen and let him off the hook. Two months for this stage.

You have now entered "Jeopardy." Now Boyfriend must fish or cut bait, and the real pressure begins. You watch him writhe like a trout on a hook, knowing you have the power to release him, but is that the best thing? As you watch the struggle, you begin to wonder, Do I even want to get married enough to strip this guy of his . . . his, heck, I don't know what I'm stripping him of, but it must be important if it's worth all this squirming.

So as it stands, Seth and I are in the Jeopardy phase. He's afraid to be alone with me, afraid I might pressure him to ask "the" question. The romance is gone. Only fear remains, and what's the fun of that? I've almost forgotten why we started dating in the first place. I remember knowing, at the time, that it was God's will for my life. Now I know it was probably God's will because I had some great life lesson to learn. I hope it's learned by now. I don't want to go through this again.

My best friend Brea is reading my first attempt at poetry now, *How Do I . . . ?* Brea is married. She adopted a baby and poof! she has another one in her tummy. Being Brea's best friend is truly impossible because she lives a charmed life. It's like little fairies drop rose petals alongside each of her steps.

Brea looks up at me from my poem. "What are you planning to do with this . . . this *poetry*, and I use the term loosely?" Brea waves the paper around. Her little baby Miles grabs it and gums the edges of it. "'How Do I Avoid Commitment?' Ash! Kinda pathetic. If this is how you feel, I think it's time you just broke things off."

Okay, not the reaction I was expecting. "What do you mean, pathetic? I think it's a deep and truthful allegory about Christian men and commitment."

"Um, if you're Sylvia Plath, maybe. Ash, this borders on the mentally deranged." While Brea sounds all concerned, she is actually giving equal time to Oprah, who is blaring over me.

My cell phone is ringing, and I just want to throw it across the room. "Give my *poem* back to me." I rip the paper from her hands, and little Miles forms a pout you could perch a bird upon. He begins to howl. "See, I can't make men happy at any age! And this," I wave my paper again, "is not mental. It's just my attempt to show Seth there's nothing to be afraid of when it comes to marriage."

Brea is now cracking up, while Miles continues to scream and Oprah offers an indispensable fashion tip. Meanwhile, my phone is still trilling. "Oh yeah, this will do it," she says. "Seth will be completely ready for commitment after this. Just rushing to the altar because he wants a wife who lives part time in the institution." Her laughter slows. "Ash, let's put it this way, if you sent this from jail? You wouldn't be getting out anytime soon. Oooh . . . oooh! Move out of the way, here's the 'after' part." Brea faces the television and her eyes are wide with excitement at a stay-at-home mom transformed into a glamour queen.

I cross my arms. "Are you listening to me?"

"Could you turn that cell phone off? It's really annoying," Brea shouts over Miles's screaming and Oprah's enthusiasm. "I want to hear this."

"I have to leave it on, in case my boss wants me. It will ring differently if he calls."

Brea laughs. "We all know your boss wants you."

"This isn't about Hans. This is about Seth." I am seriously annoyed now. "You never dated a guy afraid of commitment. You got married young, when you weren't 'bus bait.'" Bus bait is my brother's term meaning that I have more chance of getting hit by a bus than getting married over thirty. I'm thirty-one and counting. I take crosswalks seriously.

Brea rubs her belly thoughtfully, like all pregnant women do. "I know you're getting frustrated with Seth, but he's fearful, Ashley. He can't help but worry about whether you're the right one. And there's no real way to know for certain, so he's stuck. It's harder for men as they get older. They don't want to make the wrong choice. I think you should move on. That'll teach him."

"Meanwhile my clock is ticking. Brea, he is thirty-four years old, he's bald, and he dresses like an engineer. I love the man dearly, but who does he think is coming along to rescue him?"

"That only makes him more fearful, Ashley. What if he's wasting your time? He's worried about that, too, I'm sure."

My mouth is dangling open. "Are you kidding me? Whose side are you on? You're saying that Seth is so concerned about me and my biological clock that he cannot force four little words from his lips?"

Brea nods. "Seriously, I talked to John about this. He says men get nervous to date women over thirty because they feel too much pressure. What if things don't work out?"

"Thank you, Oprah. Things *are* working out. Well, I thought they were anyway." I scratch my head. Little Miles is still screaming at me and my cell phone is ringing again. Oprah is squealing about the makeover's gorgeous results, which Brea is craning her neck to see. I reach out for the baby. "Come to Auntie Ashley."

4

Miles scoffs at first, but begins to quiet as I cuddle his warm head against my chest, walk, and bounce him. We both calm down. He smells like heaven, and for the moment all my angst is forgotten and my heartbeat slows. There is only this angelic creature and his sweet new scent in my arms. I realize with trepidation that I want a baby. Who woulda thunk? Maybe Seth senses this. Maybe that's what is forcing his retreat.

Brea takes her eyes off Oprah. "Miles just loves you, Ashley. He doesn't take to anyone like you."

"You're going to have another baby soon. Why don't you just give me Miles?" I wink at her, lifting Miles above my head and back down. "You said you wanted a girl, remember? I've changed Miles's diapers, and he is distinctly a boy. So I think you should give him up."

"The doctor *said* he'd be a girl." Now Brea reverts to child gibberish. "But Mama got her perfect little prince, didn't she?" she coos.

"Do you mind? We want the boy to be a healthy adult."

"Well, that's gonna happen with you telling him I wanted a girl." Brea says, rubbing her belly.

Even pregnant, Brea looks like a fashion model. She's got her thick dark mane pulled into a ponytail and from behind you can't even tell she's expecting. Right before I started dating Seth, Brea had a miscarriage. It about broke my heart. For one thing, I couldn't stand seeing her in such emotional pain; for another, there just never was a woman meant to be a mother like Brea.

Of course when it happened, she freaked out like she'd never be able to have another child, and while operating in crisis mode, adopted little Miles from an unwed teenage mother. Which, of course, turned out perfect, but now the tables are turned. Now that it's my turn to obsess about my own marital status, she's the epitome of calm. I know better than to listen to her Dr. Phil tones. She's a drama queen too. Just not at the moment.

John, her husband, enters the house and stops at the sight before him. His house is complete chaos: Baby toys everywhere, Oprah on full-blast and my cell phone still ringing. He looks at the scene and, for a moment, I think he's going to turn around and leave.

"Brea." John shuts the door behind him. "What's going on?"

"Ashley had the afternoon off." Brea is biting her lip and I can't say I blame her. This place looks like a train rushed through, and it sounds like the locomotive is still in the vicinity. How does Brea handle it? Like a mature wife. She points at me as though I made the mess.

"That's great," John smiles. "Did you girls have a good time?"

Brea nods.

"There's probably no dinner then, huh?" He pauses for a moment, then reacts like all men would. *NOT.* "You want to go out?" John asks. Then he looks at me. "You're welcome to join us, Ashley."

And ruin my manifesto on single men. Forget it. "No, thanks. You two have a good time. Do you want me to stay with Miles so you can go somewhere nice?"

Brea giggles. "Nah. They always hold him at the Chinese restaurant while we eat. But I'm glad you came by. It was nice you got a day off." She smiles at me.

"Yeah, the first one in eighteen days. I don't know what I'm whining about, I can't commit to Seth anyway, I'm currently married to my job."

"You're whining because you love the man, and you know you want to get married. It's not a crime. That poem, however—I think *that's* a crime."

John walks into the kitchen, and I lower my tone. "How long do I have to pretend that this doesn't matter to me? That I don't want to be with him for the rest of my life? It's one thing to monitor what I say, but my heart is beginning to betray me. I love Seth, and yet he continues to hurt me every day by telling me that I'm not good enough to be his bride." I snuggle Miles closer.

"It's only been nine months. You have to be patient."

"He'll come around," John offers as he reenters the room.

"I didn't get my law degrees by being patient," I say.

"Yes, you did. I would have taken a sawed-off shotgun to school by the time you finished."

"Point taken, but Brea, would you have married John if he took that long to make up his mind? At some point, wouldn't you have thought, If he doesn't love me enough to ask me to marry him, he can stuff it? It's not like we're children, or we haven't known each other for years."

Brea pauses for a long moment and then looks at her husband with an expression on her face most of us only dream about. "I can't imagine John doing that to me, Ash," she finally says. "I know a lot of guys take forever to ask women to marry them, but they're usually sleeping with them. It's different with Christians, when they aren't doing that. Nine months is more than enough time considering how long you and Seth have known each other."

Knife to the heart. "I can't imagine John doing this either, Brea, and now you see my dilemma. If I have any self-worth at all, is sticking around the best thing? Or am I enabling him?"

"I am here," John says.

Brea's quiet. Miles is sucking on his lower lip, and I am about to burst from his cuteness. He's got a shock of auburn hair that sticks straight up in a baby Mohawk. He even looks like he belongs to Brea. He's got her big, dark brown eyes and a ready smile. The disparity suddenly grips me.

"You're going to have two babies in less than nine months, and I'm going to travel to Taiwan again, worry that I've called Seth one too many times, maybe have dinner with the Reasons . . ."

The Reasons are the singles group at church, I call them that because they all have some particular reason that they aren't married. Some of them choose their status. I obviously don't. "This is not what I thought my life would turn out to be," I continue. "I was doing fine until I made the romantic decision to be with Seth. Before that I had made up my mind to be independent and forget about men. Now I think it's time to move on with my life."

"Maybe it is. Ashley, I hate to see you pining away like this. Seth is a great guy, but what he's doing to you is criminal. Every time you start to venture out on your own, he gets scared and pulls you back in with some fleeting romantic gesture."

I'm nodding. What else can I do? It's true. I've become codependent without even realizing it. I have turned myself into a Dr. Phil show.

"So you think I should break it off?" This is not an easy question for me. I love Seth. With all my heart I want to be his wife, but not if I have to wait till I'm fifty years old. Seth takes an hour to make up his mind on a lunch beverage. I just don't have his kind of time. Maybe there's a little pride mixed in as well—I'm embarrassed that Seth hasn't asked me by now. The Reasons are all waiting, and if our engagement doesn't happen, Seth will just be rotated back into the open market.

"What do you think God wants you to do? Are you forcing something that isn't meant to be?" Brea's face looks pinched.

"Now, there's the age-old question. I don't know what God wants me to do. From the looks of it, He wants me to drone away my life in a high-tech company, writing patents that don't matter in the grand scheme of things."

"That's not true. You made your last company a fortune with that last patent."

"I didn't invent it, I just wrote it up, like the scribe I am. I have everything I thought I wanted. I have my Audi convertible, I have a great place living with Kay, and I'm well on my way to my own condominium. I have succeeded in the Silicon Valley, one of the hardest places on earth to make it, and yet I don't have the one thing I really want." I hold up baby Miles like Simba on Pride Rock.

"I didn't know you ever really wanted to be a mother, Ash."

"Neither did I."

Brea's husband pouts and kisses his wife like something out of a soap opera. *Oh yeah, this is helping me.* He notices Miles in my arms and reaches for the baby. "I'm going to go upstairs and get ready for dinner."

Brea reaches up and kisses his cheek. "I'm sorry the place is such a mess, John. You deserve better when you've had a hard day."

"You're entitled to your fun days." John winks and kisses her cheek. "Besides, I feel like Chinese food, anyway."

There was a time when I was content to be single. What I'd give to be back in that place. To not feel with every breath that my life is missing something. Seth changed that for me, but unfortunately, nothing else about him has changed—including his ability to make a commitment.

2

I live in a great little bungalow in downtown Palo Alto. It's got two bedrooms, two baths, and an anal-retentive owner: my roommate Kay Harding. Kay is a perfectionist who gives Martha a run for the money. While Kay doesn't hold down a conglomerate by day, she does manage engineers, and that alone makes her a mother by nature. Once, by accident, I opened her toothpaste drawer and everything was lined up like a dentist's tool table. I slammed it back shut when I thought I heard the music from *Twilight Zone* playing.

I used to live alone, but that's a long story I won't go into. Let's just say I had to move out quickly. Kay invited me to her place, and we've been roommates ever since. It's a good combination. She teaches me not to live like a total pig with makeup strewn on the bathroom counter (guests actually use the bathroom and it gets embarrassing) and I teach her that boiling your combs for cleanliness borders on strange. The modern-day odd couple. Of course, we both work in high tech and keep weird business hours too. That helps us understand each other.

She's home chopping up vegetables and putting them into a cut crystal salad bowl when I come in and greet her.

"Where have you been all day?" Kay glances at me. "Your boss called here looking for you a few minutes ago. Thanks for vacuuming, by the way. The place looks great."

"You're welcome. I was at Brea's for most of the day. We went to the mall and got a few things for the baby."

"Which one?"

"Miles."

Kay nods. Her perfectly coiffed hair, circa 1974, doesn't move when she nods. *It's so amazing that they still make Aqua Net.* "Listen," Kay says. "I've been meaning to talk with you about some business I thought we might enter into."

"You need legal advice?"

"No." She looks down at the salad bowl. "This is a business deal, and I think it would be great for both of us. With interest rates being so low, I'm planning to redo the house a bit. You know, expand the kitchen, update the bathrooms . . ."

I swallow hard. *Please don't let this involve a move for me.* "Really? What would you do? I think it looks great now." This house is in the best neighborhood in Palo Alto. Just having a foundation in town makes it worth nearly a million, and with the original hardwood floors in perfect condition, well, the place is a gold mine.

Kay is apparently not satisfied. "I really want a gourmet kitchen with granite countertops and a Viking stove. That kind of thing. I want to push this wall out. Maybe rip out the bathrooms . . ."

"Sounds great," I say without enthusiasm. *Granite? She still uses Aqua Net and Noxzema, but wants granite? I so do not get Kay.* "So you want me to move out?" I ask tentatively.

"No!" She laughs. "No, I was wondering if you were interested in buying half the house from me. You have the money for a down payment, and you could probably use the write-off. And this way I wouldn't have to borrow as much for the upgrades. I'd get the house appraised so the deal would be totally fair, and you could make me an offer. What do you think?"

Slowly, I find the chair behind me. Kay thinks I'm a Reason. She holds out absolutely no hope for Seth asking me to marry him, and so she's offering me the consolation prize: financial stability. Real estate in the Bay Area. *We're just two old bus baits making the best of life without men. How long until we start filling up the house with a multitude of cats?*

I finally find my voice. "Wow, that's a really generous offer, Kay. You've just completely caught me off guard. I don't know what to say."

"Take your time and think about it. I just think living together works for us: We don't get in each other's way, it's nice to have you help with the weekly Bible study, and you keep your mess in your room." Kay grabs a pair of teak forks and tosses the salad. "I think it would be good for you, too. You would have a write-off and get to keep more of your money. Maybe you'd be able to do more shopping. You seem to enjoy that."

Fear and trembling. Kay is forty-three now, and she's said numerous times she won't ever get married. She came from an abusive home and doesn't think much of the male species, in general. But her idea makes me feel icky. Like if I get too comfortable in this situation, I won't ever have the chance for another boyfriend because people will assume I don't want one. And I do want one. I just happen to want one particular person who doesn't seem to return the emotion. At least not in full.

"I'd really have to think on that, Kay. I don't mind the mess if you're going to remodel, but wow, buying part of it! Are you sure?"

"I think it's good for Christian women to help other Christian women. Lord knows, we don't get much help otherwise." Her barb sends a shiver of fear through my soul. I don't hate men. And even though God hasn't given me a particular man, I still hold out hope. Kay is well past that.

"Do you think I need the help?" I ask, knowing she'll guess I'm referring to Seth.

"I just don't think you should put all your eggs in one basket. Especially when the Easter Bunny isn't real."

Kay made a funny. Go figure. "Did Seth call me while I was gone?" I ask sheepishly, knowing full well he didn't.

"Yeah, he did. Well, he called here anyway."

Then she says nothing. For as long as I've lived with Kay, I just don't get how she doesn't share "girl" information readily. Isn't that just part of being a woman? The dish?

"Well? What did he say?"

"He actually called for me." She grimaces, as though she's sorry, but not surprised. "There's a special at Laser Quest. Three games for the price of two. Seth wanted to know if he should organize a singles' night there."

Of course he did. "Laser Quest. So Kay, I have a question. Do you think Seth will ever get married?"

"Are you asking me if I think he'll ever marry you?"

"No, I'm not asking that. Lord knows, I don't want the answer to that. I'm asking, do you think he'll ever get married at all?"

Kay shrugs, pops a bright red hothouse tomato into her mouth, and tosses the salad again. "Hard to say. You're the only woman I remember him dating for any length of time, and he hasn't asked you. Regardless, I don't think any woman should put her life on hold for a man who isn't willing to commit. Everyone else seems to date, and . . ." she snaps her fingers. "Boom, they get married. There's something about girls like us, Ashley. Perhaps we just were never meant for that kind of life."

Girls like us. I have now completely stopped breathing. I always thought I was a girl like Brea, but maybe that's just completely wishful thinking. I study Kay carefully. She's very pretty, not hard on the eyes at all. Gorgeous gray-green eyes, clear complexion, not a wrinkle on her. Granted, her clothes and hair could use the female version of *Queer Eye for the Straight Guy,* but I can't see anything physically wrong with her. I rush to the mirror at the front door. *Maybe that's why I can't see anything wrong with me, either.*

Coming back into the kitchen, I smile. "There's a singles'

Christian cruise going out of Long Beach next month. I'm thinking of taking it." There. That sounds decisive and not passive.

Kay wrinkles her nose. "That sounds fun if you're into that kind of thing. I think it would be the equivalent of a floating pickup bar. It doesn't really interest me, and I can't imagine you there either, Ash."

I lean against the doorjamb. My mouth is watering over Kay's salad. "Why do you think Seth came to Las Vegas to get me at my brother's wedding? I mean, it was the most romantic gesture, but I can't imagine him doing that now. Why did he nix that job in Phoenix if he never intended to get married?"

Kay washes and dries her hands, looking thoughtfully at me. "If you're asking me about the male psyche, you're asking the wrong person. Ashley, just tell Seth what you're feeling. Why do you put yourself through all this emotion, when it can be solved with a simple conversation? I mean, a cruise, Ash? If you want to meet the kind of guy who would win the hairy-chest contest on deck, that's great. But you can't control everything. If God doesn't want you to be married, I've got news for you . . ."

"Why do you say that? That God doesn't want me married."

"I didn't say that. I said *if* He doesn't, there's really nothing you can do about it."

I stand up taller. I am not the kind of woman who stays single. I'm just not. Why can't everyone see that? I've got a great job, an incredible shoe collection, just a million things to offer a guy, and I'm not going to be single forever. *I'm not, I'm not, I'm not!*

My cell phone rings, this time with my boss's specially programmed ring. "Hello, Hans." Jokingly, I call the man Hands because he seems to have eight of them. No, he's never touched me, but something about the way he oozes sensuality makes me feel like he has.

"How was your day off, Ashley?"

"Fun. I went shopping with my friend and her baby." And apparently, that is the end of our small talk.

"One of our engineers came up with an idea that I think has legs."

"Great! We can talk about it first thing tomorrow. Do you want to schedule me in?"

"Actually, I mean this product has real legs. I'd like you to meet me for dinner at Il Fornaio. Can you be there by seven?"

I've just started this job after being out of work for six months. Although I had a nice severance package and never feared financially, I don't care to go through the job-hunting process again anytime soon. "Sure, Hans. I'll be there." Call waiting breaks in. "I've got another call. See you soon."

"Hello." *Caller ID is not showing up. Grr.* "Ashley Stockingdale."

"Ash, it's Seth."

"Hi." I automatically start fiddling with my hair.

"You want to meet me at the Soup House for dinner?"

The Soup House. Complete meals for both of us for $11, compared to the elegant Italian Il Fornaio in downtown Palo Alto. Without question I'd rather go cheap with Seth, but I can't. "I'm sorry, but I have to work tonight. I'm meeting my boss for dinner at Il Fornaio."

"Sure, I understand." I can tell by his voice that he *doesn't* understand. He's not jealous, just annoyed that I'm not available when he has a whim. How am I supposed to know there's a blue moon tonight?

"Maybe we could meet tomorrow," I say brightly.

"I'm flying to Seattle tomorrow. I'll have to call you when I get back, okay?"

"Sure." We sound like two complete strangers. This isn't how it used to be. We had passion and desire for one another and it was a battle of wills for each of us to stay pure. Now I feel like I'm talking to my history professor, rather than the man I might have married. I guess it really is over, and this is what it feels like when nobody mentions that fact.

Nine months ago, when I thought Seth was leaving for Arizona, I was content at being a "Reason," someone who probably wouldn't get married. But now that I've been in love, now that I've felt what it's like to have someone look at me with "those" eyes, I know what I'm missing. The hole feels bigger and darker than I imagined, and I don't want to go back down there like a hobbit in the caves of Moria. With all my heart, I want to avoid that pit.

Kay's putting the finishing touches on her salad, tossing the greens with a homemade citrus-cilantro dressing and placing it on her Crate and Barrel table. The only thing Kay spends money on is kitchenware. "Are you ready to eat?" She asks me.

"I have to go meet Hands."

"Ashley! No."

"What? I was without a job for six months, Kay. I am not going that route again."

"You never wanted for anything when you were out of work. Quit acting like you were on the verge of insanity."

"Even with my severance package, I didn't feel safe to shop or go to the fancy market. I, Ashley Wilkes Stockingdale, actually shopped at Kmart," I say, like I'm at an AA meeting. "I don't ever want to do that again."

"You've spent ministry summers in Mexico. Surely you know what poverty is really like. Shopping at Kmart is not poverty."

"I was perfectly content to live the simple life in Mexico. But not here in Silicon Valley. Not where you're judged by what you do. God created me to be a lawyer. I love patents. What kind of geek loves patents? He didn't give me Ann Taylor tastes without a purpose."

Kay is laughing heartily. "Are you trying to tell me it's God's will that you should be able to shop at Stanford?"

I cross my arms. *Oh, how I hate to be laughed at.* "No, I'm trying to tell you that I am a very capable person. I tithe more than my 10 percent. I don't have anyone depending on me, and since I'm a conscientious, hard-working Christian, God enables me to do some of the things I enjoy. Like buying clothing that fits my lifestyle as a top patent attorney. I don't ever again want to be unable to do what I was born to do."

Kay shakes her head. "I'll never be hungry for couture again!"

she declares, holding up a fist. "Don't give God the control speech, Ashley. It's like saying you'll never go to Iraq on a mission. Tell Him that and you might as well just pack your bags."

"I'm going to get dressed for my dinner."

"Suit yourself. But don't say I didn't warn you."

Warn me. Oh yeah, she warned me all right. Kay warned me I'd be living in this same house with seven cats at eighty years old. We'd be the old-lady house where the kids are afraid to trick-or-treat. All I can say is *not in this lifetime.* If it's over with Seth, it is, but I refuse to believe *I'm* over.

3

There's nothing to make you feel common like parking in downtown Palo Alto. There aren't many parking places, and they are all filled with Mercedes and BMWs. I'm too cheap to pay for valet, so I'm schlepping up the street in my heels, thinking it would have been easier to walk from home. There's a November chill in the air. It's only about sixty degrees or so, but with the ocean to the left and the bay to the right, the moist air seeps into your bones. I am wearing this great white wool nautical coat, and I feel like a million, even if I am unwilling to part with five dollars for parking.

Il Fornaio is a bit "yesterday" in Palo Alto, but Hans is well-known here and likes to sit at *his* table, drinking an entire bottle of wine while conducting business. He's not married any longer. He left his wife for the nanny of his two children and I can't fathom the switch, because Sophia, the nanny, is the dimmest bulb I have ever come into acquaintance with. She makes Fran Drescher's version look like Einstein. Yes, Sophia is extremely beautiful, but so was Hans's wife, and she also possessed a brain. Sophia doesn't drive and spends her day calling Hans to tell him they need cereal or milk or bonbons. Since Hans does everything on speakerphone, it's a surreal moment when you learn that your CEO is out of toilet paper. Kind of an *I don't want to go there* place.

Now, I'm sure you're thinking Hans is a total jerk. And he is, technically speaking. But he possesses this charm that is all-encompassing and spans the limits of time and race. I've seen women sixty-plus swoon over him, as well as twentysomethings. When he speaks, he silences everyone around him, and you find yourself drawn in with an unexplainable desire and a ridiculous giggle.

I, myself, knowing he left his wife for the nanny, still find him utterly entrancing, which is so unlike me, being the "good girl." I am aware of this frailty, so I steer clear of him as much as possible. He's the male version of the adulteress in Proverbs 7, and he could rip you away from all you know to be true in a matter of moments. He looks like Mikhail Baryshnikov in younger days, and probably has the same type of reputation. Not a great feature in your boss. So I ask my friends for a lot of prayer and try to stay on guard.

I arrive at the restaurant parched and a glowing a bit, which is a nice way of saying I'm hot and sweaty. Even in the cool November weather, my trek up University Avenue has taken its toll, and I'd rip off my wool coat in a second, were it not for my pride in its appearance. The maître d' is dressed in a black suit, with an attitude, unaware that his spot is no longer hip among those who care about such things.

"I'm here for Hans Kerchner."

"Ah yes, but of course. He's at his regular table. Right this way." Grabbing a leather-bound menu, the maître d' leads me to the back of the restaurant near the fireplace. Just what I need: warmth. I take off my coat reluctantly, and the maître d' runs off with it. I watch it go, like a friend leaving for the mission field.

When I appear, Hans stands up. The fireplace is glowing behind the table, and it highlights the wine bottle, which is already half empty. "Ashley, you look lovely."

"Won't Sophia be joining us tonight?" I like to remind him about Sophia whenever I get the chance.

"She has no interest in discussing technology," he replies in his harsh German accent. "She's home watching her favorite dating show."

"Yes, *Joe Millionaire* is on tonight." I smile, letting Hans know I'd like to be home watching bad reality television too. Hans starts to fill my glass with wine, and I place my hand over the edge. "I don't drink, remember?"

"Of course, you drink. Everyone drinks. Red wine is . . ." he pats his chest, "good for the heart, you know."

"No, thank you. It gives me indigestion." Now there's an attractive excuse, but it works. He puts the bottle back on the table. The waiter comes by and I order a Diet Coke. "Listen Hans, I know you're very excited about this new patent, so let's get down to it. I can do some research tonight at home, and sketch out a patent request tomorrow. We can get moving on it by the end of the week if you think it's that big. There's no sense in waiting when you're onto something."

Hans shakes his head. "You Americans are always so business-oriented. We Europeans, we like to enjoy our lives first. We don't even begin to talk about business without a good meal in our stomach."

Which is probably how you fell into life with the nanny. "I don't mean to be rude, Hans, but I like to arrange my schedule. I like to know what's going to happen, and what *needs* to happen. It's just my nature to keep a very orderly calendar."

"See? That is what I mean. You Americans try to control everything when you really have no say in the matter. Fate always takes precedence."

"I don't believe in fate." I smooth the linen tablecloth in front of me. *Fate says you had no choice about sleeping with the babysitter.* "When you believe in fate, you can rationalize anything, so I don't believe in fate."

Hans just shakes his head. "You're so practical." *That's really the last thing I am. Maybe compared to Hans, but really, no.* He continues, "I'd like this whole product ready before Comdex next year. Meaning I want the product done, and the patent secured. This one has potential to get our company a P/E ratio and to up our stock rating."

"Not a problem on my end." I smile. Comdex isn't until September. That's nearly a year, I think with glee. My glee, as usual, is short-lived.

Hans pours himself another glass of wine. "I'm flying out to Taiwan next week to work on the prototype. I'd need you to accompany me. We leave on the Tuesday flight."

Hans flags down the waiter. "We'll start with two Caesar salads."

My skin immediately feels clammy. All I can think about is Doris Day with Cary Grant in *That Touch of Mink,* when he carries her off to be his mistress. *It doesn't matter if nothing happens. Everyone will think something has happened anyway.* And as one who has worked hard, both for my job and my good-girl reputation, I can't afford this.

Cary Grant had nothing on Hans. Cary Grant was an image, Hans is the real thing—suave, debonair, and all those things that create a good movie icon. It's been one month since I got this job, and my world already feels like it's spinning out of control.

"Tuesday?" I shake my head, willing any excuse to come into my mind. *Any excuse.* "My fiancé and I are meeting with our minister next Tuesday for our premarital counseling." I close my eyes, and clamp my teeth onto my lower lip. Not only did I lie, I lied about a minister meeting with me. *That's like double jeopardy: the lightning round, literally.*

Hans sits back in his chair. "You're getting married?"

I smile rather than lie again. I'm remembering that Bible story where Abraham tells everyone Sarah is his sister. Didn't work for him, but I'm still hoping for better results. Maybe God will have mercy on me.

"Well, I'll have to meet the lucky fellow. Why don't you bring him over to the house this weekend? Sophia makes a mean lasagna, and she's always saying we never do anything socially. It will give her a chance to show off her talents." At the word, talents, my eyebrows shoot up, but I can't say why exactly.

The rest of dinner is a blur. I know I looked at the schematics. I know I thought out the patent process, but I can't remember anything else except that by the time I leave the restaurant I have a fake fiancé and a dinner date for Saturday night. I think about explaining my situation calmly to Seth, and having him play along. But how Christian would that be, getting him to lie too?

Seth didn't like the fact that Hans and I were having dinner in the first place. Not to mention that marriage is a sticky subject at the moment. Now if I ask him to lie to save me humiliation, which I caused for myself, it's more than over. The last nine months are probably regrettable to him. The question is, do I care?

I make my way up the busy street to a coffee shop and dial my cell phone. "Brea?" I can hardly hear the sound of my voice over the noise of burring espresso machines and the chattering patrons.

"What's the matter, Ashley? Brea sounds groggy, probably from going to sleep at eight, which is what she's been doing since Miles and his two o'clock feedings have entered her life. "What time is it?"

"It's ten o'clock."

"What's the matter? Are you okay? You didn't get arrested again, did you?" she asks, making reference to one particular afternoon of my life that I'd just as soon forget.

"Hans wants me to go to Taipei with him on Tuesday."

Brea's grogginess disappears. "Well, you're not going, Ashley. He's a German Colin Farrell, and I think we both know what that means!" I can hear Miles begin to sputter, and it dawns on me that I've woken him up too. *Great.*

"Oh Brea, I'm sorry! I didn't even think about the time." I sigh and continue. "Anyway, no, I'm not going. But I needed an excuse so I kinda told him I was meeting with my fiancé and the preacher Tuesday."

She's quiet for a while, but now Miles is crying. Then I hear John. "Brea, who are you talking to?"

She muffles the phone. "It's Ashley."

He groans.

"Brea, did you hear me?" I ask.

"I heard you," Brea sighs. "Ashley, no job is worth this. You're lying now? I've known you to do a lot of things, but never to be dishonest. If anything, you're too honest. Brutally so. What's your boss going to say when you show up alone?"

"Hopefully, I won't have to. Seth is my boyfriend, Brea. It probably won't ever come up that we're getting married. It might remind Sophia that Hans won't marry her, and he's not going to have that. Besides, I ought to be able to ask Seth this favor without feeling fear." But of course, I do have fear and a lot of it.

"Are we talking about the same Seth?"

Now all my fears overflow at once. "You don't think he's ever going to marry me, either. Do you?" She doesn't answer and I continue. "Kay wants me to buy half her house, Brea. I looked for six months to find this job. I can't let Hands run me off in the first month. Maybe Kay will pretend *she's* my fiancée." The idea grosses me out completely, of course, but it's not that uncommon here in California these days. Besides, I'm desperate.

"You can't spend your life running from Hans, either, Ash. You've got to stand firm. Don't let fear control your actions. Don't you always say that to me?"

"Um, no. That must have been your other best friend." Call waiting beeps. "My phone's ringing. Listen, I'm sorry for waking you all up. I forget you're on *Murder She Wrote* time over there."

Brea clicks her tongue. "You didn't wake us up. I just fell asleep on the couch watching a movie."

"Love you, kiss that baby, and pray for me. I need it!" I press the button. "Ashley here."

"Ashley, it's Seth. Are you done with dinner?"

My heart is pounding, I feel so guilty. Do I tell Seth what I did? Or let him live under the illusion that I am a high-powered patent attorney, not a bimbo hired by the German George Clooney who coats his silken words with honey, and has the unique ability to force me to fly across the ocean with him.

"I'm done," I answer, hoping I'm not being prophetic here.

"I have something for you. I'm going to pick it up on Tuesday and I want us to celebrate. Are you up for it?"

My princess-cut ring! I exhale deeply. *My princess-cut ring is finally here! Let the heavens rejoice. I am not going to be an old maid!* "Of course I'm up to it, Seth. You name the place and time. I'll be there with bells on." And a very naked ring finger. Then guilt takes over. "I need to tell you something I did."

"You can tell me tomorrow. In the meantime, my place, Friday night, at seven." He actually sounds giddy, and I begin to remember all I saw in him in the first place. His straightforward way of looking at life. His nature to get things done. I inhale deeply while falling for him all over again.

"Should I wear anything special?" I answer happily, my smile plastered for the world to see. How on earth will I wait until Friday? Of course, I'll need at least three days to practice my surprised look in the mirror. And I'll have to get a facial. And I'll have to get a new dress. Something slinky, that isn't too showy, but lets him know he's not going to regret marrying me. Not for one moment!

"You always look great, Ashley. I'll love whatever you pick." He makes a kissing sound into the phone, and I bite my lip like an eighth grader with new lip gloss.

"I can't wait, Seth."

"Me either. I've waited a long time for this. The thought process has almost been agonizing, but the time has come."

Now mentally, I'm thinking about how to tell him about our "engagement" dinner at my boss's house. Technically, I'm not supposed to know about the ring. "Seth, if you aren't busy, my boss wants to entertain us on Saturday night. Do you think we might be free?"

"Why not? It's about time I met this Hans, anyway. He sure is doing a lot for your company's stock, and I'm anxious to see his plan for the long haul."

I'm anxious to see your plan for the long haul. I can't help but smile. *And I hope it's set in platinum.*

4

"Ashley, did you lose this?" Seth, dressed in an Armani tuxedo, holds up a Marc Jacobs pump. It's red-and-black striped. "It will fit you, won't it?"

Ashley is breathless with anticipation and nibbles on her lower lip to fight the bubbling pressure of the moment. "I . . . I don't know. If it's mine, I mean. Where did you find it?"

"I found it on my steps last night. Try it, Ashley. There's only one way for us to know . . ." Seth's brilliant blue gaze meets hers, and Ashley swoons to the rich tapestry chaise behind her. "The woman who fits this shoe is meant to be mine. Somehow, I just know it." In his other hand, Seth lifts a dazzling princess-cut canary diamond. "Will you marry me, Ashley?"

Ashley can't remove her eyes from the pump. "Where's the other one?"

"What do you mean, Ashley?"

"I mean, where's the other shoe?"

"This pump is a Marc Jacobs original. Custom made for my wife! It's just symbolic, not really meant for wear."

"Surely Marc didn't make just one shoe. There must be another around here somewhere. Symbolic or not, one shoe just doesn't make sense." Ashley rises up from the chaise looking frantically about her.

"The ring, Ashley." Seth holds the ring out toward her, but she places

her foot into the size-9 pump and twists her ankle about. "So it is yours.
Ashley, did you hear me? Will you—"

"I want the other one, Seth! Where is the other shoe?"

"I don't know, Ashley. It doesn't matter where the other shoe is. Do
you want to be my wife, or don't you?"

"Well, I do. But I want this shoe, too! Is that so wrong?"

"Ashley, wake up! You're having a nightmare." Kay is shaking me.
And I am aware, with distinct displeasure, that I've spent the night on
the sofa with a spiked heel clutched tightly against my chest. I'm too
old to spend the night on the sofa, and I feel every curvature, every
imprint of the Pottery Barn special in my hindquarters, not to mention the little divot from the pump.

"Kay, what's going on? What time is it?" I roll over and rub the
kink out of my neck, tossing the shoe on the floor.

"It's seven. You need to get up or you'll be late for work."

My laptop is sitting open on the coffee table. "I worked all night,"
I explain, as much for myself as Kay.

"I hope your boss appreciates your hard work. I thought these
hours went the way of the dot-com implosion." Kay is setting out her
Thanksgiving tchotchkes.

There's a new chill in the air, signaling that fall is here. But not
really. Not until Kay brings out the ceramic turkeys, the wax, leaf-
shaped candles, and the inevitable cornucopia filled with tiny, colorful gourds. Kay's candles are really the only fall leaves we see in the
Bay Area. This is California: evergreen country. "Oh, I almost forgot
to tell you. Your boss called this morning. Said you left your coat at
the restaurant, and he'll bring it to you at work."

"My coat. I forgot all about it. That ought to tell you how the
evening went."

"Truly. When you bought that coat, I thought you'd be buried in
it, and for the price, you probably should be." Kay smirks and crosses
her arms for a brief moment. Kay and I couldn't be more different.
The last time she bought a coat was when those Michelin-man goose-

down numbers were in, oh, about 1978 or so. It's that pale, sickly navy color that we wore in grade school, but out she goes to work in it every day like she's mushing the dogs to her office. Kay loves that down coat. You have to admire her loyalty.

"What did you do last night?" I ask while stretching and feeling every one of my thirty-one years.

"Besides answering Miss Popularity's phone, you mean?" Kay dusts off a pilgrim salt-and-pepper set.

"Do you want me to get my own line? I keep asking, and you keep saying it's a waste."

"No, I'm just giving you a hard time because I know it bugs you. Arin's back in town, by the way. She wanted to know how things were going, and to say thank you for leading her old beau to the Lord."

"Arin's back?" *Panic.* Arin, the size-2 diva/missionary that Seth once had a crush on. Somehow I sense that he could be in danger of falling for her all over again, if given the slightest opportunity.

"Yep. Arin's back."

"Does Seth know she's back?"

"How would I know that?"

"Well, what did Arin say exactly?"

"That she was back in town. That she'd talked to Kevin, or Dr. Novak, as I like to call him," Kay announces in a soap-opera tone. "And that she wants to get together with you."

"Did you tell her about Seth and me?"

"What's to tell?"

What indeed? "Is she still so thin?"

"I couldn't *see* her on the phone, Ashley. I imagine she's still thin, she was telling me about all the kayaking she did up the river in Costa Rica, and that she learned to balance a jug of water on her head."

"Isn't that in Africa where they do that?"

"I'm just telling you what she said."

"Is she coming to Bible study this week?"

"She said she'd try to make it, and that she missed us all while she was down there, but she was very anxious to speak to you."

"That's what my dream meant!" I exhale and place my hand to my forehead.

"What dream?"

"The missing Marc Jacobs pump. It's Arin, and she's come back to claim Seth. The striped heel belongs to her. It fits her, not me and my big fat size-9 foot! I'm the ugly stepsister!"

"What on earth are you talking about?" Kay puts down a rust-colored leaf and stares at me. "No, wait. I don't want to know." She holds up her palms in surrender. "I'm starting to understand you, and this makes me nervous because no one should really understand you unless they need mental help. It's Brea's job to understand you. I just have to live with you."

"I gotta go!" I rush off the couch and into the bathroom. Turning on the shower head, I wait until the warm steam fills the room and step into the sweltering tile cubicle. *Okay, Lord. I know this is about Your timing and all, but do you really mean for me to live here forever? I've been so patient. Nine months, Lord? Three years, really. You couldn't wait ten more years to bring back Arin? What if Seth looks at her and all his old feelings come back? Remember? That sad little crush he had, making him even older and balder than his years? I know the crush was short, but it was intense, Lord. So what is this about?*

God answers with the steaming shot of water out of the shower. *Ah, the silent treatment. I should be used to it by now.*

There's a pounding on the bathroom door. "Ashley, telephone!" Kay shouts.

I towel dry and find the cordless phone on the just-waxed hard-wood hallway. "Hello."

"It's Seth, Ashley." My towel-wrapped self slinks to the floor.

"Hi, Seth." His voice calms me and reminds me that I have dated him longer than any other woman. Seth and I were meant to be. The shoe dream was just a little nightmare, a little case of preengagement jitters, nothing more. Yet, there's a niggling of discomfort. "Is everything okay, Seth?"

"I can't do Friday night this week after all. Maybe next Friday."

He sounds disappointed. But not nearly disappointed enough. "Why not?" My tone doesn't even try to hide my emotion.

"I . . . I . . ." He's stammering. Not a good sign. "I can't do it because your gift won't be ready yet."

"It's only seven in the morning. Did the store call you? How do you know my gift isn't ready?"

"What store? No, Ashley. It's nothing like that. We'll do it next week, okay? I want you to be really surprised."

"I might be going to Taiwan next week, so I hope I'll be here for the big surprise. What about Saturday night with my boss, is that off too?"

"I can still do that," Seth tells me. "Your gift just isn't ready, that's all. And I want everyone to see you get it, so I'm inviting friends. Okay?"

I'm picturing myself as the ring slides onto my finger. I'm envisioning the awed look on every friend's face. "I'd love that. But I can't just show up on Saturday, Seth. Not without my . . ." I catch myself just in time. I'm praying for some of God's peace right now. Granted, none of it is deserved.

You know, I'm just not okay if God's will isn't the same as mine in this one little area. I can't help it. It's not just about being married. I'm over that whole fiasco. It's just that I am desperately in love with this man, even though I should know better. But when I see him looking at a little kid at Sunday school with his tender eyes, or taking in another out-of-work dot-commer, he just takes my breath away. This man has a heart of gold, and I want to embrace it for the rest of my life.

"Can't show up without your what?" Seth asks.

"My boyfriend," I say enthusiastically. "You know how Hans is. I want him to know I'm taken."

Seth laughs. "Of course I'll come and protect you. I promised

Arin I'd help her move some stuff on Saturday afternoon, but we'll be done by then."

"Arin?" I croak.

"She's back in town. She says she's dying to talk to you, so you should call her if you get the chance. She called here looking for you last night."

I'll just bet she did. "Why can't her Dr. Kevin help her move?" I ask, putting a bit of emphasis on the word doctor.

"He's on call this weekend. Arin was *thrilled* you led him to the Lord, by the way. She had nothing but praise for you. I told her I knew you had a missionary heart in you all along. Under that Ann Taylor exterior."

My missionary heart, as Seth puts it, is about ready to explode. "Did you two talk about anything else besides me?"

"Just your present. Arin loves the idea."

"You told Arin about my surprise?"

"It's a surprise for *you*, Ashley. Not Arin. You sound like you're disappointed someone else knows, but they'll all take part in the celebration afterwards. You just wait." He's nearly panting, like I should be excited he's talking to the size-2 blonde he had a crush on. Before she dumped him for the rain forest trip.

"I've got to get to work. So will I see you at Bible study this week?" I ask.

"Absolutely. I'm picking up Arin. She doesn't have a car now that she's back in town."

I can stand no more. "Seth, why are *you* picking up Arin? She found a way to get herself on a free trip to Costa Rica. I think she can get across town."

"Are you jealous, Ashley?"

Now, what kind of stupid question is that? "I just think if you're dating Arin, it's one thing to pick her up. If you're dating me, it's another. If you two show up together at Bible study, it sends a message." Of course, I regret this statement immediately. Because I

sound whiny and pathetic, and even if I am, I don't want to *sound*
like it.

"You and I have been dating for nine months. I can't have friends?"

"Of course, Seth." *Sure you can have friends, as long as they're not
size-2 blondes with fluttery lashes and big, innocent eyes.* "I've got to get
to work."

"Don't be like this, Ash. Arin and I are just friends. You're not the
jealous type. What's up with this?"

Does he really want the evaluation? Or just for me to shut up?
"Friendship wasn't what you wanted with Arin ten months ago, Seth,"
I accuse, hating myself in the process.

"*You* went out to dinner with the German Romeo last night.
That's okay, but my giving a sister-in-Christ a ride to Bible study has
ulterior motives?"

"Hans is my boss. And don't pull that sister-in-Christ business
with me."

"But you trust yourself with Hans. You just don't trust me with
Arin."

*No, quite frankly I don't trust any man with Arin. I've seen her oper-
ate.* I inhale deeply. "I shouldn't have brought it up. I'm sorry. I'll see
you later. I have a patent to rush."

"Fine. I'll call Arin and tell her to find herself another ride to
Bible study. Maybe she can hitch a ride with *your* ex-boyfriend, Dr.
Kevin Novak." Seth clears his throat dramatically. "Oh, but he's Arin's
ex, too, isn't he? Hmm. It seems I'm not the one with the friend/ex
issue here, am I?"

Grrr. "Seth, that's not fair. Kevin was never my boyfriend."

"Look, I don't want to fight. It's way too early in the morning,
and this is a ridiculous fight, Ashley. You either trust me or you don't.
You know how I feel."

*No, I really don't. I haven't heard "I love you." I've heard things like,
"You're very special to me," or "We have such a great bond and friendship. And my personal favorite: "You're the only woman I know like*

you. "Note to males: None of these mean a thing, because we women know you are intentionally avoiding the three little words we really want you to say.

"Maybe we can do lunch one day this week," I offer, my white flag waving limply over the phone line.

"That would be nice."

We say good-bye. Gone is my thrill over the "surprise." Life will never be what I want it to be. Perhaps my expectations are too high. Perhaps *any* expectations are too high.

I know one thing. I'm buying half of Kay's house. I want something of my own, and if it's a dash of granite with 1920s plumbing and a hefty mortgage, I'm fine with that for now. A baby would take away from my clothing budget, anyway.

5

When I walk into my office, I feel like Dolly Parton in that old movie, *9 to 5*. The admins are glaring at me, like they know I had dinner and who knows what else, with the boss. Maybe it's just my own guilt after talking to Seth. You know, the explosive inner turmoil of *The Telltale Heart?* Details from last night's bad decisions are polluting my mind. *I shouldn't have gone to dinner with Hans. I could have been with Seth. Instead, Seth was on the phone with Arin. In fact, I practically handed him over with a big, red bow. Besides, I lied to Hans . . .*

As I reach my office I lift up my chin. "Any messages?" I ask Tracy, my new admin.

"Nope. Nothing." Tracy is the office honeybee. She spends her mornings gathering the nectar of gossip, and in the afternoon she spreads her pollen with glee. She's one of those women who is married, but doesn't *look* married. She wears a ring: a great big tacky thing, but also has huge implants and wild, permed hair. Glossy scarlet will forever be her lipstick color, and flirting her native tongue.

Tracy's the type of married woman who goes to nightclubs without her husband and dances into the wee hours. While I try to understand her, I really don't. She's very sweet, but she only reminds me of my own failings. It's amazing that her husband is willing to put up with *that* behavior, but Seth is too afraid to put a ring on my finger.

Tracy's presence is like a daily slap in the face, reminding me that I have no idea what a man wants.

"Hans has a big patent in the works, so I'm going to need you to help me pull some files this afternoon."

Tracy salutes at me, and sits down at her desk to a hefty chocolate muffin. The disparity in Tracy's small stature and the size of that muffin reminds me yet again that life isn't fair, and that Arin-style sprightly figures are all you ever see on reality television. Where, I ask you, is the reality in *that?*

When I get into my office, I pull up my e-mail, intent on not allowing my social life to dip into the success of my workplace. *I need some coffee.*

There's an e-mail from Hans, and I cringe at the sight of it. He probably changed everything about the patent after I did the work. Opening the message I forget to breathe.

To: AStockingdale@gainnet.com

From: HanstheMan@gainnet.com

Re: Last Night

Ashley, just wanted to thank you for our quiet dinner last night. I think we accomplished a lot. I still have your discarded clothing. Will bring with me. See you at work. H—

Oh man, I'm in trouble. I'm in big trouble. I can't go to dinner at this man's house on Saturday. With or without Seth, Hans thinks there's something between us. At least I think he does.

Who knows with a man like him? Hans emanates sensuality like a liquor commercial, so much implied, but nothing really said. I'm too clueless for this type of subtle communication. I need an engineer. Someone to just come out and say, "Look, I'm trying to seduce you." Which, of course, an engineer never would say. And I like that feature. Being romanced with a little science fiction, or an hour of Game Cube, this is my world. I'm comfortable here.

"Ashley."

"Ah!" I clutch my startled chest. "What did you want, Tracy?"

"Hans wants you in his office."

I'll bet he does. "Okay, thank you."

Tracy comes in and shuts the door behind her. "Is he . . . you know . . . as sexy as he seems? The girls and I have a little pool going on."

Clearly, my church girl reputation has not followed me to this job. "Hans lives with a woman. If you're really interested, you should ask her, though I don't know why you would be." I laugh lightly. I don't want her to think I'm judging her. Even if I am a little. "I'm actually engaged to be married to an engineer." *Ack. There it is again.* Look how easily I'm suddenly lying. They say it's hardest the first time. Soon, I'll be telling them I'm a former Miss USA and only working for the enjoyment factor since I'm independently wealthy. I should also add that I'm a poet, which Brea will vehemently deny.

"Hans is the kind of man," Tracy wiggles her badly-in-need-of-a-pluck eyebrows, "who's too good to say no to." She comes closer. "Where's your ring?"

I pull my hand under the desk. "It's getting fitted. It's a recent engagement." Oh, I so hate myself right now. This is bad reality television at its finest, and I'm the scheming, low-down girl you root against. I don't know how I ever thought I'd get away with that whopper in the first place.

"We were all just talking about how *we'd* say yes to Hans in a minute. He only goes for you educated types, though." Tracy crinkles her nose. "To each his own, I guess. Plus, we gals think you have more of a German facial structure, so maybe he finds that attractive."

"A German facial structure?" I'm thinking this isn't necessarily a compliment.

"You know, not ugly or anything, but just . . ." she holds her fists out in front of her, "You know, squarer. Solid." Tracy obviously sees my dismay. "Not that that's a bad thing. I mean, it's sexy to a lot of guys."

"Can you get these patents filed for me?" I hand Tracy a bundle of folders. "Cross reference them by their product name and their category, which is on the side of the folders." *That ought to keep you out of trouble for a while.* I pick up the patent I worked all night on. "I'll be in Hands's, I mean Hans's, office if you need anything."

I make my way across the office floor, and I can feel that all eyes are on me. It's like my skirt is in my pantyhose. It's an ominous moment for me, because I'm never thought to be "that" kind of a girl. I'm a thirty-one-year-old virgin, for crying out loud. The fact that I'm being seen as seductress would be comical if it wasn't so eerily creepy. I knock on Hans's door, and he opens it, lifting his wheat-colored eyebrows at the sight of me.

"Ashley," he oozes. "Here's your coat." I turn around and see the admins huddled in a knowing circle. "You girls get to work!" Hans yells, and they scatter like cockroaches in the light.

You know, I have a theory, and why I was too desperate to notice it here before I took this job is beyond me at the moment. When a company hires half-dressed secretaries, it's usually a good sign that the CEO has issues. A "normal" CEO doesn't allow his company to give off that kind of a message, which really says, *our company can be bought for a price, so name it.* Sweeping my gaze across the room, I realize that Gainnet's image reminds me of bad politicians vying for the gaming lobby: guilty and sleazy.

"Thanks for my coat." I look Hans dead in the eye, hoping to tell him that I'm not afraid and that I'm not available. But inside I'm just praying, *Help me, Lord. Help me, Lord. I'm in way over my head.* All the while I suspect my lies are probably keeping me from any divine protection that might have been otherwise available.

"Don't rush off now. I want to talk to you about the patent. What I've seen so far, just last night, is genius. I know you started here as a simple patent attorney, but it's clear you're general counsel material, and I don't want to let another company figure that out first."

I let my guard down a bit and sit in the proffered chair in Hans's office. "Yes, I was offered the position of general counsel before I left Selectech. I didn't take the job for personal reasons."

"We haven't had a general counsel here at Gainnet, but with our revenue growing by such leaps and bounds, I think it's time we brought counsel in-house. Would you be interested in the job if the board approved such a position?"

I can feel the blood rising in my cheeks. "Absolutely!" By now my face is hot and red. "I'm just about to purchase half my room-mate's house, and the title would help immensely on my loan apps."

"It's more than a title I'm offering. It's an increase in your stock options, which would also help financially." He pauses for a moment. "Did you say you're purchasing half your fiancé's house?"

"Not my fiancé, my roommate." Okay, major blunder. Lying seems so easy on TV. They don't show all the other lies that have to accompany the first one.

"But I thought you were getting married."

"Well, I am, but just not presently."

"Are you going to have kids?" *Yes, this is an illegal question, but Hans cares little for American proprieties.*

"We're not sure yet about children. We're still working out the details of the wedding." *Like, whether we're actually having one.*

"These are things you have to think about as a woman with a career. Plot your course, as they say."

"Right." I'm like a Pavlovian dog at the moment, salivating over a job that hasn't even been created yet. Kay is right. No job is worth my self-respect. Do I have any of that left? "I'd like to have a bushel of kids," I suddenly blurt.

"Really?" Hans clasps his hands together on his desk. "I have four of them. Lot of work and money, those kids."

"You have four? I thought you only had two."

"Here in America, I only have two. They're from my marriage, but I was young once." He winks. "I have two that were born when I lived in France as a bachelor. I never see those kids, but they cost me a bundle." He whistles. "They're getting ready for college." He chuckles here, and I can't even force a smile. *Ewww,* is all I can think. He has kids as old as Sophia the nanny.

"Well, back to work," I say brightly. "I'd be happy to talk to you about the general counsel job when you have more time."

"I'll be in touch with the board." Hans stands up, and when I exit, the admins are huddled together again, like a high-school football team.

"Ahem," I say and they go back to pretending they're working. *I have a major headache.*

I clamber with the phone, struggling to punch in Brea's numbers, but I keep missing them. On the third try, I get her. "Hi, Ash, what's up?"

"I so need a friend. I have no friends here, Brea. They all think I'm the office . . . you know . . . but they are the ones dressed up like off-duty strippers. I'm so out of my element. I feel like I should wear a chastity belt at this job."

"You've just made a big change, Ashley. You're like the Israelites who remember the good things of Egypt instead of the slavery. Miles," Brea coos. "Say hello to Auntie Ashley. Auntie is having a bad day. Give her kisses." I hear the baby gurgling in the phone, and I just start to laugh. Brea can always make me laugh. Pretty soon, the gurgling turns into a healthy smacking sound. "No, no. Don't eat the phone, Miles. Icky. Dirty. Hello," she says to me.

"He's a doll. Can I have him yet? He's the only man I know worth having."

"No, he still remembers that you wanted a girl. He'll never forgive you for that."

"Story of my life."

"I have something to cheer you up, but you have to promise not to root me out," Brea says.

"Would I ever do that?"

"Seth invited us over on Friday night to share in a 'surprise' for you."

"No way!"

"Yep. He said he's been planning this for weeks now, and wants it to be perfect."

"This is after Arin came home?"

"Just this morning."

I scream into the phone. "Finally. Finally, something in my life is going right."

"I knew you'd have a cow if you came home with sloshy, day-old makeup, so I made up my mind to tell you, but you can't tell John. He'll call me a gossip."

"You *are* a gossip!"

"Shh. Only with you. Otherwise, I'm the perfect, Proverbs 31 woman. Miles thinks so, and that's all that matters to this mama. But I'd have a connip if John was coming to ask me to marry him and inviting people over, and I looked like I'd been at work all day. Shoot me now."

"Um, yeah." I lower my voice into the phone. "Any idea what the ring looks like?"

"He wouldn't tell me a thing, Ash. And believe me, I tried. I called John right away to tell him."

"Why didn't you call *me?* You traitor."

"Because for a few minutes I thought I could keep it from you. I thought I could rise above my personal anguish and keep a secret from my best friend. But I was wrong. As soon as I heard your voice, I knew I'd blurt it out."

"Thank goodness!"

"Listen, I gotta run. It seems Miles has been using this time productively, and the aroma is overwhelming me. Don't let that boss of yours get to you. Remember, you are a star patent attorney, and nothing he implies means anything, and the gals are just talking about what they know from experience. You'll be Seth's wife soon, and won't have to worry about this, anyway."

Seth's wife. I'll be Seth's wife soon. "See ya." I hang up the phone, and type on my to-do list.

THINGS TO DO BEFORE BECOMING A FIANCÉE

1. Tell Kay no on the house.
2. Get my nails done!
3. Practice enthusiastic facial expressions in the mirror.
4. Wax & shape eyebrows for a thoroughly surprised arch.
5. Invest in lingerie for wedding night. *I'm having a wedding night!*
6. Buy my own high-quality game controller to let Seth know I care about his needs too.
7. Make an appt for seaweed wrap, must have baby bum skin.
8. Practice hand gestures that will show off sparkling diamond!

6

Wednesday nights are the highlight of my week. It's Bible study, Reason Style! Like I said before, we all have various reasons for being woefully single. Not the least of which being that we're all weird in our own special way. We live in Silicon Valley, so I guess that goes without saying. But I digress. Bible study is a highlight because I get to hear Seth speak the Truth. I fall hopelessly in love with him all over again when I hear his knowledge of Scripture. I find myself daydreaming about what kind of husband he'll make, lulling me to sleep with God's Word. It makes me think about turning in my Audi convertible for a minivan. Well, let's not get too crazy. Maybe just a foreign SUV.

Our house is spotless, and Kay is going through her regular ritual of praying in every room before the study, and secretly, I think she stays in the kitchen the longest, hoping that everyone will love her fabulous culinary creations. She used to have people take turns with snacks, but after one too many bag-o-chips and no beverages, she gave that up. You know that saying, "He's all that and a bag of chips?" Well, that was our group: all that and one bag of measly, half-priced, grocery-store-brand chips.

(California is health conscious, so if you're going to buy chips here, you'll find they generally are made with expeller-pressed safflower oil, not hydrogenated oil, which is so artery-clogging. Normally

6# she's out of control

Californians buy the fancy stuff for themselves. But not the Reasons—
not for Bible study.)

One of the issues the Reasons share is a complete inability to
think practically. Case in point: Thanksgiving 2002. Someone is
signed up to bring mashed potatoes. I kid you not, for twenty-two
people, he showed up with a pint of potatoes from Boston Market—
with beef gravy. We had to explain that turkey is a poultry dish—and
generally goes best with a poultry, i.e., chicken or turkey gravy. *And I
thought I was lame in the kitchen.*

So now, Kay ensures her kitchen will never be tortured again: It's
a clipboard issue. Kay controls that clipboard like every other aspect
of her life. Meanwhile my life wildly spins off its axis. Tonight I feel
like a million. I feel like I am the winning bachelorette and general
counsel all rolled into one, well-dressed chick. The way I see it, it's my
last Reason Bible Study *as* a Reason. Next week, I'll have a ring and a
date, and most importantly, a fiancé.

"The bathrooms look great. Thanks for cleaning them. I love that
bleach smell." Kay inhales deeply and continues. "Have you thought
anything more about my offer? I'd like to get things started before the
rates go up."

"I have! This should be kept quiet, but . . ." Doorbell. "Hang on,
I'll get the door."

I race to the door, and my stomach flips as I see it's Arin. She's
back from the rain forest mission field, looking as emaciated as ever. *I
wish I had my ring and my date now.* Her blonde hair shines like a tow-
headed toddler. It's the kind of color you can't get from a bottle. It
makes me finger my fake auburn lowlights, for which I paid a fortune.

"Ashley!" Arin squeals and pulls me into a hug, then steps back.
"You look great. You have that glow about you. I know you're not
pregnant. Are you in love?"

I smile sheepishly. "Seth and I are dating. We've been together
nine months now."

"Nine months, you're kidding? I feel so old being away that long.

42

You have to fill me in on everything." She spots Kay. "Kay, it's so good to see you. Kevin told me a lot, but clearly not everything if you're living together, and Ashley is dating Seth and not Kevin."

Kevin is her ex. Well, he's mine too, but we won't go into that. Suffice it to say, it was brief and completely unrealistic. Kevin looks like Hugh Jackman, and he's a pediatric surgeon at Stanford Children's Hospital. Way out of my league, and quite frankly, that's okay with me. I have morning issues anyway. I don't want to wake up next to someone prettier than me. I've seen those women on Oprah whose family hasn't seen them without makeup. It's too weird for me.

So I'm still talking, unable to stop my blatant oversharing, trying to compensate for my feelings of inadequacy. "Seth came up to Las Vegas at my brother's wedding, and we've been dating ever since."

"Well, good. Those blue eyes of his are too precious to waste. They would be so pretty on a little girl." Arin is completely sincere. You want to hate her because she's so darling, but she makes it impossible. Generally she's pure of speech and motive, but Lord forbid if she wants something and you're standing in her way. It's that one little tick that makes you keep an eye on her, just in case.

"We're hardly at the point to discuss children." I laugh, but you know, come to think about it, we never have discussed children. That's kind of strange, isn't it? After nine months, shouldn't I know if Seth wants children? I have no idea.

"He must really be something, though," Arin practically sings. "You broke Kevin's heart over him. And Kevin's the sort of man who gets what he wants."

"I did *not* break Kevin's heart. That's completely laughable."

Arin sighs deeply. "He thought when he became a church boy . . . all that was left was the proposal. Then he got a phone call from you. A Dear John phone call . . ." Arin shakes her head. "I've known Kevin a long time, Ashley. He's very sincere and very focused. He doesn't even date lightly. That's why I got rid of him. He way far too marriage-minded."

It's getting hot in here. "Kevin has to have a list of women waiting longer than my arm, and he's too intellectual for me. He needs a woman who can throw a good soiree. Someone who can plan for more than tater tots and weenies in a blanket." Kay comes in and sets up a vegetable tray and I wave my hand. "Someone like Kay."

"His parents didn't like you either, huh?" Arin leans in. "Did they push you to join Mensa?"

"It wasn't ever an option for me. I'm not the Mensa type of person. I'll get the tea," I say, frantic for an exit. I go into the kitchen, only to feel Arin hot on my heels. I open the fridge and rummage for nothing in particular, hoping she'll go away. But she's standing in front of the swinging door, ensuring our privacy.

"You really did break his heart, Ashley." I turn around and face her, noting that a single tear is suspended on her lower eyelash. "He's on fire for the Lord. Are you sure there's nothing left between you? That this Seth thing is going to take off? Because someone's faith might be dependent upon it."

I slam the fridge shut. "I imagine you broke his heart too, Arin, when you left for the jungle. I didn't mean to hurt him, but you never told me he wasn't a Christian. I was seeing him under false pretenses. And I'm with Seth now. So none of this really matters. It's just water under the bridge."

"Kevin is a Christian now." Arin smiles, shrugging her narrow shoulders. "Missionary dating. It's one of my weaknesses. But guys never fall for me seriously like Kevin did you, Ashley. I'm the cute one they take out to nice dinners. You're the one they take home to mother."

Somehow I feel the sting of that comment. I move over to the sink, and proceed to scrub the spotless counter. "Arin, what are you, twenty-four? You're an otter, and you naturally want to play. I'm just more serious-minded. Parents think of me as a way for their sons to grow up. It's the lawyer thing. It makes people think I'm reliable." Which is a joke in itself.

"Kevin doesn't need to grow up. He's eighty inside if he's a day. You're not taking his feelings seriously." Arin's cutesy tone is gone.

Now she's making me nervous. "What's this about, Arin?"

"I just came from Kevin's house. He thinks Seth is something you need to get out of your system. Frankly, I agree." She crosses her gangly arms and waits for my reaction. Which I'm trying very hard not to give.

Breathe. Breathe. "You told him that wasn't true, right? You told him how long I've had this crush on Seth, and it's more than that now. I love the man." But I must admit, I'm totally flabbergasted. I hadn't thought Kevin gave me a second glance after we parted ways. Come to think of it, considering the source, I'm not sure he did.

"Kevin is praying up a storm, and he has the faith of a new Christian, Ashley. He believes with his whole heart that God is going to grant him the desire of his soul. Not to mention the fact that his parents never denied him a thing. How would he know what failure even feels like?"

"Ashley! Seth is here," Kay calls from the living room.

"Listen, I need to go. I'll have a talk with Kevin, okay? I promise I'll let him know I meant what I said. That there was never anything like that between us."

"He's a Christian now, Ashley. Just be careful. I hate to see a brother fall because . . ."

I don't wait for her to finish. Do I need this kind of guilt? I have serious issues to contemplate, like how I'm going to get a promotion without stepping in my boss's erogenous zone, and how I'm going to react when Seth Greenwood actually asks for my hand in marriage.

In the living room, I just stop at the sight of Seth. He's chatting up a storm with the group, but stops when his eyes meet mine. My stomach swirls at the sight of him, and a huge smile fills my face. His gem-blue eyes are sparkling, and when he looks at me from across the room, I feel it deep inside. My heart pounds, the back of my knees sweat, and I have to physically think about breathing. I close my eyes to avoid the surging emotions pounding in my heart. It seems like years since I've seen him, but it's only been three days.

He walks over to me. "Hi," he says with a wink and kisses me on the cheek. *Did you see that, everybody? He kissed me publicly. I am so getting engaged!* "You look happy tonight."

"Why shouldn't I be? I'm dating the handsomest guy in the room, and he's about to teach me Nehemiah. It doesn't get any more sizzling than that." I wink back at him.

He leans in, grabs my hand, and whispers, "You are one strange girl, you know that?"

"Of course I do."

"Let's get started, everyone." Kay commands the room to silence, and we all take our regular seats. *We are so boring.* Same seats, different night. Hopefully, Seth has some great pearl of wisdom to offer us.

Arin has sauntered back into the room, and Seth's eyes brighten at the sight of her. "Arin, you're back!" Seth rushes to her side and kisses her on the cheek. *Yes, that's right. PDA in my own house with another woman. Claws extending now.*

"Seth, you look fantastic." She runs her fingers over his slight hair. "Never better, in fact." Then she looks at me.

Seth sits beside her and opens up his Bible. He sits beside her, as in a different place, and I notice that all eyes in the room are on me. Well, I'm not giving them the satisfaction. I refuse to react. I open my Bible and begin to silently pray. Actually, it's kind of a vengeful prayer, but that doesn't matter now.

We're led in a fascinating study on the minor prophet, and his wisdom and complete assurance upon the Lord. *Oh ye of little faith,* is all I can think. When we're done, Arin smiles at Seth and walks into the kitchen. But surprise. I'm the one following her.

She turns around and smiles coyly, but her joyful expression disappears at the sight of me.

"What's going on?" I nod back at the door.

"What do you mean?"

"We're friends, Arin. You're a Christian. I'm a Christian, albeit not a very good one lately. But you've always said you didn't want to get married. Why are you playing with Seth's heart when he may want to marry me?"

She shrugs. "There's just something about him I find completely charming, Ashley. It's just a little innocent flirtation. When you're married, you and he can laugh about it."

I fail to see the humor here. "Not to accuse you of anything, Arin, I know your heart is generally pure in these situations, but I'm a little raw when it comes to Seth. It's been a long road, and you have a way of making him forget about our relationship. I'm not talking behind your back; I'm telling you straight up. It makes me uncomfortable."

"If that's what you're thinking, do you really want to marry some-one so easily swayed?" Arin's lagoon-blue eyes are wide, and I'll admit I don't want to dwell too long on her question.

"No, of course not," I say automatically. "But I don't want you pretending that a beautiful woman like you is going to whisk him off his feet either. Seth is very innocent in matters of the heart, and he doesn't understand that women sometimes play games."

Arin shakes her head. "I'm not playing. And I'm not the one who has two wonderful guys fawning over me, so if there's anything to be jealous about, well . . ." She flails her hand about.

My bearings are completely off. Arin has always demanded male attention just by walking in a room. But this is something I haven't seen from her before, and my mind can't help but reel trying to inter-pret her motives. Sprinkles of distrust spray down my spine, and I want to shake them off like a Labrador at a lake, but I can't.

"Do you want something to drink now?" I ask Arin.

"No," Arin's eyes widen. "There he is, the master of the hour."

I turn around and see Seth. "Hi, great job tonight."

He kisses my forehead, and then leans against the counter coolly, crossing his ankles. "Thanks. So Arin, how long are you home? Or is this for good?"

"That all depends. If I can find a reason to stay, who knows? I'm a leaf in the wind."

"What would a young gal seeking adventure possibly do for excitement in the Silicon Valley?" I ask.

She looks directly at Seth, then me. "You tell me, Ashley. You're a woman of the world. What keeps you here?"

Nothing at the moment. "I'm going to help Kay with refreshments. You two have a good talk." And I exit. I've been a Reason for thirty-one years, and God knows I'm not fighting for any man. This is not *The Bachelor,* and I am most certainly not desperate.

But when the doorbell rings, and Dr. Kevin appears in my vision with a bouquet, I realize I am desperate. Desperate and pathetic with nowhere to run.

Dr. Kevin Novak is disarmingly handsome. He grew up among the pony set in Atlanta, and now lives among the "casual Friday" crowd that is the San Francisco Bay Area. It's been months since I've seen him, but gazing at him now, I have two thoughts. One, I'm thrilled he's a new Christian (he's been attending a large, local Baptist church). Two, I feel like I've become the goal line, and regardless of his true feelings, his fierce competitiveness has taken hold. While we all want to be swept off our feet, no one wants to be captured.

Kevin holds out the flowers to Kay. "I'm sorry I'm so late, but I haven't had a Wednesday night off in months, and I wanted to come by and say how much I appreciate you all." He nods toward me. "Hello, Ashley."

"Hi, Kevin. It's good to see you." *Now, would you go into the kitchen and get Miss Pixie away from my boyfriend?* As though on cue, the swinging kitchen door opens, and Seth appears. He sees Kevin and glances at me. This is so *90210.*

"I'm going to give Arin a lift home," Seth announces.

"How did she get here?" I ask, this uncharacteristic shrew voice coming out of my mouth.

"I walked," Arin says.

Now, I'll admit, I'm really confused. Arin is a sweet girl. She has a huge heart for the Lord, and she knows I'm dating Seth. I know she lives to flirt, but it's always seemed perfectly innocent. This is strange, and while I'm uncomfortable with it, I'm not jealous. Not yet anyway. Seth would give Jack the Ripper a ride home, and soon Friday will arrive. My naked finger becomes wrapped in proprietary platinum.

"Drive safely," I say, as I pick up an empty candy dish.

Arin looks directly at Kevin and says nothing as she exits. Something is not right in the state of California. And it's more than our politics.

Calgon . . . take me away . . .

7

Just as the last hot massage rock was removed, Ashley basked in the warm California sunshine. Her table overlooked a forest-green valley of vineyards, and the scent of warm grapes and summer foliage filled her senses. The soothing sprinkling of the outdoor waterfall vied for attention with the call of the mourning doves.

"Mrs. Novak, would that be all?" A tall, slender aesthetician leans over Ashley.

"Yes, that will be all. Please send Dr. Novak out to the patio when you leave." Ashley turns herself over, under the blanket of towels, and places Ralph Lauren sunglasses on her face.

"Of course, madam. I'll send him out immediately." The aesthetician curtseys and disappears into the luxurious hotel suite.

Kevin saunters onto the patio, wearing a Stanford baseball cap. "There's my beautiful wife." He places a kiss upon her lips. "How was your massage?"

"I feel like Sleeping Beauty being awakened by my handsome prince."

"What shall we do with our day? Horseback riding? A swim in the pool? Maybe bicycling along the beach? Shopping in downtown Santa Barbara? What sounds good to you, my love?"

Ashley reaches up and kisses her husband. "Anything sounds good with you at my side."

"That's what a honeymoon is all about, Ashley."

"Indeed."

"I'm sorry?" I'm blinking wildly as I've just realized the real Kevin, not my idealized version, is talking to me. My face is heated from that strange daydream, starring *him* and not Seth. What was that about?

Kevin is looking at me, waiting for an answer to a question I didn't hear. He shakes his head. "I asked, what do you think about Saturday? Sailing on the Bay? My friend owns this incredible yacht with three full-time crew. He's a member of the St. Francis Yacht Club at the San Francisco Marina. Have you been there? Sweeping views of the City, and the entire Bay and the Golden Gate Bridge. It's just magnificent."

"I think I went to a wedding there once." I rub my forehead, which is pounding. "You know, Kevin, Seth and I have been dating for about nine months. I don't really think it would be appropriate for you and me to go sailing together."

Kevin looks at the door, his eyes insinuating the obvious question: Didn't your boyfriend just leave with another woman? "Aren't we friends, Ash? Just like Seth is still friends with Arin."

"I guess two wrongs don't make a right for me, pious as it sounds." I smile gently. Now, keep in mind, I am only Miss Popularity because I have a boyfriend. I have had months of dateless nights. Too many to count, but now that I have a boyfriend, well, all the other Silicon Valley drones wonder what is so exciting about me. It's the boyfriend mystique.

"I think you misunderstand me, Ashley. Your giving me that Bible and explaining it on an intellectual level helped me to see God. I just feel I owe you." He shrugs his wide shoulders.

I try to mask my utter humiliation here. Wasn't it enough that the entire Bible study got to watch my boyfriend leave with another woman? No, I had to top it off by refusing a man who wasn't really asking anything of me. This is Arin's fault. Why would I listen to her? Why would I actually believe that this gorgeous man (dressed in 501s and a button-up—be still my heart) actually wanted to sweep me away on a yacht? I'm telling you, this thing with Seth has me so uneasy, I'm cracking up. I'm suddenly thinking I'm Beyonce and men can't resist my charms.

I brush the hair off my face. "I sure appreciate the invitation, but Jesus paid your debt. Let's forget about it, okay?"

"I think you'd really like sailing, Ashley."

Granted, I'd like *shopping* for sailing. I love nautical wear, but no. Definitely no. *I needn't go on the Bay to be marooned.* "My boss is anxious for me to go to Taiwan, and meet our managers there. You know, to get a patent department up and running there. I doubt I'm going to be able to sail across the Bay regardless. I need to be available."

"Cell phones work on the Bay, Ashley. This isn't Timbuktu."

I meet his intense eyes directly. He's going to know I mean business. "Kevin, you don't owe me anything, all right? It's really nice of you to ask me, but I don't need your pity date!" *Sounding a little bitter here. Baggage anyone?*

He scoffs at me. "I'm not Seth, Ashley. Why do you assume the worst of me? Have I ever said anything to you that wasn't true?" He pauses for a moment here and forces me to look into his unrelenting gaze. "Do you want to know my true motives?"

I nod.

"I love your laughter, your light, and your energy. I'm attracted to that. Really attracted to that." He puts a palm to his chest. "I think it's great that shopping is a sport for you, and that you can't see me without pointing out your new shoes. I love how you toss all that material stuff aside when you're singing at church, or at the Food Kitchen, or working overnight on a patent. I love how you can tackle a theological argument with the tenacity of a good lawyer and a missionary. You are such a complete enigma to me, and I just find you absolutely fascinating. You're everything God left off of me. I'm plodding, deliberate, and driven, but I haven't stopped thinking about you since we were seeing each other."

Alrighty then. I'm looking around the room for something, any-

thing, to pull me away from this fiery conversation. *This is very bad.*
I remind myself that I have a boyfriend, but who wouldn't be flat-
tered? And maybe, just maybe I'm a little more moved than I'd like
to be.

I'm holding the candy dish. As Kevin reaches for my hand, he
slowly brushes his fingers along mine before grabbing a lone M&M
in the bowl and popping it into his mouth. I'd like to say it has no
effect on me, but it does. Our eyes connect and I can feel the energy
pulsating between us. I force myself to remember that Kevin is out
of my league, and that his interest will most certainly pass. I am
interrupted by another thought: his eyes are green, and I heard once
that was the hardest color to make DNA-wise. But God mixed up a
special palette for these. They are a combination of jade and army
green. Just gorgeous, and absolutely mesmerizing. Dangerously
mesmerizing.

I pull my eyes away, and as I'm looking at his shirt collar, I realize that something within me stirs when I'm with him. It's something
I haven't wanted to admit to, but I literally *feel* him near me. Being
in love with Seth should quench that fire. *Lord, help me to quench this
fire. Seth,* I think to myself. *Seth.*

I clear my throat. "It's too bad you missed Bible study. Seth led
a fascinating discussion on Nehemiah and honoring God in all that
you do."

He nods. "You're not answering my question about sailing."

"I am. You're just not liking my answer." I venture a small glance
at his eyes, and there it is again, that warmth in my chest.

"Fair enough. I'm sorry if I was out of line."

I shake my head. "It's all right. Seth and I are going to be engaged
soon. We're more serious than we appear." But even as I say it, I don't
know if I truly believe it. I want to *make it so*, but I'm not Captain
Jean-Luc Picard, and I may not be capable just by willing it.

Kevin puts the candy dish back on the table, and I notice the
room has completely emptied of people. Even Kay is nowhere to be

found. Kevin breathes in deeply and exhales as though about to say something profound.

"Seth doesn't seem like the type to commit, but then, you're no ordinary woman, I suppose. If I see that, why wouldn't Seth?" Kevin envelops my hand in his, and I feel it everywhere, along with the prick of guilt that follows it.

My smile fades. "Really, Kevin, it's not right for us to have this conversation." I pull away my hand.

"I understand. Please accept my apologies." And then, he does the oddest thing. He bows his head. Almost in a Mr. Darcy manner, and I'm completely awestruck by the movement. I look around me to see if maybe I've been transported back to the seventeenth century. Stranger things have happened.

"I want to marry Seth," I say meekly, but it's meeker than even I could have hoped.

Kevin's cheek flinches. "When he doesn't even care enough about your feelings to say no to Arin? Why do you want a man like that?"

And here's the question of the day. "I can't explain it in words, but I have so much history with Seth."

Kevin nods his head. "People who don't study history are doomed to repeat it." And then he clears his throat, like he regrets his words. "You're a brilliant woman, Ashley Stockingdale. I'm certain you know what you want. You'll figure it out."

But as the warmth in my stomach permeates the rest of me, I'm not certain of anything.

Kay walks into the room. "Well, you two scared everyone off early tonight."

"I beg your pardon?" I say.

Kay puts her palms up, as is her custom. "Don't get defensive, but people scuttled out of here like you were throwing daggers." She points to Kevin and back at me. "What's going on between the two of you?"

"Nothing!" We say in unison.

Kevin zips up his leather jacket and grabs the doorknob. "I've got to run. I'm on call later tonight. It had just been a long time and I wanted to check in and say hello."

"Thanks for the flowers, Kevin," Kay says.

"You're welcome, and I won't miss Bible study next time, I promise. Thanks for your hospitality. You are one amazing woman, Kay." He looks at me and whispers, "As are you." Kevin gives me a searing look that feels like lightning to a rod.

He exits and Kay is staring at me. "What's going on?"

I cross my arms. "I don't think Kevin believes Seth is going to ask me to marry him," I say, and I watch Kay's eyebrows lift. "I know, you don't either, but even if he doesn't, I can't shut my feelings off like a light switch. Or just transfer them to another guy." *Can I?*

Kay nods her head. "It looked like your light just switched on there, but it's none of my business. My offer is still good. And you don't have to marry anyone for it." Kay smiles knowingly.

"I don't know yet, Kay. Everything feels completely out of control right now. I don't know if I'm the new general counsel at Gainnet, or going to be looking for a job to maintain my innocence. I don't know if I'm getting engaged next week. Or if Seth has something else in mind. Basically, I don't know if I'm coming or going, and I hate that someone else has control over my destiny. Someone with a commitment issue."

"Ashley, you are a born drama queen. If you're waiting for Seth to calm your life down, you've got a long wait."

"What's that supposed to mean?"

"For most of us in the real world, it means that the last pair of heels at Bloomingdale's does not constitute a crisis. And if I had a friendly hottie of a doctor offering me an alternative, I'd at least be open to the idea. You're so loyal to Seth, and I don't really understand why, Ashley. Why *should* Seth make any movement toward commitment? You're going to be around regardless. He knows that."

That's not true, I protest silently. "I'm calling Brea," I announce.

"It's nine-thirty."

"She'll be up." I dial my best friend's number, anxious to hear about Seth's phone call, and his plans for our romantic surprise party for me. She's wide awake. It's *Bachelor* night, and she's watching bad reality television, reminding me there's a reason I'm so petty. Brea and I are soul mates. "Hi, it's me."

"He's getting ready to nix someone; is this important?" Brea is so into *Bachelor*.

"Um, yeah! Tell John to Tivo it."

"Go ahead," Brea moans. "I already Tivoed it."

"Arin was here, she told me Kevin is still interested, but I think the truth of the matter is that she's interested in Seth. She proceeded to flirt with him right in front of me and hitched a ride home. Then, Kevin showed up, looking as hot as ever I might add, and pretty much said Seth probably wouldn't *ever* ask me to marry him."

I hear her TV click off. "This all happened at Bible study? Did it ever occur to you people to actually study the Bible at these events?"

"So I need to know exactly what Seth said to you, Brea. Do you really think he's going to ask me to marry him?"

"He drove Arin home?"

"She asked him to."

"Sometimes your boyfriend drives me crazy. We should practice saying 'no' with him before this goes any farther. There's nice and there's clueless, and he is entering the realm of clueless."

"Regardless, he took her home. Now what?"

"Ashley, personally, I think he's going to ask you. No, I'm sure of it. He asked both John and me to be there, and said he had something he wanted to share with all of us. What else could it be? This thing with Arin is probably his last hoorah, like a shout that he's still in-dependent. Why else would he ask us all there?"

"Who knows with Seth? The *Lord of the Rings* has a new install-ment? There's a big X-box online event? You can never be too sure with my beloved."

"Just tell him that his days with Arin are over. If he's going to ask you to marry him, he should have no problem with that promise."

"I'm not going to police him, Brea. If he wants to spend time with Arin, it's better to know now. But she just wants to feed her ego, and he'll end up nursing his wounds."

"This is not right, Ash! He's not just a friend anymore. He's sup-posed to be somebody who understands exactly how you feel. He's been your boyfriend, your Christian boyfriend, for nine months. Would you accept this behavior if you were married?"

"Heck no."

"Then start being the businesswoman I know you are and grow a brain." I hear the TV click back on. "Oooh, it's getting good. Call me back." She hangs up on me, and the phone immediately starts to beep.

"Hello?"

"Ashley, it's me."

"Seth! How's Arin? Is she home safely?"

"She doesn't really have a home. She's staying with different friends. I think she was looking for a night on my couch."

"And?"

"And I told her I had a girlfriend. Sheesh, Ashley."

Oh yeah, I'm the dumb one. "So you're home now?"

"Yeah, I'm missing you. I feel like I barely got to see you tonight, and it's been too long." His emotion doesn't stir me like usual. I'm hurt. Maybe it's childish, but I'm still hurt.

"If you could go on any vacation, where would it be?" I ask, fishing for ideas. Maybe my honeymoon daydream was on the money.

"I don't know, maybe on a houseboat, or cross-country in an RV."

"An RV?" Tell me my supposed soul mate did not say the initials that have come to signify camping with a television set. "You don't maybe want to go to Hawaii or a beach somewhere? Or a spa?"

He laughs. "What would I do at a spa? I don't want some guy touching me. Gross."

Okay, no spa. I can deal with that. "What about a cruise? That's kind of like RVing."

"Are you going on vacation, Ash?"

Sigh. "No, just daydreaming, I guess."

"I just wanted to let you know I was home, and that I'll see you Saturday for your boss's thing."

"I'm trying to get out of that. Of course, I still want to see you."

"Why?" He laughs. "I mean why are you trying to get out of it, not why do you want to see me."

Um, I think Hans wants my bod. "I just don't want to set a precedent that I do things socially with my boss, that's all." The truth overtakes me. "And I think he wants me. You know, in *that* way."

Seth is quiet.

"Did you hear me?"

"What makes you think that?"

"It's not important."

"Ashley, sometimes I think . . . well, I think you live in another world sometimes."

My stomach lurches. He doesn't believe it's possible for someone else to be attracted to me. "I want to be general counsel before I leave. I need to be general counsel, or all the companies are going to think I'm poison."

"You haven't been there that long. It's your chance now to say it didn't work out. Hans is probably just a friendly guy, though, Ashley. Don't think about that anymore. You're protected by the law."

"There's another reason to keep the job. Kay was hoping I'd buy half her house as an investment." I throw it out there. Let's see how completely shocked he is.

"Really? That's a great idea, Ashley."

There's a huge lump in my throat and shadows descend over my lighthearted mood. There's no marriage proposal forthcoming. There's only me and my dog-eared copy of *The Rules.* "You really think it's a good idea, huh?"

"Yeah, it's a no-brainer to get some equity. My condo is worth three times what I paid for it."

"I don't want to make any immediate plans for the future," I say.

"I know how you feel."

Clearly.

8

What was I thinking? It's the only mantra that comes to mind when Sophia, my boss's latest live-in, opens the door. I think Seth's jaw physically dropped. I know mine did. She's like a swimsuit model *after* the air-brushing. I actually find myself feeling a little sorry for her here, because she's so fabulous looking, you can't think of a thing to say. And I wonder what her conversational life is like. You're just completely stopped by her beauty. What pressure she lives under, and who needs that? By the end of my inner turmoil, I'm convinced average is good.

Seth looks at her, then he looks at me, and I can almost hear his comical commentary. *Oh yeah, your boss wants you, not this Italian model who's living at his whims. Earth to Ashley. Rein in that incredible ego.*

"Ashley," Sophia's Italian accent leaves both Seth and I gaping. Kind of like, *hey, she talks.* "And you must be Seth." Seth nods. And I clumsily hold out the plant I've brought. "Oh, it's beautiful, thank you." Sophia says as she takes the pot.

"It's an African violet. They grow well if you have a window box." I've seen Sophia before, but I've never seen her with makeup, and boy, she cleans up good. I always thought she was gorgeous, but just how gorgeous should really be equally divided among the women of the world. She's like Kryptonite—you can't gaze directly upon her.

"We do have a window box. Well, come in. Hans is putting the shrimp kabobs on the barbecue and I have made a fabulous pesto to go with it." She looks to Seth. "Can I take your jacket?"

He shakes his head. Apparently, he's still dumbstruck.

"This is a great place you have here," I offer.

"It's nice, but small, no? Hans has to pay for all those children of his, so we're lucky to have a roof, I suppose." She lets out a tinkling laugh, and sits on a long red velvety sofa, planting the violet on a glass table beside her. She pats the seat beside her. "Come and sit."

My eyes wander as I take a seat. The house itself is very old-world. Although it's a flat-roofed Eichler, it's decorated with travertine and marble pillars, like a Tuscan villa. A baby grand piano sits beside the ornate fireplace, and the flocked wallpaper appears to be fabric. There is one exception that bolts me back into the present day: the modern, wild art that graces the walls. Everything is quite elegant except the art. It's like something out of a mental-patient gallery. Colorful and angry.

"The artwork is nice." Seth says tentatively.

What? Come on Seth, there is an entire room of beautiful things here! You have to go for the psycho art?

"Thank you. I did it myself." Sophia stands up and walks around the room. She's wearing espadrilles, linen slacks, and a flowing silk shirt—all in cream. She looks like she's never worked a day in her life, like she was created to be an ornament. Sophia points to a painting. "I call this *Pressure* because it represents the time I came to live with Hans's family. I never knew such angst could exist until I lived with children full-time." She talks with her flattened hand slicing the air for effect.

Um, maybe stealing their mother's husband had something to do with that angst. "Did you come over to America expressly to be a nanny?"

"I did. Only to discover that I don't particularly care for children."

Again, a tinkling laugh. "They're quite filthy. They always have food on their hands, and they're just little bags of noise." She grabs her ears. "Oh, the noise!"

I can see from Seth's expression that she's just lost a little of her mystique with him. "So you don't want children?" Seth asks. Odd. He's never asked me that question.

"Absolutely not. Hans has populated the world enough, and I believe in population control. A very rare, how you say, stance in my Catholic country, but I believe it." Sophia moves to another painting, her hands flailing in typical Italian fashion.

Hmm. How would I describe it? The painting is skeletal in nature, covered in red, to give the effect of stringed muscles like you'd see in an anatomy book. It's surrounded by black, and the eyes bulge out like something in a Halloween haunted house. Sophia continues, "I call this one *Death*. It represents the end of a relationship and your feelings about that other person. How you are simply raw and laid . . . how you say? Bare. Laid bare."

And Brea thinks my poetry is frightening? This gal should be locked away with her paints and a full-time Freud. "Interesting," I say. What does one say when you've just been assaulted by something unsightly referred to as art. *Um, this is called* Straightjacket?

Seth's eyes are huge, glowing orbs. Sophia is like a fantasy beer commercial, until she slaps you across the face with the harsh reality of her inner life. Judging by his furrowed brow, if I thought Seth was fearful of jewelry stores before, the news that a beautiful woman can harbor this kind of dark emotion obviously has him thinking *monastery*. He stares at me like *I've* betrayed him. We're never getting married. He now thinks I'm the *Portrait of Dorian Gray*, hiding some hideous self in the closet.

Hans comes in, much to the relief of us all. "Ashley, you look gorgeous!" He embraces me and stands back to gaze at me, lifting his eyebrows. "No patent attorney should look like this. How do you expect me to get any work done?"

Seth comes forward, and thrusts hand towards my boss. "Seth Greenwood, Ashley's boyfriend. Nice to meet you."

"Boyfriend? I thought . . ." Hans looks at me questioningly and continues. "I thought any man smart enough to date our Ashley would rush to the altar. No ring, huh?" Hans picks up my hand and shows its barrenness to Seth.

"We were just admiring Sophia's art." Seth says, avoiding the marriage conversation. As is his custom.

"She's incredible, isn't she? Such talent, and it goes unrecognized in America. In Europe, they understand her art and pay big money for it." Hans kisses Sophia on the cheek. "So, what can I get you to drink? Wine? Martini? What?"

"I'd just like a diet soda if you have one," I say, and Sophia looks at me as though I'm from another planet.

"Wine is good for the digestion," Sophia says. "Americans put too many chemicals in their bodies."

"I'm afraid it's not good for my digestion," I shrug.

"Seth, what about you?" Hans asks.

"Water, if you've got it."

"You Americans!" Hans says as he trots off to the kitchen. He returns to the silence of the room with two glasses in hand. "What do you do during the day, Seth?"

"I'm a director of software for Mitel."

Hans purses his lips and nods, as though impressed. "Their stock has been up. I hope you took a bit of your salary in stock. You'd be doing well."

"I've got a bit." Seth gives a half-smile. He has more than a bit, I can tell by his grin.

"Sounds like you're doing well for yourself." Hans stands suddenly. "I've got to turn those kabobs over. Ashley, why don't you come out so we can talk shop? Seth seems interested in hearing more about Sophia's art."

Reluctantly, I step out onto the small patio. Subtle lighting illuminates a lion's-head fountain and gleams on the water pouring from its mouth. I suddenly think of Daniel and the lions' den. The heat of the BBQ hits me, and I feel like Meshach heading into the fiery furnace. My heart begins to pound. Hans turns around, his handsome face lit by the fountain's glow.

"I've booked us on a flight for Tuesday," Hans says.

"But I told you, I have to—"

"Meet with the preacher?" Hans laughs.

I feel the sting of tears in my nose. "I *am* marrying Seth."

Hans looks down to the stamped concrete. "Of course you are. But you're going to be general counsel first. You can play the wife anytime. Seth is in no hurry. I can tell."

"Don't placate me, Hans. What does that mean, that I can play the wife anytime? Does that mean you expect something in return for my promotion?"

Hans laughs aloud. "Do I look like the sort of man who needs to expect anything, Ashley?"

Well, he's got me there. "No, but I don't understand your sudden interest in a general counsel."

"I'm not going to lie to you; I find you incredibly beautiful. Stunning, in fact. Is that what you want me to admit?"

I cross my arms. "And?"

"And it has nothing to do with you being the sharpest patent attorney I've ever met. I can explain a technology to you, and boom, I know right away what the chances for patenting it are. That kind of information is the key to rising stock." Hans lifts the lid on the BBQ. "Beautiful women are a dime a dozen. Good patent attorneys are a needle in the haystack. I don't know why more CEOs don't realize that, but when you control the patent, you control the technology. And with twenty years in this business, the product is obsolete by the time you lose the patent." He points the BBQ tongs at me.

"So why do we have to go on Tuesday, if I'm so quick? Can't I be quick after Tuesday?"

"I have a meeting there with some Chinese nationals, and I want you with me. You know how the Taiwanese and Chinese feel about canceling meetings. What is so important here that it can't wait?"

I look back at Seth in the house, who's trying to stay as far away from Sophia as possible. "I have something special planned for Friday."

"Then you have to make a choice, Ashley. I understand you're young, and you've never been through marriage before, but success is what lasts, Ashley. It lasts, and it's security in the bank." He looks in toward Seth and then back at me. "You're going to gamble on something that may never happen, and I'm offering you the opportunity to make it happen for yourself."

So why does it make me feel so terrible? "I'm not like Sophia, Hans. I want to be a wife and mother. I'm not content to be slaving over patents for the rest of my life."

"Only because you haven't been a wife yet."

"Why do you have so much against marriage? Won't you marry Sophia?"

Hans laughs. "I'll never get married again. Marriage is like cutting an open wound and allowing it to bleed until you're drained completely. I've got no more blood left to give. Unless they call in the Red Cross, I'm permanently off the market."

"Sophia seems to feel the same way, judging by her artwork." I stand and stare at him before crossing my arms.

"I guess you could say we're soul mates then. Who says opposites attract?"

"You two need Jesus. You'd feel more hope if you viewed the world from a different standard. And that's all the preaching I'm going to do." I lean against the brick wall.

"Good thing about your preaching, because it's illegal to proselytize in the workforce."

"No, it's not. Only if you're in a position of authority over an employee and they don't want to discuss it. Sexual harassment, however, is illegal."

He laughs. "Fair enough." Hans takes the kabobs off the BBQ.

"How did you know I wasn't really engaged?" I ask, knowing it's completely futile to pretend that Hans doesn't know I lied like a rug.

He hands me the plate full of kabobs. "In my lifetime, I've learned one or two things about women."

"That doesn't answer my question."

"It does if you think about it. I don't want to be accused of harassing you." He winks and closes the top on the BBQ. "You're too smart to be married to Seth, Ashley. He doesn't understand your complexities. Take my word for it and save yourself the heartache." He holds two fingers up and speaks, like he has a cigarette in his hands. "And that, my dear, is free advice."

"You're too smart to avoid listening to God. Take *my* word for it." I point at him. "Right back atcha on the free advice."

Hans smiles at me and winks, and we enter the living room, where poor Seth looks comatose. His eyes are glazed over, and I'm wondering when the last time he blinked might have been. "Hi, Seth, did you get the gallery tour?"

"Bon appétit!" Hans grabs the platter from me and puts the food on the table, where Sophia has set out her pesto and beautiful crystal goblets. He tries to pour us all wine and smiles when he passes our glasses. He fills Sophia's to the brim, and she chugs it down like grape juice.

She takes the bottle from him and pours herself another glass. "Seth was telling me he does software. I have no idea what that means, but I'm assuming it's computer stuff. You three would have quite the conversation if I'd let you, but I won't." Sophia flips her long dark hair behind her back and gives Hans a heated look. "Let's talk about something interesting."

My mind reels. What is interesting to the enigmatic Sophia? The beauty queen with wicked art taste. "I don't want to talk about software either, Sophia. I live computers all day long. Sometimes all night long. What shall we discuss?" I ask excitedly.

"Puppies. I love puppies," Sophia says. "I like little black ones, and cozy, furry brown ones. Puppies of all sorts."

I start to laugh, but I quickly realize she's not trying to sound like Cruella DeVil. I clear my throat. "Yes, puppies are wonderful."

"Do you really think so, Ashley?" Seth asks.

"Of course I do. What kind of person doesn't like puppies?"

"I'm just glad to hear you say that. I wasn't sure if you were a pet type of person."

"I like kittens, too." Sophia says. We all look at her like she's Rainman.

"Yes, well, Ashley, what do you think of Gainnet so far?" Hans says.

"I think I'm getting the hang of it. I think we'll have some key patents in place by early next year."

"That's what I like to hear. Seth, you picked a winner. When's the wedding?"

I give Hans the evil eye, as much as I can master without Seth noticing. "What kind of puppy would you want, Ashley?" Seth asks.

"A cute little one. Something that could come with me to work in a great handbag, and hide under my desk."

"That won't work while you're in Taiwan," Hans points out. "We'll be making at least three trips to Taiwan in the next three months."

Three trips. That's one a month! "I have nowhere to keep a dog, Hans. I'm renting."

"But I thought you were buying part of Kay's house?" Seth asks.

"I thought so, too," Hans chimes in.

Suddenly, the men in my life have such great recall. "I haven't actually made up my mind yet on that." We down BBQ as we talk, and I feel like I've probably got it all over my face, and I'm trying to be dainty while licking my fingers. There's more chattering, and my attention is drawn back to Hans.

"We're leaving for Taiwan on Tuesday. Did Ashley tell you that?" Hans asks Seth.

"But . . ." Seth begins to protest. "I thought . . ."

"I never agreed to leave on Tuesday. Seth and I have plans that were made in advance of this trip for Friday. Don't we, Seth?"

Hans continues, "I'm sure that was before he knew about your impending general counsel position. Did she tell you about that, Seth? That I'm talking to the board on her behalf."

Seth's lips mold into a straight line and the blue in his eyes has darkened visibly in the candlelight. "I had a bit of a party planned for her Friday night, Hans. She's been working very hard lately."

"You can have the party when she gets back. She'll be back on Saturday, and at that point she'll be able to celebrate that she's general counsel," Hans says, and serves up more French bread.

Seth puts his napkin on the table and pushes his chair out with a squeal. "If you'll excuse me . . ."

"I told you we should talk about puppies!" Sophia says, and she, too, stomps away.

I've never seen Seth lose his cool before. It's a fascinating dance to watch, and for a brief moment, I believe I even saw jealousy in his eyes. How is that possible exactly? That he can avoid being alone with me for weeks, and then get angry that I should dedicate myself to work, or to buying a place of my own? I mean, what exactly are my options?

"We'd better go. Hans, thank you for having us, and please give our appreciation to Sophia. Her pesto was lovely."

I follow Seth out the front door, and see Hans standing in the hallway, the light outlining his muscular physique. He's got a smile all the way to his eyes, and I'm left to scramble after my boyfriend like the beggar I have become.

"Seth, wait for me! You're walking too fast."

"I'm moving too fast?" He slaps himself on the chest. *Yeah, go figure; never thought I'd say that. "I'm* moving too fast? Hans seems to be
moving pretty quickly and I don't hear you complaining."

"What's that supposed to mean? I tried to tell you, and . . ." I
look down at my hands.

"Friday night. I have everyone coming over to my place. This surprise for you was something I worked on for a long time, but your job
has ruined that too. It's all about your job."

"My job? *My* job?" I can barely contain my anger. "You, who
work 24/7, have the nerve to pick on my job? What am I supposed
to do, Seth? You think it's a good idea for me to buy part of Kay's
house. What do you think that tells me? You practically laugh when
I tell you Hans is interested in me in *that* way, and yet when I make
a move to get out of that position, to actually become a general counsel, you're mad at me because I have to change my schedule. I don't
understand you, Seth." I stop walking after him here. "I guess I'm not
meant to."

Seth steps forward, and I feel his closeness to my toes. As angry
as I am, this man moves me like I'm his rag doll. He brings his hands
around my face. "I don't know what I want, but Ashley Wilkes
Stockingdale, I care about you and I don't like to see you treated
that way."

Which I find really odd, because doesn't he treat me "that way"
too? I don't have time to think about it. He kisses me in the dead of
the November night, and I'm pulled into the moment, but I don't feel
anything. I feel numbness, like someone who's been hit too many
times and ceases to feel the pain.

Hans is still in the doorway when Seth and I separate, the two of
us looking like pathetic high schoolers, kissing on the sidewalk. I can
hear Brea chanting in my ears: *Never kiss by the garden gate. Love is
blind, but the neighbors ain't.*

9

As I stand in front of my house in the darkness and watch Seth's taillights disappear around the corner, I suddenly remember a few words scribbled in my history. When I was in college, there was a poem written in graffiti, along the several campus columns I passed on my route home. It was written in chalk, but stayed there for years, probably because the janitor was a romantic at heart. The poem read:

> *I wish to*
> *Make a lot of money*
> *With which to*
> *Buy her cute shoes.*

So it's not Yeats, but there's something about that sentiment that has stuck with me through the years. What is more personal, more romantic, than quality footwear for your loved one? And Seth is never going to buy me shoes, because to him, it's like buying me jewelry, which he has no use for either. It defies the practical and enters the realm of romance. And romance is one thing he has become an expert at avoiding.

If you follow this equation to its natural end, he's never going to marry me because he cannot imagine giving up the practical for the sake of furthering our relationship. He's satisfied with that red stop sign at each corner of our courtship. And I'm not.

I'm not. And there it is. Could this be the first time I've thought about what I wanted in this relationship?

Seth supposes that I'll be happy with our junior high going-steady gig for a lifetime. Marriage gets in the way of his life, and he's not willing to share that part of him. Giving up Seth is starting to feel like giving up any other unhealthy addiction. I love him, but he might not be the best thing. When Seth kissed me, he wriggled uncomfortably, kind of like the spider the old lady swallowed. I don't inspire romance in the man; I inspire fear. And that's just not good enough for me.

I'm beginning to view the world slightly differently. I can't help but wonder: If I cleared Seth out of the way, would God bring me something better? Could he bring me something where I didn't feel so desperate and tentative? I mean, insecurity is not a natural state, is it?

Kay is in the kitchen making candles when I arrive home, and the house smells like cinnamon-spice-scented wax. She peers up over the deep red liquid she's pouring. "Did you have fun at Hans's house?"

I shrug. "I guess."

"Well, that sounds convincing. You should have stayed home and made candles with me. I invited the singles' group, but they decided to see a movie instead. In the meantime, I'll be ready for Christmas while they're scrambling at Macy's to get the last of the preseason holiday candles."

"I've decided to buy part of the house," I blurt, looking straight at Kay. "If that's still all right, of course."

"You have?" She stops pouring wax and thrusts a fist to her hip. "Why? Is this some emotional outburst you're going to resent tomorrow?"

"No." But part of me wonders. "Well, I don't think so anyway. I'm not backing out, regardless. I've waited around long enough, don't you think? I can't put my life on hold forever."

"What if Friday is about an engagement, Ashley?"

"What if it's not? I don't want to make every decision based on my romantic aspirations. It's pathetic. Here." I hand her the contract she gave me weeks ago. I've been carrying it around in my purse while I contemplated the future. "I'm serious this time. It's signed. We can have it notarized tomorrow after church."

"Are you sure you want to do this?"

"I'm so sure. And I haven't told you how appreciative I am of you, that you would offer it. You're a fabulous friend, Kay. This house will force me to keep the job at Gainnet and make it work until I'm general counsel. I need real motivation. I seriously need to stop living in this dream world."

"You're one driven person, Ashley. Does this mean you're calling Dr. Kevin?"

"It means I've given up on romance as an escape route. Whenever I feel a craving coming on, I'm going to run to the Bloomie's shoe sale and avoid men like the plague. If you still love the shoes when the credit card bill comes, you know true satisfaction. The idea that I'll ever feel that way about a man is laughable."

"You could get out your Bible," Kay suggests. "It sounds like your theology is a bit off, if you don't mind my saying so."

"Are you about to give me the contentment sermon? Because I could throw it right back for the granite countertops and travertine bathrooms, you know. Your lack of contentment is feeding mine." I smile, and we start to giggle.

Kay goes back to pouring the blood-red mixture. "Touché."

"Ah, I'm sorry, Kay. I don't mean to jump at you. You deserve the kitchen of your dreams." There's pumpkin-spice bread on the counter, and it's calling my name. I'm trying to do the Atkins diet, but it's the holidays. And Kay bakes. And the flesh is weak. "Can I have some of this?"

"Go ahead." She offers me a knife and a napkin. "So what did Hans think of Seth?"

"Doesn't think he's worth my career," I answer with my mouth full. "Hans has his own motives though, since he still wants me to fly to Taiwan on Tuesday. But I worked it out. I'm going Saturday morning."

"You don't think Seth is going to propose, do you?" The way she asks the question is more like, *You're not inane enough to believe Friday's the day, are you?*

"Why do you ask?"

"No reason, but I don't get your boyfriend. Let's put it that way."

I gobble down the last crumbs of Kay's mouthwatering spice bread, ignoring any and all Atkins ambitions, and say good night. I walk into my bedroom, which is strewn with the many outfits I debated before I left tonight. I look in the mirror over my dresser, and there's a photo of Seth and me, dressed up for the Harvest Fair at church in our jeans and plaid shirts. I take the photo down and study it. I'm struck by the thought that we don't look happy. We look uncomfortable. Maybe even a bit suspicious.

I've wasted nine months and how many great outfits on the wrong man. Arin is back now, and perhaps that's God's timing. Maybe she'll inspire romance in the man. As for me, I'm a bigger person for about two seconds, then the claws come out. *I hope their babies look like rain-forest monkeys and call Arin back to her previous missionary lifestyle.*

I look around my room at the crisp white crown molding and the bright sunflower paint against the mix of antiques and Pottery Barn furniture. You know what? I have great taste. This room makes me happy. Seth just makes me nervous.

That night after my brother's wedding, when Seth came and swept me off my feet, I thought it would last forever. Now I'm pretty sure that nothing lasts forever except Jesus, and in the earthly realm, I'm better off with the solid foundation that is Palo Alto real estate. Authentic woodwork, and original hardwood floors, and a desirable zip code—be content in all circumstances, as Paul reminds us in the

Bible. So I flop on my bed and put my hands behind my head. *I'm content, I'm content,* I tell myself until I fall asleep.

Friday, after a day of not really being at work mentally and getting ready for Taiwan the next day, I arrive at Seth's condominium anxious for my surprise, but cautious. I'm very cautious, unsure of what my answer will be if the question does turn out to be about marriage. The last time Seth "surprised" me was on Valentine's Day, when I got a Lucite paperweight with a Scripture quote written inside it. Now my heart is pounding as I knock at the door. I'm dressed like I'm ready for anything, in an Ann Taylor tweed skirt with a chocolate suede blazer, so I can be considered casual or elegant depending upon what the moment calls for.

Seth answers the door wearing holey jeans and a Stanford sweatshirt. Not a good sign, and I feel my smile evaporate.

"Hi," I say as enthusiastically as I can manage.

"Hi, yourself. Are you excited?" Seth asks.

"Should I be?"

"I think so. I waited weeks to find you the perfect match, and I've found it."

"That's very cryptic."

"All the better to surprise you with, my lady." He takes my hand, and helps me slip out of my suede jacket, which he hangs up in the closet.

"Is anyone else here yet?"

"Brea and John were waiting for the babysitter to get there. Kay's on her way. I also invited Sam, Kevin, and Arin. I hope you don't mind."

I think my heart just stopped. "You invited Kevin and Arin?"

"That's okay, isn't it?"

"Since I don't know what the surprise is, I guess I don't know the answer to that question."

The doorbell rings. It's Sam. Sam is big, burly, and constantly worried about where his next meal is coming from. Especially when he doesn't have to pay for it. "Hey, Ash." He nods a chin my way. If he was smaller, I'd check him for furry feet to see if he was a hobbit. "What's for dinner, big guy?" Sam asks Seth.

"I'm ordering pizzas."

Half of us are on Atkins, but I don't mention that. Let's all just have a gluten fiesta because I have a feeling carbs are going to be the least of my problems tonight.

Kevin is the next to arrive, and he's got a bouquet of peach-colored roses. "For the guest of honor." He holds them out toward me and winks as I take them. Our gazes catch, and I pull mine away. Like the good, almost-engaged girl I am.

"Thank you," I say, as I take the roses, careful to avoid further eye contact. "You must own stock in a florist." Eye contact is very dangerous with a man who looks like Hugh Jackman and talks like a romantic lead. Kevin fulfills all my romantic fantasies, but none of my practical realities. He's too perfect, and I think he's looking for a breeder rather than a mate. This scares me and my astounding SAT scores: Chivalry is to men in Silicon Valley like manners are to the straight guy on TV.

Kay comes to the door next, and she's wearing a dress. Go figure. I never knew she owned one. She takes one of her pumpkin-spice loaves and hands it to Seth. "I thought you might like this for dessert."

"Forget dessert, breakfast for me. You all get your own," Seth says, his blue eyes sparkling with mischief. He is really in his element here, and whatever he has in store for me, it has him giddy. I haven't spent much time around a giddy Seth, and it's disconcerting, but kinda cute too.

Brea and John finally arrive, and she looks like *she's* expecting an engagement ring. She's wearing Lilly maternity cords and a hand-painted top around her bulging belly. As usual, she's gorgeous. Arin hasn't shown, and most likely she's too busy flirting with some non-believer somewhere to grace us with her presence.

"Hey!" Brea's smile dies the moment she notices Seth's sweatshirt. "Seth, are you dressed for the occasion?"

He looks down at the Cardinal-red letters emblazoned across his chest. "I'm dressed for anything. Stanford rules!" He lifts his arms up. "Okay, everyone, I know you're dying to know why I've asked you all here." He does a little dance with his legs. "I can't wait to tell you!"

Seth reaches for me and looks into my eyes. "Ashley, we've been dating for some time now, and in that time, I've heard you mention more than once that the quiet of your house is driving you crazy. That you longed for some companionship and excitement."

I shake my head slightly to imply the rudeness aimed at Kay here, but Seth doesn't get it. He just keeps blabbering.

"Come on, what's this about, Greenwood?" John asks.

Yeah, what's this about, Greenwood?

"Okay, wait here." Seth runs to the back room of his condo, and comes out with—no, it is definitely not a black velvet box. It has two eyes, a wet nose, floppy ears, and it's wearing a blue bow. "I looked forever to find you a purebred boxer; that's why I had to cancel the last time, but then I found this guy at the pound, and he has a little boxer in him. He's part terrier, too, and they assured me he'd be no bigger than fifteen pounds." He looks at Kay. "I hope this is all right, Kay, but I just knew Ashley needed someone to keep her company."

Someone, Seth. Someone. And what's Kay, raw beef?

He thrusts the puppy at me. "What do you think?"

Searching for words here. "I don't know if I can take a pet. I'm leaving for Taiwan tomorrow," I stammer.

"That's the best part. I'll take him when you're gone. This is a no-brainer, Ash. You'll see." He hands me the puppy, and I feel the tears welling as I hold this precious puppy. He's warm and quivering slightly. His sad, brown eyes look lost and abandoned, and I see he's familiar with pain too. Maybe we have more in common than I thought. It takes everything within me not to burst into tears. *A dog.*

He bought me a dog. Our commitment is not marriage, but duel custody of a puppy.

Kevin comes besides me, puts the flowers aside, grabs my hand and squeezes, and I feel a tear escape. *No, no, please don't show me any kindness. I will definitely lose it.* Brea knows me well, and that's why she won't look at me.

I pick up the puppy, and he licks my face and settles into the crook of my arm. I wish everyone wasn't here staring at me for my reaction because I want to take this dog and just be done with the whole human aspect of my life. I cuddle close against him, trying to forget where I am.

"He's gorgeous." I finally say, and everyone breaks into applause, which scares my little puppy and I tighten my grip so he'll know he's safe.

Brea's eyes are filled with liquid, and she's shaking her head. John is holding her by the elbow. I fear for Seth. If she had a blunt object, he might really be in danger here. She moves closer to Seth, with John at her heel. "Did you really buy Ash a dog without asking her?" she demands.

"I adopted it from the pound. Isn't he perfect? Look, they already love each other."

The puppy and I are clinging to each other for life, unsure of the foreignness surrounding us. Kevin approaches me again. "The dog is sweet, Ashley. The kids at the hospital will love him if you ever want to bring him by."

I look at Kevin and feel tears running down my cheeks.

"I think the puppy needs some fresh air." Kevin opens the door and yanks me out onto the walkway.

I can't speak for a moment, then I look at the dog, and my true feelings burst forth. "How could I be so stupid?"

Kevin's jaw tightens. "Why do assume it's *you*, Ashley?"

"I should have known. Why didn't I know, Kevin?"

He places his hand upon my cheek, and wipes away the tears.

"Because sometimes it's easier to pretend." He picks up the puppy. "Let's go back in. Don't let him see you fall apart."

I nod and straighten my shoulders, opening the door. Kevin deposits the puppy in the foyer, and waves good-bye, offering me a last look of support . . . and disgust.

"Don't you want to stay for pizza?" Seth asks him.

"No, and Ashley's on Atkins; order her a salad." With that, Kevin leaves and I wish I were going with him.

Brea and John are next. "It's a cute puppy, Ashley," Brea says quietly. "Call me." Those are her actual words. But what she's really just said is, *"Kill him, Ashley, and then call me and tell me the grisly details."*

Kay looks disgusted too. "See ya at home. Considering our hardwood floors, I don't know where you're going to put that thing." The door slams behind her.

So now, it's just Seth, me, the puppy, and Sam waiting for free pizza. You know, I guess I knew it wasn't an engagement party, but why did it have to be a public humiliation in front of everyone I'm close to? I could have done without that. I hand Seth the puppy.

"Thanks, but I don't think I can keep him," I say, sorry I'm taking my anger out on the poor innocent animal.

Seth has rejection written all over his face. I want to ask him how it feels. At least all his friends weren't here to witness it like mine were. Only Sam, and his sole concern is extra sausage. I exit without my Ann Taylor suede jacket, but with my dignity intact. For the moment.

10

I'm haunted as I drive away from Seth's, not just by guilt and Seth's devastated expression, but by those big, brown puppy eyes peering up at me and the immediate connection we made. It's as if the dog's licking my cheek sealed the deal. I can still see his white socks against the rust and black of his coloring. He is so tiny. *He needs me.* That is *so* my dog. I turn my car around on a dime and squeal back to Seth's door. I can hear my heels clicking as I run up the walkway, which only reminds me how great I dressed for this nonoccasion. What a waste.

I pound on the door, and Seth opens it with crossed arms. His bright blue eyes are clouded, and I feel like he can barely look at me. It's as though I have rejected his firstborn.

"I've changed my mind," I say. "Can I have my dog now?"

"Oh, so it's your dog now?"

"Yes."

"I don't want to give him to someone who doesn't appreciate him."

But my puppy comes bounding out and nips at my ankles, and I pick him up and place his warm face against my cheek. "See, he knows who he belongs to. Hewo baby."

"Do you want to know his name?" Seth asks with his hands on his hips.

"His name? He has no name yet. I'm naming him."

"His name is Bounder, according to the shelter."

"No, his name is . . ." I lift him up and his little legs scamper for security, and I gently place him back into the crook of my arm. "His name is Rhett Butlah. He has that Clark Gable look, don't you think? Handsome, romantic, and masculine . . ." Rhett and I Eskimo kiss to seal the deal.

"Rhett Butler?"

"Not Butler, Butlah, so you get the whole southern thing going on. Get it?"

Seth's got that confused look. "I think being named Ashley Wilkes and having a dog named Rhett Butlah is a little over the top, don't you?"

"If you had gotten me a girl, it would have made more sense to call her Scarlett. Then Ashley and Scarlett would have finally been together." Rhett licks me again. "But I don't want any old girl. I want Rhett." I coo and am rewarded with a wet snuggle into my neck. If this don't beat all. Why was I trying so hard to get married when a dog was exactly what I was looking for all along?

Sam comes lumbering in to the foyer and shows his disappointment that I'm not the pizza man. "You're taking the dog now? Thought he wasn't good enough for you?"

"It's my dog," I say with simplicity.

"You didn't act like you wanted it. Seth's been looking for just the right dog for weeks now and you were ungrateful."

Yes, well, Seth should have been looking for diamonds, but he's forgiven.

"I didn't think I wanted a pet. Too much responsibility and all that. It's generally good to give a girl time to get used to an idea. With my new job I never know when exactly I'll be home."

"Well, if you can't handle a dog, how are you going to handle a kid? That's what Seth wanted to know, and it looks like he's got his answer."

Seth socks Sam in the arm and I'm glaring at both of them.

"You're testing me? Rhett is just another test?"

"No, I'm not testing you. I've just never really seen you with a baby, well, besides Miles occasionally. Do you even want kids?"

My eyes are tearing up, and this makes Rhett whimper. "Why didn't you ask me, if you wanted to know my thoughts on children? It seems a straightforward question when you've been dating me nine months." *What if it turns out I can't have kids*, I think. *What then?* "I can't make everything perfect for you, Seth. I'm not perfect."

"It wasn't about that, Ashley."

"There are no guarantees in life, Seth. I don't come with a warranty. You can't kick my tires, and I can't assure you that I'll be rich, healthy, or thin for the rest of my life." I turn on my heels with Rhett tightly clasped.

"Ashley, wait." Seth reaches for my arm, and when our eyes meet, mine are filled with tears, but I'm not feeling sad. I think rage would be a better word.

"How could you do this to me?" I look back at Sam, who seems quite pleased with himself. Getting his buddy back for free pizza and burritos is all he cares about. Me? I'm dispensable.

"I don't want a guarantee." Seth is shaking his head frantically. "But I want to know that we're going to work. I don't want to invest in this and have it fall apart."

Sam is polishing off a bag of chips, watching us like we're the evening sitcom.

"Do you mind, Sam? This is kind of personal," I say, putting Rhett down at my feet.

Sam shrugs and falls onto the couch and clicks on the TV with one fluid movement.

"Rhett is as much of a commitment as you can make, isn't he?" I ask Seth. "When Kay offers me part of her house, it's more than you're willing to do, and she's just a Christian sister, Seth."

Seth clasps his eyes shut. "I don't want to get married, Ashley."

Hah! I knew it. "I'd make a terrible husband and a worse father. My dad shipped us off to an all-boys English school while he preached in China, and I don't know the first thing about women. I keep trying to blame you or find faults in you because it's easier, but it's my problem, and it isn't getting fixed. Not even for you, and I love you, Ashley."

I can't breathe. I love Seth, but he doesn't fear being a bad husband any more than I fear being a bad wife. But this is about him. This is about him giving up freedom and autonomy and the ideal woman that he thinks might still be waiting for him. *Bad husband, my bum!*

It never dawned on my woefully neurotic mind that it might not be me with the mental issues. Maybe it should have. Maybe that's what Kevin had been trying to tell me all along. A marriage won't fix Seth. And I'm not going to be one of those nursemaid women who spends her life whining about the mistake she made. I can do that single.

"I don't know what to say, Seth." *No, I do know what to say. But what I want to say is that we can get married and work it all out. How stupid is that? So much for higher education.* "I'll never be perfect, and you'll never be happy until you get over this fear. That's fine if you're happy with this life." I nod toward the permanent couch ornament of Sam. "I suppose we need a break. Maybe you could talk to Pastor Romanski and see if there's anything worth fighting for."

"Counseling? I don't have a problem, Ashley. You're the one with the problem." *Oh, trust me.* "I just don't want to get married because I'm just not sure this," he motions his hand between the two of us, "is right."

I look at Sam, whose looking at the TV like a zombie. I just nod. I can't think of a thing to say that I won't regret.

The doorbell rings, and Seth takes out his wallet to pay for the pizza, but it's not a delivery man. It's Arin, and she tosses her long blonde ringlets to announce her cuteness. "Hi!" She steps in the door.

"I'm sorry I'm so late, but I got caught up in this Italian movie playing over at Camera III." *Camera III is for those who like to be tormented by French subtitles.* "Who died in here? You all look so sad."

Rhett starts to growl, and Arin looks down as a puddle appears beside her off-season flip-flops.

"That's my dog." *Who obviously shares my good taste in people.* "Seth bought me a dog to keep me company."

I look at my ex-boyfriend's gorgeous blue eyes, and they don't touch me like they normally do. My body doesn't react physically at the sight.

Seth has a rag and some cleaning solution at the ready. *That's definitely not a good sign. Perhaps my puppy has potty issues.* Seth runs into the nearby guest bathroom and washes his hands.

"Why don't you stay and have pizza with Sam, Arin? He's in the living room." Seth nods toward the sheet glass window. "Ashley and I are going out." Seth grabs my suede jacket and puts it around my shoulders. "Sam, will you take Rhett out in a half an hour? Don't wait up."

He slams the door behind us, and then he kisses me. He kisses me like he's never kissed me before. Without fear, without trepidation, without the false belief that I have cooties.

"What was that about?"

"Marry me, Ashley."

"What?"

"Marry me." I have waited how long to hear these words? And yet, it's nothing like I hoped for. There's not an ounce of romance in them. It's like Seth has succumbed to his fate and is willing to be sacrificed.

"You know, I don't think you mean that." Now, I'd like to think Seth has turned into an outrageous romantic, but my fear is that he's only trying to prove something. Prove he *can* get married, and that he *can* commit and he's not like the other Reasons. I don't think he *is* like the other Reasons, but he's not like this either. "With regard to commitment, I think it's better not go cold turkey on this one." I crinkle my nose at him, and he presses a kiss there.

"You don't think I *can* get married," he says like we're playing *Truth or Dare*.

I picture myself standing at the front of the sanctuary alone, with only Rhett the puppy as my hero, showing up for the ceremony. All my friends crying and seething.

"This isn't *Fear Factor*, Seth. This is our life."

"You want to do Fresh Choice?" *Salad bar where Seth dumped me for Arin the first time.*

"Um, no, I don't. I'd like to celebrate Rhett." *And maybe my emancipation from you.* "Let's go somewhere nice." *Where you don't have to break out the coupon you're carrying in your wallet.*

But really, I don't want to go anywhere with Seth, and I wonder why my mouth doesn't say so. It's not like I'm the shy type. We get into his car and drive downtown. Not a word passes between us.

Once in the restaurant, a quaint little Italian place, I'm gazing across the table at Seth with the weirdest mixture of desire and anger. I mean, when I look at him, I just think he is so gorgeous, and I'm so anxious to plop those blue eyes on our future kids. And yet when I think about his fears, I just want to force him at gunpoint to the local diamond broker and run up his Visa to high heaven.

"You know," Seth says, wringing his hands like Lady Macbeth, "I may have spoken out of turn earlier."

Here it comes.

"I think it's a good idea for me to talk to Pastor Romanski first before we talk serious commitment." Seth is nodding his head, wholly agreeing with himself.

"To save you from the gallows one last time?" I mean, I thought we had broken up, but Seth hasn't arrived in this place with me yet.

"What did you say?"

"Nothing. I think that's a good idea, Seth, for you to talk to Pastor. Maybe God is calling you to the mission field." I give him yet another out, and he nods. "I signed the contract for half of Kay's house, finally." *In other words, I'm moving on.*

"You did? So you're really going to do that?"

"Can't see any reason why I wouldn't. It's a great house, great neighborhood, and soon, Rhett will think of it as home."

"Do you really like the dog, Ash?"

"I love him." *And he actually seems to want to be with me.* Our soup arrives, and Seth searches for yet another topic where we don't have to discuss the next step. I've been enabling a commitment-phobe for nine months. I can't be healthy. In fact, I'm probably worthy of my own Oprah show. And most importantly, I miss my dog.

I get up from the table, and ask the maître d' to call me a cab. There comes a day in every girl's life where she has to face the music and stop being pathetic. This is my moment.

11

Which is worse? To suspect your boyfriend is avoiding commitment, or to actually know it for a fact? At least in my ignorance, there was the bliss of possibility. The imaginings that one night (like last night for example) Seth might show up with an engagement ring and a bent knee. I laugh aloud thinking about the puppy. A puppy! I've lost a boyfriend, but gained a four-legged friend with a free dog-sitter thrown in. Not a bad arrangement really. In fact, Rhett is with Seth right now.

Getting on the plane brings such a strange sensation of emotions. Like it was good to leave the past where it belonged, but Taiwan was not really my future either. I take out my journal, and try to plan a new direction for my life.

GOALS:

1. General counsel at Gainnet by January 1.
2. Contentment as a single. (Or marriage proposal that isn't forced.)

And I'm stuck here. Not exactly *Purpose-Driven Life* kind of stuff. Maybe that's my problem, my goals aren't big enough, or aren't eternal enough in purpose. Technically, I could have the job promotion by the end of the week, and maybe that should be my goal. Then, I can think long term and more eternally. I wad up my goal sheet and shove it into my suit pocket.

Stepping off the plane in Taiwan is always a mixture of relief and dismal reality. Relief, because anything is better than a plane for eighteen hours. Dismal reality because Taiwan is, well, Taiwan. I'm sure it's a beautiful country, somewhere, but of course I never see that. I see hotels, manufacturing facilities, offices, and fancy fish restaurants.

Business travel sounds so glamorous until you actually do it. Then, it's like, London looks like Taiwan, and Taiwan looks like India, and India looks like Paducah. You stay in American-style hotels and meet with foreign businessmen. Travel implies there's some sort of adventure involved, but unless you count looking into the eyes of whatever it is you're eating, business travel has no adventure.

Once I get into the airport, I go to baggage claim. Which I don't usually do, but my enthusiasm for this trip was showing and I thought a little time checking my bag wouldn't be such a bad thing. My red suitcase is going around the carousel all by itself, with one lone black bag on the other side of the silver monster.

"Is this yours?" a sales engineer asks. How can I tell he's a sales engineer? The uniform. Software engineers (like Seth) are the geeky ones. They're the pocket-protector kings, the ones who wear nothing but free trade show T-shirts and are the butt of television jokes. Hardware engineers come up to business casual, generally going for the collared shirt with no tie and khakis or clean-lined slacks. But sales and marketing engineers are a different breed. They are the Hollywood version of engineers, savvy and intellectual, completely aware of the life around them that extends beyond video games and science-fiction movies.

"Is this your bag?" he repeats.

I nod, and he pulls it down from the carousel. "Thanks."

I'm just standing here staring at him. My eyes say, "Are you my future husband?" Like that kid's book *Are You My Mother?*

"Well, enjoy your stay." He says and jogs off, and my stomach lurches. My life is all about unmet expectations. I must have some invisible aura that says, Run men! Run away now! Don't look back!

When I get dropped off in front of the hotel, there's a jewelry store outside the front door. It occurs to me that I've sulked here before. An Israeli man runs it, and the window is sprayed with Hebrew, Chinese, and English markings. The English says, "Sale," and I assume the others do, too.

In the window is an antique sapphire-and-platinum ring, set with diamonds, and its price tag is in Yuan, which I can only imagine. Everything about it says "expensive," but I feel like that ring has a beacon calling out to me: *Have a pity party with me!* I sigh and walk to the front door of my hotel, my carry-on bag behind me.

At the hotel, the bellman takes my bags to a room that has an elegant living room with sofas, desks, and actual square footage. *Wow, traveling with the boss has its privileges,* I think for approximately two seconds before my mouth drops at the sight of a second bedroom off the suite. The door is open and someone's suitcase is sitting there open. And there's no question in my mind whose suitcase it is.

"Excuse me, but I'm not staying with anyone."

The nodding starts. "General Manager, Hans. He always get a suite, Miss."

My heart is pounding in my ears. I am in a foreign country with a man, no, check that, with a reptile who doesn't respect the rules. No, actually he respects his own rules, which are based on who knows what. My palms are sweating.

"I'd like my own room. Can you please move my things?" I hold up my credit card. "Credit card. I pay for it." I slap my chest for effect which might work if I were talking in gorilla.

"Hotel very busy, Miss. This room paid for, already." The bellman looks at me questioningly. I know it's nothing new that older businessmen travel with younger women, but I am a lawyer, not my boss's "baggage," and I want to be treated as such.

I'm here on business, and I have to make this man, who speaks very little English, understand this.

I bow, *"No*, I'm not sharing a room with a man." I wave my hands. "No man in my room."

"Dining room. Your man in the dining room."

I march downstairs, braced to knock anyone out of my way that gets in it. Hans is indeed waiting for me at the dining room. He's smiling slyly over his standard bottle of red wine, and his sideways grin makes me more than nervous. "What took you so long?"

I must give him the benefit of the doubt. "I checked my bag, and traffic was tough. Hans, there is some type of mistake. I appear to be in your room."

He shakes his head. "You're not in my room. We have a suite. You have your separate room, I have mine, but this way we can work into the night, and we don't have to be near a bed. See? No harassment here." He stretches his arms behind his head, and just the way he moves, full of confidence and bravado, makes me even more uncomfortable.

It's perfectly practical, I tell myself. *Like getting your own meeting room in the deal. Grow up, Ashley.* My mind floats back to Sophia. He's dating a supermodel. This is nothing but my overactive imagination, but then my eyes narrow. "But what if I get tired, and you still want to work?"

"Then you shut your door and go to bed, Ashley. You have your own lock. Are you afraid I'm going to pound it down?" Hans puts his hand to his mouth and rests his chin on his palm. The way he does it, so effortlessly, reminds me of a dancer. He unavoidably captures your attention.

"I know you didn't mean anything by the room, of course. But it's hardly appropriate, even with the center room. I'm a single woman. A Christian single woman, and it doesn't look right. We enter via the same doorway. I'd be mortified if my mother saw me."

"Is your mother due in Taiwan, Ashley?"

"Well, no, but it's the idea."

"I'm a single man, too," he says as he sits back in his chair, "and I'm not worried."

"I wonder what Sophia would say to that comment about your being single. I wonder what she'd think if she called the room and I answered."

He tosses a hand and calls my bluff. "She'd think you answered our phone. Sit down. You don't want to make a scene. Sophia and I are not caught up in your American idealism. We are very, as they say, modern."

Actually, I'd say amoral. "Hans, the Bible is very clear about its position on things, and that's my guide. So if you don't mind, I would prefer my own room just for my own peace of mind."

He laughs at this. "You didn't seem to have a moral issue with mauling your boyfriend on my sidewalk the other night."

My eyes slam shut. Is there anything worse as a Christian than being reminded that you acted like less than one?

"Or should I call him your fiancé?" Hans laughs.

"Hans, I may be less than stellar in my personal affairs, but that isn't about business. I can assure you I'm an excellent patent attorney, which is why I'm here. Why don't we discuss that?" I sit down at his table, and once again he tries to pour me wine. I cover my glass.

"Come on, no one will see you here. Drink with me."

"Waiter, a Diet Coke," I say, holding up my hand. "Do you have drawings on this patent?"

"I'm a flirt, Ashley, and you're a natural. Why don't you do an old man's heart good and flirt with me?" He takes his finger and loosely points up and down my figure. "No one who spends as much as you do on clothes is anything but a flirt. What's the point, then?"

"You are not an old man and you know it, and I'm no flirt. I am a very well-dressed patent attorney, and I want the general counsel position you've offered me, Hans. But I'm not going to play games."

Though, I must admit, I have very little choice at the moment. I have a mortgage now.

"I love it when you're serious with me."

"I'm going to the room. It's nine a.m. at home, and I want to call Seth and check on my dog."

"Ah yes, the boyfriend who won't marry you. Give him my very best."

He's not my boyfriend anymore. However, I'm not exactly going to advertise this to Hans. "Excuse me." I grab my Diet Coke and take it with me upstairs. The room is truly luxurious and I try to avoid thinking about the fact that I'll soon have to leave it. If Hans were the decent sort, he'd leave me the cavernous room, but then again if he were the decent sort, I wouldn't be in this mess.

I change into my yoga pants, not that they've ever seen the light of a yoga studio, but they're comfy, and *officially*, they are known as yoga pants. *Traditionally*, they are known as the sweats I eat ice cream in. I dial Seth's work number, and he answers immediately.

"Seth Greenwood." His voice sounds harried.

"Hi, Seth, it's Ashley." I straighten my shoulders. "I wanted to call and check on Rhett." *Take that, I'm not calling you. I'm calling the dog.*

"Ashley, I'm so glad you called. Hang on, let me shut my door." I hear the door kick shut, and he comes back on the line. "You're not going to believe what's happened."

"Is Rhett okay?"

"The dog's fine, but I'm not going to be able to watch him when you travel. I can probably still give him back to the pound if he's too much for you."

"What? Why?" *I thought this was a joint custody thing.*

"In case you don't want him, the pound will probably still take him back."

"No, I mean why can't you watch him?"

"When I got in this morning, they announced big layoffs. They're taking all the software jobs to India. Just leaving the bare bones here."

"Did you lose your job?"

"No. I actually gained one." He pauses for a moment. "I'm going to India to set up the new department."

"That takes a bit of time, doesn't it?" I say, as casually as possible.

"At least three months, maybe up to six."

So this is how it is. Seth is going to India. God is actually sending him on a mission so he gets to avoid marriage. How completely convenient for him.

"So when are you leaving? Will you be home when I get there?" Before he thinks it's about him, I add, "Or do I need to make arrangements for Rhett Butlah?"

"I'll find him a kennel before I go."

"He's not going to any kennel, Seth. Tell me when you're leaving. You can leave a message on my cell or e-mail me, and I'll find someone from church to help me."

"You sound upset."

"What should I be?"

"You should be happy for me. I'm going to be going out into a real mission field."

"So I guess this means you won't be talking to Pastor Romanski, huh?" Our breakup is apparently permanent.

"I don't really see the point now. God is clearly calling me to India, even if it's only a short-term mission."

"I've got to run. I've got some shopping to do tonight."

"Shouldn't we talk about this some more?" Seth asks.

"Talk about what? I think you've said it all."

"We should talk about my leaving. I feel really bad, but I couldn't know my future. I sure couldn't have planned it any better!"

I'm not letting him off the hook. No way. What was I raised for by my mother, if it wasn't to learn how to dole out a good dose of guilt? "Once, Seth, you *knew* your future wasn't in Arizona. This isn't about me. And it isn't about God and the mission field. It's never been about anything but *you*. Tell yourself you're doing the godly thing all you want. It's the cowardly thing, and I'm just thankful I'm starting to see how things really are."

"You're not mad, are you, Ashley? Why would you be mad?"

I slam down the phone and run to the elevator where I press the button about forty times. Finally, the elevator arrives, and I'm let out on the lobby floor like a spilled bag of flour.

Hans is still lingering over his wine with some beat-up crustacean legs in front of him. He looks at me oddly, and I stare down at the yoga pants I'm still sporting.

"I know, I know. Look, I'm going out for a minute. I need to get something."

Hans stands up. "Not at night. Not without an escort, and it's my pleasure." He throws his linen napkin on the table.

"Whatever." If I'm going to be officially and permanently dumped from halfway around the world, I guess I need some international retail therapy.

12

The streets of Taipei are bustling, with horns honking and people walking. It looks decidedly like home with all the well-dressed Asians and the fine selection of restaurants, but then the heat hits you, and you know you're not in California any longer.

The hot, wet, brown heat is 24/7, but it does get a little better at night when you don't have to actually visualize the air. It smells like diesel fuel and cigarette smoke, and you find yourself holding your breath without thinking. Hans is behind me, his hand pressed into the small of my back. Europeans are very protective of women, from my experience, not that I have an extensive track record, mind you.

"Thanks for coming out with me, Hans. I have to admit, I was a little worried to go by myself at night."

"Is this going to take long? We *do* have work to do, but I do understand a women's need to shop at the first inclination. Sophia has taught me well."

"It won't take long. I know just what I want. It's just a question of whether or not I can afford it."

"Things not going well with the boyfriend?"

I look straight at Hans. How does he sense this has anything to do with Seth? "No, not really. We broke up."

To me, Hans doesn't look so much German as like an athlete:

long and lean and always dressed in the best European suits money can buy. His hair is straight, yet not stringy, and it's dirty blond in color. His eyes are pale blue-green. He's probably old enough to be his girlfriend's father, but he exudes youthful playfulness. He's not threatening in the least, which is, of course, what makes him more threatening than anyone.

"I'm going to tell you something about men," Hans says. "If they don't want to marry you in the first year, they are probably not going to."

I stop walking and look at him. "I don't know anyone who gets married that quickly."

"No, no." He shakes his head. "I didn't say they *would* marry you in the first year, but they *know* by then if they're going to marry you. If a man doesn't talk about marriage and avoids the subject, he's not the man for you. If after two years, he avoids the topic altogether, he'll never commit."

There's a lump in my throat the size of a moon cake. When I'm away from home, I feel like such an idiot for my relationship with Seth. Can you even call it a relationship? I think it's more the avoidance of a relationship. I guess because I loved Seth, I just believed he felt the same way. I saw him through my eyes, which apparently badly need Lasik.

"How do you know all that about men? Do you think you speak for all men, saying that they won't marry if they don't think of it in the first year? You're not marrying Sophia."

"Precisely. I'm *not* going to marry Sophia, and she knows that, or at least she should. I don't want to marry a woman who would have an affair with a married man."

"What? What on earth do you mean? You had the affair too! And you were the married one!"

Hans laughs and starts walking again. "True, but sleeping with her and marrying her are two different things. I loved only my wife. I still do."

"That is the most sexist, rude, arrogant statement I have ever heard! I can't believe you're admitting it."

He shrugs. "I'm only being honest. You'd do well to listen to me."

"Seth doesn't think that way." *I know he doesn't think this way.* But my pulse is deafening, and I want to throttle this man for the sake of all womanhood. "He just doesn't like change, so he can't decide if marriage is for him. It's too major of a shift."

"Things aren't always the way you hope they'll be." Hans says, like some prophet of doom. "Seth's a worker ant, not the type of man that makes a difference in the world. Like I said, you're too smart for him."

"So, if you're speaking for all mankind, tell me why Seth won't marry me." I figure as long as I've got Hans here, I'll take advantage of his thought process. Maybe there's a glimpse of something here, some fragment of truth.

Hans purses his lips in a thoughtful manner and brings one hand over his mouth, with the other crossed across his chest for support. "Hmm."

"Come on, you have a theory. Out with it."

"I think he's afraid of marriage. It's got nothing to do with you. The older a man gets, the more he thinks that settling for just one woman closes his world up. In reality, your romantic possibilities get smaller as you get older, but you don't know that. You're still waiting for the supermodel."

"This coming from a man who is dating a woman who could *be* a supermodel."

"You could be a model yourself, Ashley. This has nothing to do with you not being beautiful. Your kind of beauty is renowned in Europe."

"So I'm apparently in the wrong country, is that what you're saying? I should give up citizenship for a husband? I'm certainly not renowned in America, where the world wants a size 2." I drop my head in my hands. "I can't believe I just said that. Look, this conversation is totally inappropriate. I'm sorry I asked."

We're standing outside the jewelry store now. My eyes scan the window and settle on the ring. "Are you any good at negotiating, Hans?"

"You mean haggling?"

"I guess. You see that ring right there? If I can get it for less than $2,000, I want it."

"Done. Pretend to shop and let me handle things. Let's go." Hans escorts me into the jewelry store, and my mouth goes dry.

I feel so small buying my own ring, so insignificant. Yet I need to be strong and take control of my own destiny. I need to make a statement that I'm okay with being single. Still, somewhere in the background I think I can hear my brother cackling that I had to buy my own diamond, the so-called *right-hand ring*. Not to mention my mother. What would she say? *Oh Lord, help me.* But the Lord has nothing to do with directing my visit to an expensive foreign jewelry store. Only my fears and insecurities.

I hear Hans turn on his full German accent. "I'd like something for the lady. Something under a thousand dollars." The jeweler takes out a dove gray velvet tray with several rings upon them. All of them plain. All of them gold. None of them are going to calm my broken heart. Hans shakes his head. "Thanks for your time."

"Wait," the seller says in perfect English. "I have just the thing." He takes out another tray, this one with gemstones and jade. But the ring I want is behind us, and I can think of nothing else. I absently look at the rings before me, and try to remain calm. This is too much like poker. Not that I've ever played, but it sure feels like gambling. I start to look around the store, ignoring the immense pressure I feel in my chest. For a fleeting second, there's the voice of reason that says this is stupid, that a ring is not going to solve my problems. But that little voice is quickly hushed by another glance at the platinum.

Finally, Hans walks over to the ring I want. "What about this one in the window? How much?"

"Ah, you have excellent taste. Just 136,000."

Hans shakes his head. "Do the math for me. How many American dollars?"

"Four thousand."

"Thirteen hundred."

"No, no good."

"Fourteen hundred."

He shakes his head again.

"Nineteen hundred." Hans holds up his hand. "Last price."

The merchant nods his head. "All right. You kill my business, but all right."

I slip the ring onto my finger, and it's a perfect fit. I take out my credit card and hand it to the man, who stares at Hans with disdain. Hans takes out his wallet and hands his own credit card to the man.

"Hans, what are you doing?"

"Consider it a signing bonus for taking the job."

"Hans, no. I can't do that. I cannot take gifts from a man who is not my husband. It doesn't look right. It *isn't* right."

The merchant ignores my cries and takes Hans's card.

Hans whispers, "Shh . . . you can pay me later." He shakes his head ever so slightly and I put my credit card away.

The ring is now throbbing on my hand, like Frodo's. The ring possesses too much power, and I feel sold and soiled. I slip it off into my pocket. "I won't wear it until you let me pay for it," I say as we walk out of the store.

"You go back tomorrow and buy something of equal value for Sophia. Now that you know how to do it."

"How would I know what Sophia would like?"

"She likes red and gold—flashy. Get her something red. I can't have jewelry show up on my credit card and show up with nothing now, can I?"

"Let's take it back, Hans."

But I know jewelry here is not something you take back. And

Hans just shakes his head. "That's worse! Then it looks like I didn't get my way and took the jewelry back."

Confession: I didn't think Sophia was smart enough to read a credit card statement. But I imagine when you start your relationship off on the wrong foot, it stays there indefinitely.

We enter the hotel. Hans stops and leans against the wall, crossing his arms and ankles. "I know what you think of me, Ashley, but let me tell you something: marriage is hard work. When one partner stops working, it's nearly impossible, and you don't want to enter into that with someone who won't go the distance. You need a marathon man, not a sprinter."

"Who stopped working at your house?"

"My wife left me for another man. She took the kids and went when she got tired of my long hours at the office, and I suppose my wandering eye didn't help."

"I thought you left with Sophia."

"No, basically Sophia got left with me. No green card and no work without the kids. The rest just sort of happened. We were convenient."

"It's not impossible, Hans. If you still love your wife . . ."

"I've been married twice. I'm no good at it." He waves two fingers around in his casual way. "But you . . ." His lanky forefinger comes toward me. "You've got a chance to start fresh. Start right. Start with someone who will pay you the right kind of attention. Someone who will buy you a ring out of love."

"You've got a chance, too. Jesus specializes in second chances. He really does, Hans." I tip my eyes towards the sky.

He sighs at me. "You've done your shopping. Tomorrow, you work. No more preaching."

"Fair enough. Good night, Hans."

So here I am, sitting in my private hotel room (Hans closed both sets of doors) with expensive jewelry on the nightstand, and a lump in my chest. *Why do I try to fix things? I only make it worse. Now I look like a kept woman, who's been bought with a price. I feel even emptier than when I started this trip.* I reach for the Bible in my suitcase when the work international cell phone rings.

"Hello. Ashley Stockingdale."

"Ashley, it's Seth. Are you ready to talk about my leaving?"

I inhale thickly.

"I'm ready." I sniffle. I look at the ring on my nightstand and am suddenly faced with all my lost dreams. Perhaps they were pathetic in nature, but dreams aren't supposed to make sense. Like that shoe one, for instance.

"You didn't give me a chance to explain," Seth accuses.

"I think I did."

"Ash, I wanted to invite you along," he says, and I gasp an exhilarated sigh, when he continues. "There's patent work there too. They really need help in their telecommunications areas, and I think it would be a good experience for you."

Hans's words come back to haunt me about Seth not wanting to marry me. He doesn't even want to sleep with me, which in this culture is more than pathetic. I wish I could forget his kisses and his warm breath in my ear at the theater. I wish I could focus on making my dreams come true with someone else. Someone who didn't have all these fears and hang-ups, not to mention the bad wardrobe. But I didn't come equipped that way. I have this fierce loyalty that snaps on me like an alligator every time. I'm basically a marionette clutched in the jaws until the alligator decides to let go.

God, You are bigger than this. Please . . . fix this.

After a long pause, I find the strength to answer him with the harsh truth. "I don't want to go to India."

"Sure you do," Seth says. "You loved working for Purvi back at Selectech, and the Indian culture is great. You love the food, the people. I don't understand."

Finally, I'm annoyed. "Seth, I can't go to India with you. What would Pastor Romanski think? This is just one more extension of being your buddy. Take Sam with you if you want company."

"Sam isn't qualified to go there."

That's it. I've got nothing to lose. "When you kiss me, do you want to be my friend? It doesn't *feel* like you want to be my friend, but I'm not a very good judge, I suppose."

He pauses before speaking, and he breathes a jagged breath. "No, quite frankly, when I kiss you I want to ravage you—all of you—which is why I err on the side of safety. Our Christian faith is more important than my desires."

But there's this thing called marriage that makes that lust legal. "You're not a priest. You don't have to live your whole life that way, you know?"

"I asked you to marry me once, Ash, and you said no."

"That wasn't really a proposal. That was more of forfeiture."

"Can we talk about this when you get home? I'm an engineer, Ash. I'm not going to do this right. Tell me what you want, and I'll do it."

"You won't be there to talk when I get home. Hans says that you would know by now if you wanted to marry me. That you don't really want to get married, and I might be the good-for-now girl."

"Hans is a fifty-year-old man who left his wife and kids for the stupid nanny. And I do mean *stupid.* He's old enough to be her father, possibly her grandfather. Are you actually confiding in him about me?"

"No, but . . ."

"Ash. I know I have a lot of issues. I grew up on the other side of the world, and things are different here. I'm not like Cary Grant in those old movies you watch. I just don't know what I want. In the meantime, you need to stop talking to Hans, and don't ever take any of his advice."

"Deal," I submit. But I have to admit, my heart is more done with this relationship than I'd like to admit. I'm tired of being second-best. I'm tired of feeling inferior and waiting like a lovesick puppy for him to throw me a bone.

Speaking of which, I hear squeals and a few yelps. "Rhett's here at work with me. Do you know how ridiculous I feel telling people my dog's name is Rhett Butlah? I'm already older and single, so you know what they think."

I start to giggle. "'Frankly, my dear . . .'"

"Come home, Ashley," he says with a heat I didn't think he could feel. "At least meet my boss and talk to him about the job."

"India smells like raw sewage, Seth."

"I'll wear cologne."

"My plane gets in at eight a.m. not this Saturday, but next." I relent. Why do I always relent?

"I'll be there."

"Good night, Seth."

"Sleep tight."

We hang up the phone, and it's settled. I am Alice on the Brady Bunch. Seth knows just which buttons to push to get me running. *Lord, if he's not the one for me, please free me. Take me out from under his spell.*

13

The fog hangs over San Francisco like a thick, woolly blanket that softens the edges of everything and blots out most of the morning's rays. The airplane's wheels touch the ground with a screech, and soon Ashley emerges from the runway, flushed from her long night's travel yet sporting a healthy pink glow. She tosses her hair back with manicured nails, and her body warms at the sight of her one true love.

Seth is standing, ankles crossed, leaning against his BMW—a brand-new 745iL. Rhett is in his arms and jumps from a dangerous height to rush and greet Ashley. She scoops up the puppy, allowing him to rain kisses upon her cheek, while she breathes in the salty San Francisco Bay air and exhales deeply.

"I'm so glad to be home," she yells over the roar of the airplanes.

"We're so glad to have you home." Seth embraces her tightly. "Rhett and I missed you with a passion. Life is not the same without you."

"I don't know what to say. I'm sure you both did fine." She giggles and twists her finger into her hair.

"No, we didn't do fine." Seth bows to one knee. "We can't manage life on our own, Ashley. We need you like a flower needs the sun." He lifts his hand to the sky. "Like the earth needs the rain. We were parched without you. Desperate and dehydrated."

"I'm here now." Ashley sinks to her knees and kisses Seth.

"Don't ever leave us again." Seth holds out a ring, a spectacular *radiant cut diamond. "Marry me, Ashley. Marry us. Don't leave us again."*

"Oh Seth—" Ashley falls into Seth's arms.

"Ma'am, can you put your seat back up? We're landing soon." A perky flight attendant jars me from the perfect dream. *Parched! Seth was parched, for heaven's sake.*

"Yeah, sure." I put the seat up and look at Hans, who is smiling in amusement. "What?"

"That Seth must be quite the hero," he says with one eyebrow raised. "You had a smile on your face that defies explanation."

I rub my face, feeling the red color my cheeks. "Never mind. Did you get any work done?"

"Tons, until you decided to have an interactive dream. It was quite entertaining. You talk in your sleep, you know."

I think this is the most embarrassing moment of my life. And trust me, that's saying something. "Don't tell me what I said. I don't even want to know. Just tell me what you think of my patent work on this trip."

"I think you're a genius. A genius who is adorable when she talks in her sleep."

"That just sounds bad. Don't say that." I take out my Bible threateningly.

"Okay, I give up. Do you promise not to preach at me?"

"You'd do well to pick up this Book yourself, but I promise not to read anything out loud, at least for now. If, that is, you promise to give up the talk about anything I do in my sleep. The glass ceiling is thick enough; I don't need rumors starting around the office."

"Very well. I'm anxious to see your friend Seth again. He must be one of those guys who compensates for his looks in other ways."

"I beg your pardon. Seth is extremely good-looking. A hottie, in fact."

"Ugh, don't say that word. You sound twelve. It reminds me of Sophia and I'm not ready to see her yet."

And I thought I made things difficult. "Do Sophia a favor, Hans. Send her home." I shove everything under the seat in front of me as I feel the plane descend further. "You never did tell me what happened to your wife. Did she marry the other guy?"

"They're living together."

"With the kids?" My fingers fly to my mouth. "I'm sorry, that's really none of my business."

"Ashley, I've taken Gainnet from a fledgling start-up to a $250 million company. Let's talk about something I've done right, okay? Even something that *you've* done right is a better topic: Sophia will love the ruby you picked for her. Thank you."

"And thank you for this." I hold up the exquisite sapphire ring. "I never could have bought it without your bartering." Though I must admit the ring hasn't brought me nearly the amount of joy I thought it would. It hasn't relieved any of the pain of Seth's long, slow rejection, and the loss of my own feelings towards him.

Hans taps my finger. "You have excellent taste. That piece is classically Renaissance. It will never go out of style. Jewelry should always be like that, never trendy. My father was a jeweler in Prague, and you have a very good eye."

"I guess it's a gift," I say. "But I thought you were from Austria."

"I am. My father was a jeweler in Prague."

All righty, then. My boss's life is more complicated than a hybrid circuit board. But I'm enjoying Hans. If it's possible to enjoy your slithering yet utterly charming boss. We have this camaraderie where we dispense with formality and just lay it on the line. I love that. I don't have to hide my Christianity in a closet, and he doesn't have to try and pretend his lifestyle doesn't offend me. Naturally, it's an affront to women everywhere for him to keep a woman he doesn't love out of sheer convenience. When Hans dies, his obituary will be about what he did—*PROFITABLE GAINNET CEO DIES.* He could be so much more than that, but I fear he'll never explore his better side.

As we descend, I'm reminded that no matter how many times I land at SFO, I hate to land at SFO. When you come in over the San Francisco Bay, you can't see anything but water. And as you get closer and closer to the water, you start to panic until the wheels touch the ground, and you suddenly view cement, which by now you want to kiss with reverence.

After a fairly quick line, we exit customs. Sophia is waiting for Hans, and comes running to him, sort of like I dreamed Seth would run to me. Of course, Seth is nowhere to be found, and even though my feelings have changed, I'm still disappointed.

By now Sophia is draped around Hans like a knit shawl. She's wearing straight-leg espresso-brown leather pants with a cashmere sweater, and she looks like she just stepped off the runway. The final touch is her gorgeous glittery lip gloss—just the thing most women wear at eight a.m.

I don't think I'll ever see Sophia the same way after this trip. I'll certainly never be envious again. Maybe she's not the sharpest knife in the drawer, but she's holding on so tightly to something *so* wrong for her. In that way, I'm starting to see that she's not that different from me. The truth is, I haven't committed my relationship with Seth to the Lord in a long time. I was always afraid the answer wouldn't be what I wanted.

Hans, meanwhile, seems completely oblivious to Sophia's presence, and it grieves me like a lost relative. Will he ever value anyone? Or will he just go through life not feeling anything because emotions hurt too much?

"I'll see you Monday, Ashley." Hans salutes me.

"Good-bye Ashley," Sophia sings out in her beautiful Italian way. "Thank you for taking care of my Hans."

I wave them both off and begin to look around for Seth. After a thorough search of the international terminal, I jog outside, secretly hoping my dream has a basis in reality, but he's not at the curb either. *Come on, Seth,* I mumble with vehemence. I turn on my cell phone and see there's a message. Punching in my code, I hear Seth's voice and my eyes close.

"Ashley, it's me. I'm really sorry, but I unexpectedly had to go to India this morning. I waited as long as I could, but it was the only flight I could catch before Wednesday. Rhett's at home with Kay, and Sam is going to pick you up. I'll call you as soon as I get in." I'm trying to make this register. *Seth is in India. He went without me. Who says you need closure?*

I drop my bags around my feet and look at the line of cabs. Hans is driving away in the company car as we speak, and I'm waiting for Sam. The big, mean, burrito-eating machine. I settle myself on my red suitcase, which substitutes as a camp seat, and I force myself not to think about my situation, but tears are coming unabated anyway. He left me. I've been under this delusion that I dumped him, but when all is said and done, Seth did the leaving.

A half an hour passes, and I'm still waiting without enough will of my own to get into a cab. Just as I'm about to force myself to stand up and move, Dr. Kevin Novak drives up in his Porsche Boxter. "I heard you needed a ride. Going my way?"

The sight of him causes more tears, and I rush toward him for a much-needed hug, but I halt in my tracks at the realization that I've been played. *Sam.* It wasn't enough for him that Seth was leaving the country. Sam had to do his best to thwart my chances for any future. Enter Kevin.

Still, I'm grateful for Kevin's appearance. I'm so desperately tired. And last time I had jet lag, I inadvertently hit a police officer with my Prada bag and ended up in the slammer. So I'm taking this ride, knowing that at least now I won't be headed for the pokey.

"Aren't you on call?" I ask him through the window.

"I worked all night instead. I thought I might have missed you. I got the call on my pager, but didn't check it until a half an hour ago. I guess Arin assumed I'd get the message."

Arin?

"We should make a great pair then. Me with jet lag, you without sleep."

"We'll stop for an espresso," Kevin says as he gets out of the car.

"Music to my ears. So how did you end up here?"

Kevin takes my bag from me. "Well, Sam got held up so he called Arin, and Arin couldn't do it, so Arin called me."

"Why didn't he just call Kay?"

"Something about a puppy and a torn rug. That's all I know." Kevin gets out of the car and opens the trunk, placing my bags in what little there is of a trunk. "I visited your puppy this week."

He opens the door for me, and I slide into what feels like a cockpit. "I appreciate this. Thanks, Kevin."

"You don't sound like you appreciate it." One eyebrow of his goes higher than the other, and I'm fascinated by his uncanny ability to mimic an actor's look.

I buckle my seat belt and stare straight ahead. "No, I really do appreciate it. It's just that I had other ideas in my head. Expectations and all that. So why did you visit my puppy?"

"One of my colleagues has this little cancer patient, and she loves dogs. Unfortunately, while she was in for chemo, her dog died at home. Her mom doesn't want to tell her, so I brought Rhett in to keep her spirits up. I didn't think you'd mind."

"No, not at all. Did she like Rhett?"

"You should have seen it, Ashley. She loved Rhett, and Rhett didn't want to leave her side. I think he's a very intelligent dog, too, because he went sniffing right where her cancer incision was. It's like he knows where she's sick."

"No kidding?" I nod my head. "I knew he was a great dog."

"That's a beautiful ring." Kevin grabs my hand. "Did you get that in Taiwan?"

I nod.

"I was going to say, I think I'd remember that."

"You remember everything, like that I am on Atkins."

"You're looking great, too. But it's my job to remember. I couldn't have gotten through med school without a memory. I remember everything, so be careful what you say. If, for example, you tell me those boots cost $400, don't try and tell me later they were $200."

I lift my foot, laughing. "They're knockoffs—$75."

"I didn't know you had it in you to bargain hunt." His smile is absolutely gorgeous. I find myself utterly entranced by his profile as I turn and face him in the car.

"The secret is to never overwhelm with an outfit. You saw my Kenneth Cole suede jacket?"

"I saw your suede. I'm not much of a tag reader."

"The designer jacket is the focus of today's outfit. If I go buying Prada boots with the jacket, then I'm like saying, 'Look at me' instead of 'Look at this great jacket, my focal point of the day.' Like any great room, a great outfit should have a focal point."

Kevin's gripping the steering wheel while he laughs. "It's frightening how you say that like it's the most normal theory in the entire world. No wonder you're a lawyer, you have that ability to justify anything."

"Justify? I'm not justifying. I'm merely saying that today the jacket is the star of the show. Tomorrow, it might be my great new handbag from Taiwan."

He's still laughing. I love how he laughs. It's with his entire being, and the fact that he finds me so entertaining gives me a ripple of pleasure. My ego needed this today.

"So are you ever going to write these fascinating theories down?"

"Absolutely. If I could write a book about fashion overkill, I'd just be doing the world a favor. I mean, Paris Hilton? Complete fashion overkill on a daily basis. She's got a great body, but let's leave a bit to the imagination, you know? Overkill. Mariah Carey? Satin is just *so* over. And she needs to invest in some undergarments the world doesn't see."

"Ashley, I have no idea who you're talking about, but my world is so much bigger with you in it." He ventures a look my way, and I see he's not teasing me. He actually enjoys my ramblings on nothing. My mind started to wander. "Ashley, did you hear me?"

"Huh?"

"I asked you if you got the general counsel job."

"Oh no. At least not yet, but Hans and I got a lot done in Taiwan. I think we're going to have a really solid team in Taipei. The better the engineers, the better the patents. The more foolproof." I look out the window. "By the way, what were Arin and Sam doing that she was too busy to pick me up?" *Seeing as how they don't have jobs and you're, like, a surgeon.*

"She's packing to go to India. Apparently, she's picturing herself the next Mother Teresa."

I gasp so deeply that poor Kevin thinks I've choked, and he whacks me on the back. *Calm. Be calm.* India is an enormous country. She probably won't even see another Caucasian, much less Seth. "She's leaving the country again?"

"She needed to find a sponsor to join up with FoodVision, and she found one."

"Only one?"

"Seth. I guess he's paying for it from his trust." He sees my face, and shakes his head. "I'm sorry, Ashley. I assumed you knew."

My head is shaking of its own volition. "What trust?"

"Seth's trust fund."

"Seth's trust. Where would Seth get a *trust?*"

"I don't know. He told Arin he'd pay for it from his trust. Actually, he announced it during Bible study last week. They both seemed happy about the arrangement."

His parents were missionaries in China. Where would he possibly get a trust? *Unless, he invented it.* I rub my temples. *I wonder if there's an award for being the most naive person on the planet? American Idiot.*

Kevin pulls the car off the freeway at nearly the first exit, and we drive into downtown Burlingame, a wealthy, elitist suburb of San

Francisco. He stops the car in front of a small roasting company, and the aroma of coffee fills my senses. "Are you hungry?"

I nod. "Yeah, I think I am."

Kevin seems to sense that I'm not all here and his brows furrow. "Arin and Seth share a vision, so Arin tells me. He has the money. She has the heart for missions." He speaks softly and covers his hand over mine. It's probably the same move he uses to tell someone a patient is dying. "It's a match made in heaven, and Ashley . . ." he looks straight into my eyes. "It's still going to be all right."

Only it's not. "I feel like such a stunningly fantastic idiot. I am a complete idiot, aren't I?"

He doesn't answer for a moment. "Did you not just relay the theory of focal point dressing?" He grins. "No one," he turns to me, and uses both hands for emphasis, *"no one* who understands the intricacies of focal point dressing is an idiot. Seth wears the Mitel T-shirt and jeans nearly every day. It's just too obvious for my tastes." Kevin shrugs and looks away with the utmost severity until he falls into laughter. "Those are the facts as we know them. I let you be the judge on where the idiocy lies."

Kevin's ruggedly handsome exterior is just that. On the inside he's soft and chewy like a marshmallow. He feels things deeply, unlike most doctors I've met, but I don't trust myself any longer. "I just want God's will." But that's not really true. I want what I want when I want it. And unfortunately for me, God's onto me.

"Seth's leaving you for a rat-infested country, Ashley."

I wring my hands together. "I work too much anyway. It was wishful thinking to try a relationship in this town."

"I work a lot too." His expression softens, and I realize he's talking about being more than friends. But no. I just got dumped. I'm on the rebound. And Kevin is too stinkin' perfect, have I not mentioned that?

"Work's a good thing sometimes," I say to avoid any relationship discussion.

He brings my hands together and clasps them in his own. "Can't you give me a moment's credit that maybe there's something here?"

But I don't want to face that. I don't want to jump off this precipice and start again. I want to hang back with Seth, where it's safe and comfortable, even though I know it's a lie. "Kevin, you could have any woman you wanted. There's not one thing settled in my life: not my job, my mortgage, my pet ownership. If you thought Arin was flaky, I'm a king-sized croissant."

"You think I know what's happening? I don't know if Stanford will keep me on. I don't know if I want to stay a pediatric surgeon. Watching all these sick children every day hurts my heart like I never imagined. I'm too soft to be a doctor. Trust me, Ash, your life's dramas don't scare me."

"Well, they should."

We all have faults, and as I look at Kevin's gorgeous façade, none of his faults are readily apparent. But then, Seth seemed a little like that too at first, but now . . . . If I fall for someone else, will I have the same results? They say that's the sign of mental illness, when you do the same thing and expect a different result. What if I spray Kevin with Ashley-repellent, too? Then what?

14

As I look at the breakfast menu, I just get annoyed. California is such a freak show. It's ten dollars a plate for ingredients like feta, tarragon, tofu, and fresh baby greens. I just want eggs. Well, really I want pancakes, and they market them like they're Atkins-approved: high-protein, whole-wheat hotcakes served with a side of fresh strawberry yogurt. Really now, can yogurt actually be fresh?

"What are you having?" Kevin's sage-green eyes peer over the top of the menu, and I have to admit they give Seth's tanzanite eyes a run for their money in decadence.

"Pancakes," I state with conviction. "With strawberries and whipped cream."

"As a doctor . . ." he says deeply.

"As a doctor, you know when to keep your mouth shut, right?"

He laughs. "No, I learned that as a son of a vain mother. Besides the fact is that you don't need to lose weight. Do you want to look like Arin?"

"Yes, actually."

"Arin looks emaciated, Ashley. You look healthy. And quite gorgeous, I might add. That's my professional opinion."

I smile to myself. They did a survey on whether men liked Renee Zellweger's look when she ballooned up for a role, or when she is emaciated and toned as she normally is. The men voted for round, though it involves a difference in cleavage, so it may not be a fat/skinny thing. And Renee is gorgeous regardless of her weight, so I guess the study actually has no take-away for me.

Kevin is still smiling at me. He's so much like Greg Wilson—the ideal of my youth. I had a crush on the redheaded Greg in high school, but he was entirely out of reach. He went to Woodside Priory, an elite prep school, lived in a mansion in Atherton, and even wore Cole Haans to youth group, though I had no idea what they were called back then. Greg Wilson was so quiet and reserved. You just knew he had so much going on inside, and you wanted a key. Alas, he stayed in his tower, and I went out with the boys who wore Nikes. I sneak a look at Kevin's shoes: *nice, good quality loafers.*

The waitress comes at this point, the point where I'm deliberating on my thighs and pancakes, and on the vision of wispy Arin on Seth's nickel in a foreign country. "Eggs over medium with a side of vegetables. Can you use olive oil for those?" I start to ask if the oil is cold-pressed, but realize I'm sounding more and more like Kay. And anal-retentive is not the direction I'm heading.

The waitress nods at me, but suddenly focuses on Kevin, and seems to realize he looks like Hugh Jackman. She sputters for a moment, then recovers. "And for you?"

"Pancakes with strawberries and whipped cream." He smiles. "Lots of whipped cream."

"Do you want the high-protein whole-wheat pancakes?" the waitress asks, and Kevin looks to me. I nod slightly.

"I sure do," he says, and the waitress goes off with a skip in her step.

"What's it like to have that effect on people?" I ask him.

"What do you mean?"

"I mean that charm that gets people to do your bidding without even asking. What's that like?"

"I don't know what you're talking about." He holds up his hand. "Excuse me, can I get a refill on my coffee?"

The waitress practically giggles and puts a tray down to bring him his coffee immediately.

"You don't notice that this kind of service is unusual?"

"They're charging $10.95 for pancakes. It ought to be good service."

I cross my arms. "You live a charmed life. How is my puppy doing?"

"Your puppy is fabulous. He's been carrying around an old T-shirt of yours that he attacked to remind himself of your scent, I suppose."

"An old T-shirt?"

"Bright lime green thing. He's ripped it to shreds."

I tap the table. "That's a Lilly pistachio tee," I look down at my hands. "It wasn't old."

I look up and Kevin makes a face. "It is now. Maybe you should teach Rhett about focal destroying."

I pretend to punch him across the table, and he grabs my fist and places the hottest kiss on my hand. He opens my palm and places one there as well, and I feel my entire body come to life. Kevin looks away and says nothing about the kiss as he places my hand gently back onto the table.

"The décor here is really fabulous." Kevin says. "I need to hire a decorator, or at least that's what my mother tells me. She says my house looks like *Trading Spaces*—after Hilda's been there. Do you like decorating?"

Kevin's townhome would be a dream to decorate. The singles went there for movie night. It's got great coffered ceilings in the dining room and simple crown molding everywhere else, a granite kitchen, but absolutely no wall color besides white. And the furniture? He's obviously inherited classic pieces from his mother, but against the white, it all appears way too Ikealike. "You need some color. Doesn't it bug you to be in a white box? Colors make you feel. Bright yellow? Happy! Red? Sensual. Blue? Carefree and relaxed. Green?

Calm. Whenever I've been to your place, I've wanted to come in wielding a paintbrush."

"So why don't you?" He shrugs. "You could paint it whatever color you think I'd like. I trust you."

"You seem like a midnight-blue guy to me. You know, deep and strong like the night sky."

He starts to growl and we both start to crack up. "So, what else did Rhett do while I was away?"

"Let's just say Bible study wasn't the same with your puppy joining us."

"So Kay's had the puppy since Wednesday?"

"Seth's been working around the clock. Kay felt like she had to take care of him because Seth almost took him back to the pound. I had Rhett a couple nights after I took him to see Brianna."

"Brianna's the little girl with cancer?"

Kevin nods. "You'd love her, Ashley. She's just got the fire of life in her, and I just feel with my whole heart she's going to beat it. She's not my patient, but we've all fallen in love with her on the ward."

"Small wonder. She sounds fabulous. I'm sorry about Rhett being so much trouble. I guess I should have admitted that having a dog is too much for me. Kay's going to kill me when I get home. Why didn't you tell me before that Rhett's been with her that long?"

Kevin focuses on a Howard Behrens painting. "Kay *is* going to kill you." Then he looks straight at me. "But if I told you, I wouldn't be having breakfast with you right now. Would I? I'm no fool. My mama didn't pay for a fancy education for nothing."

I start to laugh. "Charming me is not fair. You realize that I'm very impressionable. That I've just been dumped for a promotion."

"For now." Our meals come, and Kevin takes my hand. "Let's pray. Dear heavenly Father, we just praise you for this time together. For Ashley's safe trip home, and for her possible promotion, Father. We know you hold it in the palm of your hands. Bless this meal, and bless our ride home." Kevin takes the plate with vegetables from in front of me, and slides over the pancakes. "Enjoy yourself for once, will you? Atkins is gone, and you don't need to lose a pound."

"They've done studies that show . . ." I look at the slathered whipped cream and the pancakes, and my mouth stings like a Pavlovian dog. "You're really going to eat the vegetables instead of this?"

"You don't seem to understand *me* at all. Do you, Ashley?" He takes a huge forkful of zucchini and shoves it into his mouth. "For you, I'd even eat rabbit food."

After chowing down the pancakes like I hadn't seen food for a week, Kevin helps me back into the Porsche, and we start down the freeway. Along with a cash tip, he left a tract for the waitress and a small Gideon-like New Testament. Poor thing, she probably thinks it's his phone number, but hopefully, she'll be interested enough to read the Book. I have to say he's a powerful witness, because he possesses this mystique that's indescribable. Who wouldn't want to own that?

"So you missed your puppy?" Kevin asks.

"I did. I got this great new bag in Taiwan to carry him to work in." Kevin starts to laugh.

"What's so funny?"

"Nothing. What kind of bag?"

"It's a Versace knockoff, and it's beige and black. Just gorgeous. Rhett is going to be to-die-for in it. It was between that and this great Dooney and Bourke tassel tote. Well, there was a Deborah Lewis sailor bag in lime that got my attention, too, but then I saw the price and, hey. But she had an incredible mock-croc doctor bag. Do you think that would be write-off for you?"

"Did you actually work in Taipei? Or just shop?"

"I sorta shop when I'm nervous."

"Then it sounds like you have an anxiety disorder, Ashley. Should I prescribe something for that?"

Sure, your paycheck. "I got a bonus for traveling."

"Did the bonus cover the ring and the purse?"

"What are you, my mother?"

Kevin tosses his head back in laughter and punches the gas pedal. "I'm just thinking it's probably cheaper for Seth to support Arin's mission for a lifetime than your weekly shopping habit."

All humor disintegrates with this comment. Seth has watched me spend a lot of money. Maybe he worries I'm like a slow-moving waterfall, constantly draining his supposed trust until it isn't there.

We pull up to my house, and there's a pile of wood in the front yard—an obvious diversion from Kay's normal *Better Homes & Gardens* look. I can hear Rhett barking continuously and I run to the gate before getting my bags. Opening the gate, I see this much-bigger-than-Rhett dog come lurching at me, and I brace for impact. The dog and I tumble to the hard concrete. Deep brown eyes stare at me, my cheek is under the blanket of a huge pink tongue, and I realize it is Rhett. He's obviously been eating well.

Kevin comes around the back and helps me to my feet.

I look at the dog suspiciously. "Rhett's a big terrier, don't you think?"

"Actually, the pound called Seth while you were gone. They made a mistake. The neighbor didn't know her breeds too well. He's half-boxer, half-shepherd. Not terrier."

I mull this over a bit. "Who doesn't know the difference between a terrier and a shepherd, Kevin?"

"The same type of person who doesn't get his dog neutered and lets him hop over the fence, Ashley."

"Look at him, Kevin." I reach up a hand, and Kevin helps me off the hard ground. "He's a lot bigger—he fit into my Lilly bag before I left! And those feet! He hasn't stopped yet."

"Is this the bag you were going to put him in?" Kevin holds up my new Versace.

"That's it. I guess I've got about a week before he's out of it, huh?" We both break into laughter before I realize this is *so* not funny. I have a dog who, judging by the size of his gargantuan paws, is going to be the size of a Great Dane and I own a yard big enough for a terrier. "I guess he's not a frou-frou dog, is he?"

"Are you going to give him back?"

I instantly cover the dog's ears. "Never! Do you give back your child when he throws a tantrum?"

I notice something new in the yard, and realize that Kay bought him a doghouse. How sweet is that? But she's going to be beside herself when Rhett is full-grown. Kay, the woman who has her Tupperware sorted and numbered, has been looking after the future Conan the Dog for the week. I glance into the garage and there's an enormous bag of dog food beside a brand-new, giant dog bed. Clearly, she's noticed his paws. I'm in so deep.

Meanwhile, Kevin's still smiling. "Look at the size of that dog bowl. It's like its own lake." Rhett is right at my heel, as handsome as ever. I rub his ears until he lies down on my feet. "It's okay, Kevin. He can't get much bigger."

"You've only been gone two weeks, Ashley."

Clearly, Rhett has hardly begun to blossom. I start to bite my nails, and I don't even bite my nails. Exhaling deeply, I know it's time to face the music. "I better find Kay. I think we need to have a discussion." Rhett comes in behind me, nipping at my feet like a tiny Pomeranian.

I go into the house, and it's covered with dust and there's this frantic, consistent pounding. I walk to the noise: my bathroom, but it's not there. It's a few sparse two-by-fours and a dusty Kay in the middle of it. Rhett is barking. "Shh, Rhett. Kay, what's going on?"

"You're finally back, huh?" Kay is whacking the wall with a sledge hammer. "Demolition. It's cheaper to do it by myself, and with your little pony out there, he's done enough damage on his own, so I figured I'd get started." Kay is covered in the chalky white dust of broken Sheetrock, and the toilet is lying well away from its rightful place with only a metal ring marking its previous location.

"So we're sharing a bathroom now?"

Kay's eyes thin into slivers, and I could swear she's about to utter, *"I'll get you my pretty, and your little dog, too."* But she doesn't say anything; she just goes back to taking her aggression out on the wall. My bathroom wall. My *former* bathroom wall.

"If you need a place to stay . . ." Kevin says behind me, and Rhett has found his way onto my bed, which is covered with a layer of dust and dog hair.

"That's the bathroom I just purchased, Kevin. There's a mortgage attached to that nonexistent toilet. She could have asked."

"She's probably saying the same thing about you and the dog."

"Don't you have a life to save somewhere?"

"Yes, and she's standing in front of me," he answers plainly. "If you want to stay at my place . . ."

"Oh yeah, that's appropriate." I roll my eyes, wondering what I invoke in men to make them think sharing a room with me is an option. My clothes clearly say well-bred and sophisticated. They do not read on-the-make.

"I'm never home, Ashley. I can sleep at the hospital. I didn't mean I'd be there. Besides, you have some painting to do there anyway, don't you?"

He actually means I can have his place, and I'm struck by his devotion to me, which is so undeserved. So completely mystifying. Whatever he sees in me, be it Mensa material or some strange preoccupation with the average-looking, I wish Seth saw it too. It would have made my life so much less complicated. Kevin is not an option. Doesn't he get that?

I look him straight in the eye. "Am I the type of woman who gets married?" I whisper to avoid Kay's overhearing. "Or am I the type you think will grow old gracefully and alone? Perhaps bitterly?"

Kevin lifts a single brow. "I think you're whatever type of woman you want to be. You just have to be quiet and hear God's voice." Then he turns away from me, and I hear a whisper trying to mimic the voice of God. "You were created to be a doctor's wife."

He steps closer, and I feel a warm breeze, like a Hawaiian evening. A mist of comfort overcomes me, and for the first time, I wonder if he actually feels anything for me. I always thought Seth was a practical choice. Kevin is everything but practical.

I clap my hands together to break up our proximity. "Go, rescue someone who needs rescuing." *Marriage? We don't even know each other.*

A mortgage on a bathroom that doesn't exist, a puppy that might grow into a Clydesdale, the wrong man's attention, a recent boyfriend supporting another woman, and a boss who has too much going on in his personal life to think about my promotion. What exactly is it about me that attracts toxic mold? Why am I my own science experiment?

15

I am not, by nature, a weight lifter, or really even a gym girl. This is why owning a medium-sized (um, potentially large) dog is a whole new experience. Once the dog food in the garage is gone, I go to the pet store, which is as nice as Bloomingdale's if you're a dog, and scout the aisles. I now know why they let you bring pets in here. It's like Disneyland for Rhett. He sniffs the cats for adoption, goes down the doggie treat aisle eyeing everything, and finally halts, twisting his head in confusion at the sight of turtles climbing over each other.

"I know. Weird, aren't they?" I say to the dog, offering him reassurance.

Which brings us to the dog food aisle. As I look at all these dainty bags of dog food, I think, *That won't last two days at my house,* and then, with horror, I see the appropriate size for us. I look out at my Audi TT in front of the store, and this bag o' chow before me, and I think, is it physically possible to even get that bag in that car? I'm coveting Brea's minivan, and that's just frightening in its own right.

Rhett keeps staring and sniffing. I'm in the dog food aisle while he questions life as he knows it, in the vision of a turtle totem pole. I'm still gazing, open-mouthed, at these enormous cement bags full of kibble, wishing I'd paid more attention to the Cal-OSHA guy at work when he came to speak on lifting. I hear his mantra, *lift from the legs.*

But unless I've suddenly sprouted Vin Diesel calves, I don't see this happening.

"Can I help you?" A little teenager who makes me *feel* like Vin Diesel stops in front of me.

"How do I get this to my car?" *And then, more importantly, how do I get it out?*

"Just let me know what you need. It goes on a flatbed, and we take it to your car."

"I think you need to diet," I tell Rhett. A flatbed? Really now.

The kid looks at me. "So what kind do you want?" Lamb & Veal, Lite Formula, Senior Formula, Puppy Formula, Chicken Blend, Organic, Vegetarian. *Vegetarian? What are his teeth for?* Now, I am a person who doesn't generally panic over a shopping choice. I'm decisive. I'm brand-conscious and yet value-oriented. But I stand here without a brain cell to my name because I don't know what to buy this dog. Honestly, does it really matter?

"I don't know yet. I'll call you when I'm ready."

"I can help you if you're confused."

"I'm not confused." *He's questioning my mental status?* I'm just thoughtful here. "I need to ponder a minute."

"I'll be in the reptile section when you're ready."

I look over, and yep, there is a reptile section. Lots of green things crawling about. There's a visual I could do without before my coffee. Meanwhile, Rhett has grown tired of the turtles and he's found the food section with interest. Duh? Let the dog pick. So Rhett goes along, sniffing the bags, and stops at . . . everything.

"Big dogs generally need less protein," the kid says to me as Rhett heartily inhales the pleasures of a Beef and Lamb combination.

"He's not really a big dog," I say hopefully.

"Look at those paws. He's going to be."

Can I bind these feet like they used to do in China? No, probably not. "I'll take this one." I point to a bag, and the kid gives me that *Really?* look.

"What's wrong with that one?"

"Nothing," he says unconvincingly. He relents. "You probably want something lower in fat to keep him from growing too fast. It's hard on the skeletal system."

"You know what? You pick." I give him free rein and walk to the counter to pay.

"Do you need a storage bin for the food?"

"The bag's not good enough?"

"It will stay fresher in a bin, like Tupperware."

"Oh, by all means. The dog needs Tupperware." Kay ought to like that.

"And a scoop."

"Actually he needs one of those blue sparkle collars." My eyes get big at the sight of the cubic zirconia fashion for dogs.

"They don't come that big. How about a silver stud in the shape of a diamond model?" He lifts a blue nylon collar with cowboy studs on it.

I nod. "Perfect. A little bit country. A little bit rock 'n' roll."

We get to the register and I hear, "$64.53."

"Sixty-four dollars?" I clarify.

A roll of the eyes and an outstretched palm. "Credit card or cash?"

I look down at Rhett. "That's a great pair of marked-down shoes. Are you worth it?"

His brown eyes meet mine, and I could swear he's saying, *I feel for you, babe.* So I hand over the credit card and watch as they load my TT to low-rider status. I race home and leave the car loaded until later. Church starts in five minutes!

Sitting in the front row of church feels like a light down comforter surrounding me. It seems eons since I've been in a body of believers, and it's like warm honey to my soul. The familiar music takes me to a place I'd forgotten existed: wrapped in the security of my God's warmth. Worship is such an integral part of my life, and when I come home, it seems like my best friend welcoming me like the constant prodigal I am.

Naturally, there's a sense of sadness, too, because Seth is missing, and Arin is singing her heart out on the altar. I don't know what to think of Arin any longer. There's the human part of me that just wants to hate her guts, but then the Christian within me hopes she'll eventually get things figured out.

Arin definitely has a missionary heart, but it's hard to see it beating under her Juicy! sweatshirt. Up on the altar, despite her DKNY jeans, she is just completely with Jesus. Her eyes are closed, hands raised to the sky and an expression that is lost to Him. Unfortunately, I'm reminded I'm no better or worse than her. Arin's long blonde hair is swept up into a loose bun, and she doesn't wear a stitch of makeup except for a clear lip gloss, and you're still distracted by her beauty. I realize she loves the Lord, but she also wants what *she* wants. And isn't that the human in all of us?

The sermon is "Living Out Loud," about living your faith out in the real world, not just at Christian potlucks and social events. I can't remember the last time I had time to live *in* Christian fellowship. Silicon Valley is stripped of religion, unless it's transcendental meditation, Islam, or Buddhism—something politically correct for the time. I don't know how you live anything else but *out loud* here. Just the fact that you own a Bible makes you suspect.

I try to imagine what Hans thought in Taipei. Did he assume I was more shopper than Christian? Faith should do more than highlight your faults, so I take out my notepad and I scribble furiously. Hans's name is on my heart. He needs the Lord, and so does Sophia, and my soul grieves every time I think about her eager welcome at the airport, and his apathetic response. It's so easy to see in someone else. I suppose I look just like Sophia to Seth, and his trademark retreat is evident.

Just as the last worship song is ending, my cell phone rings. I look around, mortified that I forgot to turn it off. How utterly tactless and Silicon Valley. I run out of the church like the loser I am and notice it's Brea's cell number. And Brea should be here.

"Brea?" I say into the phone.

"It's John, Ashley. Brea's having early labor pains. Her mother's at home with Miles, but she wants to be at the hospital. Can you go stay with Miles?"

"Absolutely!" My heart is pounding. "Can they stop the labor?"

"We don't know, Ash." I'm mortified because I don't remember how far along she is, and I don't want to ask. What kind of best friend forgets these things? It's been ages since I've seen her, and with the puppy and the trip . . . "She's only thirty-two weeks, Ashley," John says and then starts to break up.

"She's going to be fine," I say with conviction. "I'll get everyone praying." Brea's miscarriage is fresh in our minds. The idea of her losing another child is too much to bear, and I'm going to tell God so. "Tell your mother-in-law I'll be there ASAP." My stomach lurches. "John, I hate to do this, but I've got to stop and get Rhett."

"Can you get Miles first? I've left his car seat for him."

"No problem. Oh wait, there is a problem. I have an air bag. I can't put Miles in my car. Look, never mind. I'll figure it out. I'll be right over. You just get to the hospital." I run back into the gym we call a sanctuary, and everyone is walking out. "Wait. Wait!" I jog up toward the stage and ask everyone to pray. Arin is beside me and she seems intent on arresting my attention.

"Ashley, I really need to talk to you." Arin says.

"Not now," I tell her bluntly. The last thing I want to do is relieve Arin's guilt. If Arin has guilt, let her wallow in it. My best friend needs me. I race my car to Brea's house, and Mrs. Browning, her mother, is waiting at the door, with Miles in her arms facing out toward me. I take the baby, and he looks up at me nervously. His little lip is protruding, and he's working up a good scream. "Don't cry, Miles. It's

Auntie Ashley." I take his binky from Grandma and put it in his mouth. "Any instructions?"

"He just ate. He should be ready for a nap soon. The dogs need to be in their crates if you take Miles out for a walk. They are in there now."

"Lucy and Ricky," I say aloud. Brea's pugs. I never thought about the pugs. "Mrs. Browning, would you mind if I took your car so I can take Miles out?"

"Where would you need to go?" Her tone is such that I feel like she's asking me why I would need to eat.

"I have to get my dog. He's been home alone all morning, and my roommate has had it. She's doing a lot of demolition work, and I don't want the dog hurt."

Mrs. Browning purses her lips, and I brace for the barrage. "You know, Ashley Wilkes Stockingdale, ever since you came into our lives, you've had one event of theater after another. Why don't you get married and have yourself a real crisis for once?"

"It's not for a lack of trying," I mumble.

"Maybe if you'd think of someone besides yourself once in a while . . ."

Brea's mom has never exactly liked me. And I guess that doesn't need explaining. I was always the little urchin who followed her charmed daughter around. The portly girl, who never seemed to have a home of her own. Which I did, but my brother Dave lived there too, so I avoided it. While Mrs. Browning ran a Christian household, outreach wasn't exactly her focus. She wanted her daughter to grow up and imitate her life and grow other little Christians. That's where her evangelism started and ended.

Mr. Browning loved me though, and he took me everywhere he took Brea, much to the missus's chagrin. We went to ball games, Pizza & Pipes to see the Wurlitzer organ, we hiked the Golden Gate Bridge, and we fed ducks at the Baylands (before that was environmentally wrong). And when I graduated from anything, Mr. Browning was there in the front row shouting my name, with Mrs. Browning by his side, assuring his loyalty to her. When he died of a stroke this year, I felt it as acutely as if my own father had gone.

But here is Mrs. Browning, bringing up the selfish single argument when her daughter suffers. I've heard the selfish thing more than a few times. She could at least be original, don't you think?

"I am thinking of Brea, Mrs. Browning. That's why I'm here." Miles cuddles into my chest as if to tell his grandmother to can it, and I hold him tightly. "This is my baby, my sweet baby Miles."

"Don't hold him like that. He likes to look out," Mrs. Browning dictates.

She's upset. If there's anything I've learned in twenty years of this family, it's not to push Mrs. Browning when she's upset. I turn Miles around and hold him across his chest, and his little roly-poly legs and arms flail in deliberate kicks.

"There's Grandma's boy," she says with cheer; then her demeanor changes, and she stares at me coolly. "The dogs have colds. Keep Miles away from them, and if you take him out, be sure and put his jacket on, and a blanket in the stroller."

"Remember all those years Brea and I played with dolls?" *Like way past the age of acceptability. Geeks that we were.* "Well, we learned a thing or two about babies," I say.

"I also remember the huge messes you made." She sweeps her hand across the perfectly picked carpet as if to show me what a clean house looks like. "Brea is going to have enough stress, so could you do your best to keep the house maintained the way Brea would?"

Now, I love Brea, but she is the worst housekeeper on the planet. It's not unusual to find a folded-up dirty diaper on her dinner table because she got distracted on her way to the garbage can. And her laundry area usually looks like a dorm room, with wrinkled clothes in chaotic piles that fail to define themselves as clean or dirty. Trust me, keeping up with the housekeeping by Brea's standards would not be hard. Mrs. Browning's standards, however . . .

I suppose John has finally deciphered her laundry method, either that or he's found a good dry cleaner. The house is extremely organized now, and Mrs. Browning thinks I should believe it always looks like this. Brea's house looked cleaner before Miles came along, but now I guess it's too much effort, with his being the daily fashion-model baby. Anyway, her old ways are back in spades.

Mrs. Browning marches out the door and turns with one last cold stare. "If you must get your dog, use John's car. The keys are on the hook near the garage door. Don't keep Miles out gallivanting on your wild schedule. He's a baby. He needs his rest, and you could do with a little relaxing yourself. You look entirely too haggard for your age."

I'm waiting for a plastic surgeon's card, but she walks out without another word. When I see her drive off, I take Miles in and set him on his homemade quilt that Brea designed for him. It's green with little roads, and cars and airplanes everywhere. I put him on his tummy, and immediately he rolls over to his back, kicks his legs and arms, and giggles.

"Oh, so my big man is turning over now." I put him back on his tummy, and he turns over again, giggling like a slumber party attendee. We do this for about ten minutes, and he starts to rub his eyes with a balled-up fist. "You're getting tired. Now's a good time to go get Rhett. Do you want to meet Rhett?"

I get a gummy smile. Which must mean yes. Buckling him into the car seat of John's SUV, I hand him his quilt, and he leans into the car seat, smashing his face against the wall of it for comfort. I place the binky with him, and by the time I get the car packed, he's sleeping peacefully. Wouldn't it be great to sleep like that? His stomach is expanding and contracting, and he is just contentment personified. I just wish I could watch him up front, but he's facing backwards and the little mirror in front of him doesn't do him justice in the rearview mirror.

The dogs are yapping at me from their crate when we back out of the garage. I leave the garage door open an inch or two for their comfort and away we drive. I'm dying for an espresso. My mind is racing in constant prayer for Brea, and I can't focus on everything I need to accomplish. It dawns on me that I can't just stop for an espresso with a baby in the car. Simple concept, but really frustrating when you're dying for a caffeine high. I remember the drive-thru in the next town, and go three miles out of my way for bad espresso. *So this is parenthood.*

Once at my house, my gorgeous little bungalow now sporting holes and an angry roommate, I wonder how I'm going to get Miles out of his car seat without waking him up. It isn't going to work. In the driveway, I'm so close to the house. It's just right there. And I'm right here, but how do I get there? I scratch my head. I'm a smart girl, but this one eludes me. I have to make a choice. Do I wake a sleeping baby? Or do I dare leave him for a minute? Which is really no choice, because it's um . . . a baby.

I dial Kay on my cell phone, and pray she's home playing Bob Vila. After about twenty rings, she answers the phone. "What? Did you know you left the dog in the house? Luckily, it was your Steve Maddens he chomped. Apparently, he has your taste, because my L.L. Bean loafers are perfectly intact."

"I came home to get Rhett. I've got baby Miles asleep in the car. Can you bring him out?"

"You bet I can bring him out." Soon Kay appears in the doorway, holding Rhett by the collar and dragging him to the car, until he sees me. Then he bounds like the sweet puppy I know. "You are planning to take that dog to obedience school, aren't you?"

"Of course I am, but I didn't know I had a dog until a few weeks ago, and I haven't exactly been here to get him going on it." Rhett jumps into the car, and it dawns on me again that he's a big ol' dog, and that Miles is asleep. I yank him back by his collar. "No, boy. No!" But it's too late. Rhett wipes a wet sloppy tongue across Miles's face. The baby's expression wrinkles up, but he stays asleep. Apparently,

Miles has a bit of food on his face, because Rhett takes another swipe. *Yum.*

Kay is standing with arms crossed, judging my lack of parenting skills. For both the dog and the baby. "No, Rhett. No." I pull him into the front seat and take a baby wipe to Miles's face. Mrs. Browning would freak.

"Brea is letting you watch her baby?" Kay finally asks.

"Why does everyone assume I'm such an idiot? Weren't you in church? Brea is having contractions."

She shakes her head. "I left early. I had to get the water turned off."

"So we have no water?"

"Just for the day."

"It's Sunday. The day of rest and all that."

"Tell that to your dog. His bladder never seems to take a rest, and I'm nearly out of Pine-Sol. I still have yet to figure out how that is your dog. Seeings as how you have yet to take care of it." Kay glares at me in disgust. "Tell Seth to give you jewelry next time. A living thing is not your strong suit."

And a personality isn't yours, I think before apologizing silently, but sheesh, what is it? Pick on Ashley day? "I'll be at Brea's if you need me."

"Her pugs are going to be scared to death of your monster."

"I doubt that. Brea's pugs tend to think they're mastiffs."

"I'll be praying for Brea," Kay finally says, "and for baby Miles, too."

I drive around the city, hoping that Miles will eventually wake, but he's snugger than a prince in happily-ever-after. Rhett starts to get antsy and starts barking, which wakes Miles up in a frantic state of confusion. I stop the car, and let him know it's me, Auntie Ashley, and the furry snout in his face is friendly. But he's scared to death and screaming appropriately.

I quickly get back into the car and drive to Brea's. I get Miles out of the car, and Rhett bounds out with glee, going straight for the pugs' crates and barking. The phone is ringing in the house, and Miles is still screaming. I take him in my arms and race to the kitchen. "Hello, Wright residence."

"Who is this, Ashley? What's wrong with Miles?" Mrs. Browning asks.

"He just woke up." I want to tell her the phone woke him, but I decide lying is not something I want to add to my résumé today.

"John asked me to call. They've stopped the contractions for now with medications."

Oh, praise God.

"But she's got to be on complete bed rest for now. And they're keeping her here overnight for observation."

"Well, that's good though, right?"

She gasps like I shouldn't be trusted with a goldfish, much less her grandchild or pertinent information on Brea. "We'll be home in the morning."

My eyes go wide. "The morning?" *But work? Rhett? Miles?* "Brea told me you've just gotten back from around the world again. Surely, that job can give you a day of your own life."

Well, yeah, but a baby overnight is not exactly my own life. Now I really am afraid that Brea trusted me with Miles. Maybe everyone's fears are well-deserved, because the idea of watching him for a long period kind of scares me.

"Ashley, neither John or I want to leave Brea. She's very anxious, and we're trying to keep her calm."

Then please leave and give her a break. "Miles is anxious too." Not to mention my own fears. A baby, three dogs, and me. Four living things depending upon me, and they don't really care if Stuart Weitzman or Blahniks are a better heel choice. They actually want to eat, and do other things. *Oh Lord, give me strength.*

132

16

Exhausted. Not tired, like when I've watched one too many movies on Saturday night, not even like jet lag from an international trip. I'm dead tired. Bone weary, to the point I've become aware of my bones and they're shouting at me like a bad Halloween nightmare. The constant juggling of keeping Lucy and Ricky away from Rhett, and Rhett away from Miles, and Miles away from Lucy and Ricky and their snubbed-snout doggie colds has given new meaning to the word *multitasking.*

As if the social circle time management isn't enough, all of these cohabitating beings want food incessantly. Food and attention, and— Ack! Just shoot me now. I cannot believe I wanted to be a mother. Did I actually utter those words? Because I'm so thinking this life is not for me, and that I'm better off as a patent attorney. If Kevin could see me now, I'm sure his fantasies about who I am would dwindle away along with his belief that I could pass the Mensa test.

I didn't realize all those nesting instincts essentially mean dropping baby worms into a gaping mouth. There's a disgusting side of mothering that no one tells you about. And if you had energy to accomplish these foul missions, that might be one thing, but you're already dead-on-your-feet because you're running a never-ending marathon, and I'm not talking about the twenty-six-mile marathon that has an actual finish line. The idea that Brea actually exercises is hilarious. What the heck is this, if not Pilates, yoga, and aerobics wrapped into one constant job?

Miles finally falls asleep, and I put Rhett outside and the pugs in their crates for the night. I fall onto the couch like I'm recovering from a battle. The minute my face hits the cushion, my cell phone rings.

"Go away," I groan. But it keeps ringing. The voice mail beep comes on, but the phone just starts ringing again. "Hello."

"Ashley, it's Seth."

"Seth." Just the sound of his voice makes me start to cry and revisit the baby issue. But I'm too tired to think straight. "Where are you?"

"I'm home, Ashley."

"You're home? Palo Alto home?"

"I'm here, Ash. I told you I wouldn't go without saying good-bye. I'm back for our official good-bye, which I hope won't really be a good-bye. Have you thought about talking to my boss about a job?"

"I don't think . . ."

"I've been flying for twenty-one hours straight. I need to sleep, Ash, but I didn't want you to go anywhere without knowing I'm here. You're not taking off to Taiwan tomorrow, right?"

"No, I'm at Brea's. She's having early labor problems, so I'm staying with Miles. They've stabilized her, but she's going to be on bed-rest from here on out."

"Ash, I'm so sorry. I'll be praying." He pauses for a moment. "Can I come see you?"

I don't want to see him. That's the first thought that floats into my wee mind, and there's a brief celebration as I contemplate that perhaps I've moved on. "Now you want to come over? I thought you were exhausted."

"I am. But . . . I just need to see you, Ash."

There's a hint of desperation in his voice, and naturally it's the *perspective effect* taking place. I learned in art class that as something gets farther away, it appears smaller to the human eye. As I walk away from Seth (or in this case, he flies away from me) his perspective changes. Suddenly he craves me in close proximity because he's worried he's made a terrible mistake, that his viewpoint was off. He needs to get closer to determine that his perspective was right. I'm not in the mood to give him the opportunity.

I swallow hard. "Not now. The baby's sleeping, and I'm exhausted."

Perspective shrinking (think helium balloon released into the sky). "Please, Ash. I need to see you."

This is the first time I can ever remember Seth doing something spontaneous. I don't have my makeup bag, or clean clothes, but I figure I look like what a housewife is supposed to look like—weary. I run to the mirror and pinch my cheeks Scarlett-style, but it's of little use. I still look like Melanie Wilkes on a bad hair day. "Fine, but just for a minute. I need to get to sleep." I hang up, thoroughly ticked that I didn't hold my ground.

Rhett starts to bark uproariously. "Shh. Shh. Rhett, you'll wake the baby."

But it's too late, Miles is screaming like a rock star in two seconds flat. I run upstairs, and when he sees I'm not his mommy, he starts to really wail.

"Miles, it's Auntie Ashley." I pick him up and bring him to my chest, and bounce around the room with him. "It's okay, Miles," I soothe him nervously. "Auntie is here. Auntie is here."

Miles is screaming himself into a fit, and soon, he's sick all down my front. So now, I have bedhead, no makeup, and I smell like baby vomit. My dreams of romantic encounters are quickly dashed. Okay, maybe not a romantic encounter, but at least a little remorse on Seth's part. I am human, after all, and I would like to see him wallow a bit.

At least Miles didn't mess up his sheets. But then I look and see. His sheets are messed up. The poor little guy is sick.

"Oh, Miles, baby!" I run him a bath, and try to figure out how I'm going to get him into it when I decide it's just easier to get in with him. I strip down to my undies and step into the tub, using my shins to keep him upright. I take some baby shampoo to his body, and he's still whimpering, but the warm water calms us both. His face screws up into a bevy of wrinkles, not understanding why he's sick, and why I'm doing this to him.

When I step out of the bath, and towel us off, I notice there's a baby tub sitting on the sink. "So that's how you do this, huh?"

Miles stares at me, clueless imbecile that I am. I just get him dressed in a fuzzy blue sleeper when I hear the doorbell ring. I have no pants on, and there's still baby barf on the sheets.

"Just a minute!" I yell. I throw my church skirt back on, find a clean T-shirt of John's, and lift Miles over my shoulder. "You poor baby," I say again. As we're heading downstairs, I brush his full, auburn locks, and he looks like the most respectable little man in his footsie pajamas, with his hair so perfect and parted. I arrive at the door, and Seth is standing there. He's wrapped in a scarlet-and-gold scarf, and the blue of his eyes looks right inside me. Those eyes render me . . . well, they used to render me powerless. At the moment, they look kinda freaky.

"For you, mademoiselle." Seth takes the scarf off and wraps it around Miles and me. Then he comes toward us both and plants a kiss on my lips. Miles is looking up at me questioningly.

"This is Seth," I explain to the baby. "Miles is sick," I say to Seth. "I need to finish cleaning up his crib, and I don't want to leave him in case he gets sick again."

"So what you're saying is I'm competing with a man who has a full head of hair."

"You're not competing with anyone, Seth. You've made your choice." *Ooh, sounding a little vicious here.*

His smile disintegrates. "Please come to India with me."

"Don't you say hello first?" I put a fist on my hip. "Why do you have to do this, Seth? What about India is so fascinating?" *Besides seeing if I'll follow you like a lost puppy?*

"I just feel the calling to do it. I can't explain it. I just know I'm supposed to be there. When the Arizona job opened up, I hemmed and hawed, but this was different. I knew immediately."

"I just started this job, Seth. I feel like it's important that I'm there, and in general proximity to the mall. And restaurants, and church, and my life as I know it." I feel a little mercy for him here and exhale my angst. "Look, Seth, Hans has really come to trust me. And if I abandon him now, he's going to think all Christians just serve their own purposes. Contrary to what you think, I appreciate that your ministry and life is in India. But mine is here, Seth."

"It's only for three months. You can come back to Hans."

"To start. It's only for three months to start. I've seen what these companies do to get you settled in other countries. You live like a king on nothing, and your salary comes back here tax free, while you live the luxury lifestyle gratis. You'll get used to it, and you probably won't ever come back."

"Are you worried about being somewhere with me?"

"I'm worried about being anywhere without good espresso and shopping malls. You can't change who you fundamentally are unless God allows for it." I sweep my hand in front of me. "Look around you, Seth. This is a mission field, ripe for the picking and the workers are few. I'm called to be here."

He holds up the red scarf. "They have shopping malls in India, and they're outdoors like Stanford. Better than Ann Taylor. Cheaper, more feminine." He wiggles his eyebrow. "And you could buy all the scarves you wanted. I'd love to see you in them."

I stare him down and for the moment, I soften. *Are you asking me to marry you?* Dr. Laura always says to get a ring and a date. *A ring and a date.* I mean, how do I ask this question, and really it's not my question to ask technically, now is it? Going off to another country involves such a level of commitment, and I sincerely doubt he's willing to make it. But I have to know for certain just for peace of mind.

I'm imagining the future, where I'm haggard from the sun and

I've lost my ability to dress well after wearing nothing but Indian saris. Then, like the thirsty to an oasis, I come back to America, only to discover patent work has changed immensely since my absence. My bank account has dwindled with new tax laws and I can no longer afford Botox. Or worse yet, it's no longer even offered, the Food and Drug Administration has outlawed its use. And right here is where I have the epiphany. *I cannot change at the cellular level for any person other than Jesus.*

"I know you love me," Seth says, his voice deep and clear. He leans in and presses his lips to mine. "I know you love people and being a patent attorney and Indian food and cheap clothes. India has it all." He kisses me again softly, and I feel myself pull away. "And it has me."

It has me? Is he tripping?

"First off, let's get one thing straight. I do not like cheap clothing. I like quality clothing at an affordable price. So I just need to understand this, Seth. You want a commitment from me without having to commit yourself, am I understanding that right?"

"If things work out in India, we'll—"

"And if pigs fly, and if the stock soars, and if Frodo gets the ring back to the Mount of Doom. If. If. If! If any of these things happen, you still won't be able to commit!" My eyes close, maybe to make him disappear.

"My parents are coming tomorrow." Seth takes my hand. "Will you at least meet them?"

As what, the keeper of his dog? His on-again, off-again girlfriend who inches closer to the altar only to be dashed like Charlie Brown and the football each time? "Let's talk about it tomorrow, Seth."

He sighs. "I'm going home to bed. I'm sorry, Ash, I just need to know the woman I love would follow me anywhere."

Apparently Arin will. I guess that answers our question.

17

This is Jen Jenkins reporting from Telecopter Seven at the wedding of Indian Princess Ashley Stockingdale."

The studio's Rick Ramirez breaks in with a Spanish-accented laugh. "Now, Jen, she isn't really an Indian princess."

"No, but the Indian people have certainly grown to love her here in Punjab. She's had her traditional ritual bath with herbs, and she should be emerging shortly. Her groom, Seth Greenwood, waits with visible anticipation."

A roar from the gathering crowd rises, and Ashley appears to her fans. "Ashley's arriving now. Oh, look at her, in the traditional red wedding gown and her hair gold-leafed. She's magnificent. We've been told even her raw silk shoes, designed by Giuseppe Zanotti, are topped with handmade beaded uppers by Indian craftsmen. She is, indeed, a sight to behold. Our sources here tell us she has followed all sixteen traditional accoutrements of an Indian wedding, from the Bindi forehead dot to a perfume created especially for her."

"What's the groom's reaction, Jen? Can you see his expression?"

"The groom appears to be inspired, Rick. His mouth is agape, and he's watching mesmerized as Ashley walks to his side. Although the wedding will follow traditional Christian vows, there's nothing traditional about this wedding, Rick. Back to you in the studio."

I wake startled and unnerved. An Indian princess? Why do my dreams make me so pathetic? I can't even dream normally.

It's Monday morning. Three dogs and a baby. Wasn't that a movie? I think about calling in sick, but I can't do that. Hans gave me that hefty bonus for traveling because I was reliable. I sigh and do what any smart-thinking career girl in Silicon Valley would do. I pack up the crew. I've found a cage for the back of the car, and I've got everyone's leashes.

Once I pack up all the supplies baby Miles might need this side of eternity, I get into the car. I realize that everyone looks great. The dogs are fed, the baby is cleaned and dressed-to-the-nines in a little navy Tommy Hilfiger outfit I bought him, and I'm feeling downright accomplished. But I take a gander in the rearview mirror and realize not only am I sans makeup, but my hair is sticking straight out and Brea's tiny shirt is stretched to capacity across my chest. I look like an unkempt streetwalker.

"I've got to stop at home," I explain to all my occupants, who, of course, don't understand a word. We drive across town and once at my house, I realize the only way to do this is to bring everyone inside. Because Rhett can't be trusted with upholstery. I bring the baby, his stroller to sit in, and all the dogs follow me to the front porch. Lucy and Ricky can't get up the steps, so I have to open the stroller, put the brake on, set Miles in his seat belt, and lift the dogs physically. Meanwhile, Rhett is giving Miles a tongue bath.

"Ack! Get off the baby, Rhett." I finally open the door.

Kay's gone, but her disapproving presence remains. There's a white layer of dust over her normally pristine house, and my bedroom is a graveyard for everything Rhett has apparently chewed up. There's a pair of Kay's cheap sunglasses, a few Thanksgiving knickknacks including one mangled stuffed animal turkey, there's a wooden rolling pin munched with teeth marks, and a holey pillow that used to read, "If friends were flowers, I'd pick you."

I look for something to wear, but notice everything is covered with dust and dog hair. Looking for a light color, I decide to avoid the no-white-after-Labor-Day rule, go with calling my suit winter white, and set a new fashion precedent at Gainnet.

I can't take a shower because Miles is already in a strange place, and if one dog can leave a toy graveyard, I don't even want to think about three with a baby. So I do my best, matting down my hair with water and a mixture of gel and leave-in conditioner. Now I look greasy and helmetlike, but I'm going to make it to work, and today, that's the only goal I'm looking forward to accomplishing.

After primping for an hour, I pile all the dogs and Miles back into the car. Then I remember. I didn't bring any bottles for Miles. I drive back to Brea's house, kill the car in the garage, and close the door, running in to get formula and baby food. It then dawns on me that the pugs should stay home, and I put them back into their cages, feeling like Cruella herself.

"We're ready to go," I say. Finally. I look at my watch. It's 9:30. I started this process at 6:30 and I'm not even at work yet.

Finally I walk into work and put Rhett in the dog area. Yes, we have a dog area. It's one of the ways that Silicon Valley geeks pretend to be relational. We have dogs. Marriage may be out of the question, but living together and dogs, they can do that. It's all so forward-thinking. Not. I'm quickly realizing that this myth of doing it all is just that. And I'm a complete moron to bring a dog and a baby to work. Does my brain function at all? Mensa, hah! I wouldn't pass the SATs at this rate.

Hans meets me on the gated back porch for dogs. "What's all this? Who is this?"

"This is Miles, my best friend's baby. It's a long story, but he's here with me today. I've brought blankets, toys, videos, you name it. This baby is going to enjoy my job, even if it kills my back."

My cell phone rings and Hans's eyebrows lift. "I hope I'm not getting in your way," he quips.

I answer the phone anyway. It might be Brea. "Hello?"

"Ash, it's Brea. Can I talk to my little man? His mama misses him like nobody's business."

"It's my girlfriend," I whisper to Hans. "The baby's mother. She wants to talk to her baby."

Hans tosses his hand at me. "When you're available." He places his palm on his stomach and bows. "At your leisure, naturally." Then he walks away and slams his office door.

I put the cell phone next to baby Miles's ear, and he starts to giggle and chew on it. His baby slobber is everywhere, and I'm wondering how on earth any mother stays professional.

I wipe the phone off with my jacket. "Brea?"

"Please bring him here. Please. Please. I'm going crazy without him. John doesn't want me lifting him, but if you held him up to me . . ."

"You're asking me to bring contraband to the hospital?"

"Please, Ash. I'm begging you. Miles can't forget his mama."

I look at Hans's closed door and quickly see my promotion dwindling, but then there's my best friend begging. It's not pretty. "All right. Do you want anything else?"

"Will you stop and get me a Jamba Juice? Miles and I like to share them."

"Where's John?"

"He went to work."

He went to work. Did it ever occur to him that he could take his son to work with him? "Where's your mom?"

"She had her Christian Ladies' League at the Country Club. She'll be back this afternoon, but she said it was important for her to go because they're planning the craft fair."

I want to explain that a country club appointment is, like, not a *job*. But I doubt I'd get very far, and Brea's feelings would be hurt. Besides, I don't want her to think I don't love Miles. I love Miles like my own. I just have no natural affinity toward this mothering thing.

I knock on Hans's door softly. "Come in!" he shouts harshly. I open the door and his eyebrows are lifted, as though waiting for my excuse. "What now? Ashley, I've got stockholders breathing down my neck and a product to get to market. Do you think you could try to focus on your work?"

"We've been in Taiwan for two weeks. I've done everything I can to get this patent out, but I need some time for myself." And here it comes. "Do you think you could keep an eye on Rhett in the pen outside? I have to run really quickly to the hospital. I'll be right back, I promise."

He crosses his arms. I won't bother to describe the look on his face. "Are you really asking me to babysit a dog while you gallivant around, coddling a child who's not your own?"

I want to suggest that Sophia could do it instead of him, but I doubt that's going to help my case. "You see, my friend Brea is having pregnancy complications and—"

Hans holds up a palm. "Do not say another word! I don't want to hear about women's issues. I have enough women issues in my life. Just go and come back when you're a man."

"Huh?"

"Once you have morphed back into the genius patent attorney I hired, come back to us."

"So is that a yes on the dog? Because Rhett, my puppy, is really active and—"

"Ashley," he says evenly. "Do you suppose I care about your dog's personality?"

"Um, no." I shake my head. "Not really, no."

He points at the door. "Just go!"

I take Miles's balled-up fist and move it to motion bye-bye. Hans is not the least bit amused and I cut my losses, rushing out the door. One thing I learned about Hans when in Taiwan is that his patience level goes from zero to ballistic in seconds. He can be the epitome of European charm, then *Bam!* He's like the Third Reich unleashing its fury. I honestly wondered when we were in Taiwan if he was bipolar. In his mind, it's completely rational to scream an obscenity at a helpless Taiwanese employee in a meeting. And speaking of helpless employees . . .

We stop at Jamba Juice, an overpriced smoothie store, and get Brea her fruit drink. My back is killing me from all this in-and-out with the car. What a complete pain in the neck. Literally.

We get to the hospital, after a million stoplights and mall traffic at Stanford. I suddenly realize I have no warm water for Miles's bottle, and he's not happy about it. I put him in his stroller, find him a binky, which I pray is clean, and head to the cafeteria. He starts screaming. Soon I am pushing the empty stroller, carrying him on my hip, and trying to shove the binky back into his mouth. All while I'm juggling a diaper bag the size of Brazil.

Sitting right beside the hot water dispenser is Kevin. He stands up immediately, his face a study in amazement. "Ashley, what are you doing here?" He's wearing his white doctor coat and just looks yummy, though I know I shouldn't notice. *I'm on the rebound. I'm on the rebound.*

"I brought Miles to see Brea." I hold him out. "Will you hold him for a minute so I can get his bottle ready?"

"Sure." Kevin holds Miles and the baby immediately calms.

"Wow, you've got the magic touch. I wish I'd had you last night." *Did I just say that?* My hand flies to my forehead. "I mean . . ."

"I know what you meant. Kay told me you were at Brea's. I figured you had your hands full, but I've been on call nonstop anyway."

"You called?" *I suddenly need call waiting?* It's like I'm fighting them off with a stick, I tell you. Not really, but it does my heart good to pretend.

"I wanted to bring Rhett to the hospital to see Brianna last night, but Kay said you had him."

"Why didn't you call me on my cell? You could have picked him up." *I'd trust you with my dog. And maybe a tiny piece of my heart.*

"I wanted to give you some space." He shrugs. "I tend to run roughshod over people when I want something. I'm trying to tame that." He stares me down with those gorgeous green eyes, and *tame* is just not the word that comes to mind.

"Next time, call. It's about a child, not me. Okay?"

I turn toward the water spout and try to ignore the underlying current between us—that neon blue electrical force that I feel with my whole being. I'd forgotten how attracted I'd once been to Kevin. How his kisses had literally swirled my stomach and rocked my world. I'm staring at him while reliving the moment. I think I'm blushing now. He hands Miles back to me and my heart races at his proximity. He stays beside me, intimately close, just a moment longer than necessary, and it unnerves me.

"I've got the night off Wednesday. Will you be at Bible study?" Kevin asks.

"If Brea's okay with the baby, I will be." This is awkward. The most stilted conversation I've had since my last bad job interview.

"Could we get a cup of coffee afterwards?" He looks down at me with an austere look. *So Mr. Darcy. Yum.* "Ashley, coffee?"

My hands are flailing like one of Brea's Italian conversations. "Coffee could lead to dessert, and dessert could lead to another meal out, and then, before you know it, I am your girlfriend. And I'm a terrible girlfriend, Kevin. Ask Seth."

"Seth wouldn't know a good girlfriend if she hit him over the head. Which I'm sure she's been tempted to do. I know I've been coming on strong, Ash, but it's just coffee. I promise."

"No, definitely no on the coffee." I start to back away and finish the baby's bottle with a shake. I notice his eyebrows lift.

"If this wasn't so fresh with you and Seth, would you say yes?"

A young woman comes in and stands beside Kevin before I answer. She's got to be in her twenties, with dark brown locks cascading down her back; big, brown eyes; and the tiniest tennis bracelet gracing her petite wrist. She's holding a Bible and she smiles at me, thrusting her little wrist toward me. "Hi, I'm Kendra. Who's this precious bundle?" She is reaching out for the baby.

"That's Miles Wright, my friend's baby." *She gets no chance to ask when I'm going to lose the baby fat.* "I'm Ashley Stockingdale."

Her expression changes. I could swear there's an instant change of mood, and her chirpy demeanor is clouded over by a dark, contemplative stare. "I'll be waiting over here for you, Kevin." Not so much as a good-bye smile for me.

I look at Kevin's apologetic eyes and wonder what I've stepped into. "I'm sorry, did I say something wrong? Are you two . . . you know?"

He laughs. "Of course not. Would I be asking you out if we were?"

I shrug. After nine months with Seth and no boundaries, who knows?

"It's just that maybe," he continues, "I've mentioned you a time or two before." He looks away.

"Mentioned me how? Like I eat my young?"

"As the reason I'm not seeing anyone else. You know, avoiding her." He grins and the corners of his eyes crinkle just as his pager goes off. "Hang on." He picks up his phone and pushes a button. "Dr. Novak calling in." There's a pause. "No! Don't let them touch him. I'll be right up."

Kevin's smile is gone. "I've got to go. Insurance company trying to kick out a very sick child. Think about Wednesday night." He sprints off.

My head is nodding on its own volition. "Okay."

"Coffee's good." He kisses my cheek. "I'll see you then." I grab for my cheek and Kendra moves toward me. I pull Miles in closer. Kendra opens her mouth to say something, then just stalks off.

Coffee? I think to myself, *didn't I just say no?* But, really, there's no harm in coffee. Coffee is caffeine-laden. I will have a solid, clear head when I see him again.

18

I schlep Miles to the third floor and scout for Brea's room. It isn't long before I hear her uproarious giggle, and I know I've found the right place. A nurse exists, and as we enter, Brea doesn't even look at me. As far as she's concerned, I'm the post behind Miles.

She squeals like a horror movie extra. Her hands go crazy waving toward herself. "Give him to me. Give him to me!"

"You're not supposed to hold him," I remind her.

She pats the side of her bed. "Put him right here next to the rail. I won't pick him up, but I can cuddle him and nuzzle his chipmunk cheek." I lay Miles down beside her.

"Oh, Miles, how's mama's baby? Is my big man learning to be a lawyer?" She coos.

"Let's hope not," I say. "Hans will teach him to be the CEO with extensive stock options and others to do his bidding."

"Let's pray that's all Hans teaches him. How is your slimy boss?"

"They all slither in Silicon Valley. Some are just more colorful." I wink, enjoying my brief moment with creativity.

"Spoken like a true cynic."

"I'm enjoying working for Hans, actually. His personal life is completely *90210*, but he's a good boss if you can put up with the occasional tantrums." I hand Brea the baby's bottle, she starts to feed him, and he snuggles into her rounded tummy. "I guess I feel a little sorry for him, too. He's just chasing after the wind, you know?"

"What's he think of having Miles at work?"

I shrug. "Didn't give him a second glance. You look gorgeous. Are you really sick? Or just trying to get your mother to clean your house?"

Brea purses her lips. "They stopped the contractions, but I can't do anything for fear they'll start again. I'm so tired of television, I could vomit."

"Speaking of which, Miles had a little stomach thing last night. He's been fine today. Just really sleepy."

She rubs Miles's belly. "You'll make a great mother, Ash. When's Seth getting back?"

"He's back."

"And?"

"Wants me to go to Punjab with no commitment. Yep, Prince Charming awaits. I mean, I can be unemployed and manless here, can I not?"

"I don't want to hear about Seth. He's yesterday's news. What's up with Dr. Kevin?"

"Nothing. Nothing is up with Dr. Kevin, and I plan to keep it that way." *For once in my life, I'm going to behave like an adult.*

"I'm sure you do plan to keep it that way. You'll find some new engineering geek to chase. Some new guy who thinks Prada is a Mexican parade." Brea clicks her tongue. "You have the weirdest taste in men. Always did."

"It's not *my* high-school boyfriend who turned gay," I remind her.

Her laughter dies like a plant in my care. "I just hope this thing with Seth finally tells you that you can do better."

I walk around the bed and sit at the foot of it. "I thought God was pointing in Seth's direction. I think He's trying to point out what I should steer clear of, but I've got a fairly hard head." *Granite, I believe.*

"Um, yeah you do."

"I have to ask you a question."

"I've got nothing but time." She places another kiss on Miles's forehead. "The longer you stay, the longer he stays."

"Do you remember in sixth grade when we watched that contraband *Thorn Birds* tape your sister got us?"

"Do I ever! Richard Chamberlain shirtless on the beach. It lives in infamy." She points to her head.

Rolling my eyes here. "Remember how Meggie was so in love with Father Ralph, but he couldn't leave her for his God? He loved God more."

Brea's face screws up and she nods, fanning her face. "I'm *verklempt*. Talk among yourselves. It makes me emotional just to think about it." Brea starts to tear up. "And that week on the beach when he came and found her. She could never go back to another man." Brea's sniffling now, nodding her head up and down.

I'm hoping it's just the hormones.

"Putting aside all of the sin contained in that movie—which you seem to be relishing, I might add—Meggie loved Ralph, but Ralph didn't love her the same way. Oh sure, there was the temptation and the breaking of his priestly vows, but their love was bigger than that for her, right? It was a lifetime of unrequited love."

"Your point?" Brea asks.

"A tragic, yet victorious story because Ralph ultimately loved his God more."

"Actually, I think he loved himself more. Wasn't that the theme of the movie?"

"Just stay with me here, okay? So Meggie couldn't have Ralph, so she married another."

"Bryan Brown working hard in the cane." Brea whistles. "Oh yeah, he was some consolation prize."

"Brea, I'm serious here."

"You're serious about an '80s miniseries?"

"Yes. And the book was better, I might add."

"And why are we talking about this?"

"Because I think I'm Meggie. I fall in love with the wrong men. So maybe I should avoid them altogether, don't you think? I mean, the Bible says it's better to cut your eye out than sin with it, right?"

"You need a good theology class, Ashley. It's not your Scripture, but your interpretation that scares me. I'm thinking muddling Scripture with *The Thorn Birds* might be where you're off."

"Come on, Brea. Help me out here. Why does Kevin want to date me? Or why does God want Kevin to want to date me? Because he's the wrong man in some way and I'm supposed to figure it out, right? Wouldn't it be smarter just to say I've grown and move on before the actual pain begins? I mean, I have a vivid imagination. I can figure out what it will be like."

Brea ignores all the instructions, lifts Miles over her head, and kisses him. I yank the baby down and put him beside her again.

She rolls her eyes. "When all was said and done, Rachel Ward married Bryan Brown in real life, and Richard Chamberlain turned out to be gay."

"Thank you, *People Magazine*, 1984." I look straight at her. "I'm serious, Brea. I'm really liking Kevin, but I know where this will end. He thinks about me, and who I am. He remembers I'm on Atkins and still orders me pancakes because that's what I really want. He takes my dog to visit sick children. I love how he can perform surgery in the morning, but still be at the airport to pick me up. I love how I'm important to him. Until he catches me, and it all stops."

"You were important to Seth, too, Ash. He's just a freak."

I exhale. "He'd rather run off to a third-world country and support a missionary he barely knows than walk down the aisle with me."

"A missionary?"

"Arin," I say reluctantly. The mere name makes me cringe and feel like such a fool. I remember when Seth was first meeting her, that day in Chevys. I should have noticed that he'd never looked at me that way. Why couldn't I know that he never *would?*

"Just because Seth wasn't the one doesn't mean there will never be another, Ash. Most women have ex-boyfriends. Even Christian women. You know what they say about kissing a few frogs. Yours just have a few more warts than usual." Brea starts to giggle.

"It's been a year of on-again, off-again misery for me. I don't want to do that anymore. But I'll admit my weakness for bald men. Why waste a perfectly good head of hair on me?"

"You've got to get back on the horse, Ash. Look, I'd be careful about analyzing *The Thorn Birds* too closely. I mean, they may have made Father Ralph look so desirable, but I can't stress enough that Richard Chamberlain was really gay. Rachel Ward married Bryan Brown in real life, and they've got like three kids or something now."

I drop my head in my hands. "Did I actually start this stupid conversation?"

"You did. Is that my Jamba Juice?"

"I forgot all about it." I bring her the cup out of the diaper bag. The once-frozen drink is now sticky, warm red Styrofoam.

"Yum, that looks appetizing. Thanks anyway." She hands the cup back to me.

"Hey, I brought Miles, and that was enough work on its own." I laugh. "I can't believe a little blob of cuteness can be that much work."

"I can't let him go, Ash. Leave him with me." She pulls off his socks and plays with his bare feet.

"I've got to get back to work. Hans is ready to kill me now. He's taking care of Rhett while I'm here."

"Are you nuts?"

"I got overwhelmed this morning with the baby. I don't think clearly when I'm overwhelmed." Which seems to be consistently.

"Quit analyzing everything! You don't have to find the deeper meaning in every raindrop on the windshield, you know?"

"Kevin asked me out to coffee," I sheepishly admit.

"So you go for coffee. It's not like he asked you to be the mother his children. He didn't, did he? With you, I never know."

"I gotta get back to work." I pick up my bag and reach for Miles.

"I really can't let go of Miles. My mother will be here soon. Leave him with me."

"I can't. What if he gets sick again?"

"Then we're in a hospital. And I can call Kevin immediately. Kevin came here last night and brought me ice cream, did I tell you that? If he's trying to get to you through me, he has my vote. Come on, please let Miles stay. John just had a few things to do at the office. He'll be back soon."

I hand her the phone. "Call him and prove it to me."

Miles is at complete peace. How can I break that up? I bring all his diaper needs to her bed and wait as she makes the call, just like she used to do when asking if she could spend the night. But before she finishes, John walks in the door on his cell phone.

"Okay, you're saved," I announce, reaching for my keys. "If you need anything, call me. I've got one meeting this afternoon with Hans, and then Seth wants me to go to dinner tonight . . ." Brea rolls her eyes. "But I'll change things around for you if I need to. You know that, right?"

"I do, and you're avoiding my advice. It's time to just live your life. Not every event has to be a possible lifetime."

"Even coffee with a gorgeous surgeon who looks like Hugh Jackman?"

Her eyebrows lift. "Especially that. It was time to cut bait, Ashley. Seth needs to grow up, and that's his issue, not yours. But maybe you should try a practice date with someone who isn't prettier than you."

We both laugh. "Very comforting thought, thank you." As I stand up, John kisses me on the cheek. "Thank you, Ashley. What can we ever do to repay you?"

"Oh. Oh!" Brea raises her hand. "I nearly forgot. I had my mother get this for you last night." Brea lifts up a linen envelope. "It's for a rain-forest therapy at Provence Spa."

"Dare I ask?"

"Rain-forest therapy. It's so great, Ash. They take all these natural oils from the rain forest, and drip them on your back, and it's supposed to pull out all the impurities in your body. It helps your body recover, and your immune system be boosted, so you won't get the flu this fall."

"Did my credit card actually pay for this bit of new-age hogwash? I mean, I appreciate all she's done, don't get me wrong. But she'd probably like a good dinner out. Without Seth bringing along a two-for-one deal, you know?" John glances at me hopefully.

"No, she's gonna love it. Aren't you, Ash?"

Being basted like a Thanksgiving turkey, oh yeah, that's on the top of my list of things to do. And rain forest doesn't exactly create a warm cozy for me. It reminds me of Arin and her monkey kids with Seth.

"Of course I'll enjoy it. Thanks so much!"

19

I walk into my office tentatively, realizing that I'm not exactly employee of the year at the moment. I sneak by Hans's office to the back doggie porch. Rhett isn't there. I suck in a breath. No panicking, but my throat tightens like I'm a mother who's lost her child in the crowd. I'm sure he's right here somewhere, but the truth might be darker. In fact, the truth is that I can't even keep track of a puppy.

I run back into the office, hoping to avoid Hans, who, of course, I see immediately. He's sticking his head out his door and using a long, beckoning finger to call me. Why do I act like a four-year-old?

"Ashley, would you come in here, please," Hans asks. By the look on his face, explaining would do me absolutely no good.

"Hans, I'm sorry about this morning, but . . ." *But I brought an untrained puppy to work and then abandoned him.* Is there even an explanation? Not without going into "women's issues" as Hans calls it. I enter his office and see Rhett huddled in a corner, and a telltale puddle under my boss's desk.

"Are you looking for someone, Ashley?" Hans asks.

"Why'd you take him off the back porch?" *Like I have any leg to stand on here, but accusing really does take the focus off me.*

"Because he was howling like a werewolf, and people were complaining that they couldn't talk on their phones without sounding like they were at the dog pound."

I clamp my eyes shut. I've been let go before. I'll deal. "I'm sorry Hans. I, well, I really don't have a good enough excuse, now do I? Rhett was a gift, and I haven't quite adjusted to his presence in my life. Being in Taiwan . . ." I let my voice trail. I'm going for the pity angle, and praying for the best.

Hans sits at his desk, leans back in his chair and picks up his shiny black phone. "I'm taking the dog home to Sophia for the day. You can pick him up when you're done tonight. I am assuming you're working tonight? Since you've brought us a baby and a dog, but no patent attorney for the day."

"You're taking my dog into custody?"

"Not custody, just an experiment. I've been thinking if Sophia had some company she might not call me forty times a day. This is the perfect opportunity to find out. It will give my patent attorney time to actually do some work, and my girlfriend simply something to do."

Like the artwork isn't enough?

"Drive over with me, so the dog knows Sophia's okay." He looks at me. "Don't worry, we can talk in the car. Think of it as your weekly meeting with me. I want you to update me on the Taiwan products, anyway."

Maybe my ego needs a huge reality check, but Hans unnerves me. I feel like if he were given the opportunity . . . He's just too smooth, too sophisticated. And I'm . . . not.

"I just have to check my e-mail before we go." I jog into my office and bring up the Internet, hoping for some amazing excuse for not going with Hans. What I find is something from Seth.

To: AStockingdale@gainnet.com
From: MatrixMan@mmm.com
So, what about dinner? I know I don't deserve it, but my parents are in town, and they'd love to meet the girl I've told them so much about. Truce?
To: MatrixMan@mmm.com

From: AStockingdale@gainnet.com

Dinner would be great. For your parents! Capiche? Working late, so leave me details when/where to be. Ash

There. I don't sound too desperate, and quite frankly, I could take or leave the invitation, but I'm actually excited about it. I mean, I get to see the parents behind the commitment phobe. There have to be some clues there, wouldn't you think?

"You ready to go?" Hans hands me Rhett's leash from my doorway.

"I'm ready."

Again, Hans places his palm in the small of my back, and I notice all the admins staring at us as we walk out the door. Staring and whispering. Once we're outside, I face my boss. I can completely see how women fall for his charm. He's just so elegant. Like Cary Grant, you want to believe in Hans, that he can be turned around and tamed. Logic tells you otherwise, but logic doesn't always rule in matters of the heart. Just ask me, a textbook case of *Smart Women, Foolish Choices.*

I groan as Rhett hops on my leg, destroying the second pair of hose in a day. "You know, leaving together doesn't really look good to the office staff. I think they are wondering what's going on. And could you not touch me?"

Hans's lips curve into a slow, sultry smile. "So you're telling me I should hire a male general counsel so the admins won't talk?" His car chirps gently as it unlocks. "I'm European, Ashley. We help guide women to the car because we have manners, not because we're trying to get lucky."

I feel like I've shrunk four inches. "Let's just get this over with," I mumble, pulling Rhett around toward Hans's Jaguar.

Rhett is under the distinct illusion that he is a tiny dog, and he sits on my lap, realizing that tenth of a terrier within, which may not even exist. I certainly hope dog hair is in fashion. Hans sits in the cockpit of his classic, leather-appointed English car and inserts the key into the ignition.

"Did you tell Sophia we were coming?" I ask.

He shrugs. "Why, what's she got to do?"

"It's just polite not to surprise a woman."

"Isn't surprising her the point? I'm bringing her a dog. Surprise! It seemed to win you over for the bald guy."

"Seth. And I like bald guys."

Hans apparently learned to drive on the autobahn. We're at the house in a matter of what seems like seconds. When the garage door goes up, Sophia appears in the doorway. She's casual-gorgeous today, in a pair of navy yoga pants and a pale pink sweatshirt. She acknowledges my presence as if she'd been expecting me.

"Hello! Are you here for a late lunch?" she asks us.

"I brought you a surprise." Hans pulls Rhett out of the car, and Sophia squeals. Not happily, I might add.

"Where did you get that mongrel?" Her entire face is pursed like a closed sea anemone.

"It's Ashley's dog. His name is Rhett. I thought he might keep you company."

She smiles at me, unwilling to admit she's just insulted my dog. "Sorry, does he have fleas? I'm highly allergic to dander."

"Probably has fleas on his fleas" I say. Something about her tone makes me want to add head lice to the list, but I snap my mouth shut.

"Why can't Ashley care for him? Next thing you know, you'll be bringing me sick day care kids from the office. I'm very busy with my art, Hans."

It suddenly feels very hot, as if the garage is too crowded. Which it is.

Hans's brow darkens, and I catch a glimpse of the ruthless nature that he harbors. I've heard it unleashed on others behind closed doors. But I've never actually seen his face, and it's like a Disney villain. You can picture him rubbing the apple. "You were brought over here to care for kids. My wife seems to be doing that now. The dog is the least of your issues."

"If you had trained those kids properly, they never would have been the . . ." And she sinks into Italian here. Somehow I'm thankful I can't understand her because it doesn't sound pretty. Even in a romance language.

I must say, I don't want to leave my dog with her. This place feels dark and ugly and Rhett is just a puppy. I pinch Rhett's floppy ear slightly and he whines. I wrinkle my face up with concern. "You know, Rhett is probably going to cry all day if he stays here. He's just getting to know me, and I want him to know he lives at my house. We'll drop him at home, if that's all right with you, Hans."

My boss looks at Sophia and then at me. "Fine."

We clamber back in the vehicle so Rhett can shred the rest of my nylons. Rhett snuggles his wet nose against my cheek. "No need to thank me," I whisper. "I feel the same way." We cuddle up together.

"So she doesn't like dogs *or* children," Hans says as he races down his street.

"What's the difference if she doesn't like dogs?"

"I want the kids to have a dog when they come over. They need to have something to look forward to at my house. They hate all those ghastly death paintings on the walls."

"Why don't you take the kids somewhere else then? I don't imagine Sophia exactly conjures up warm fuzzies for them." *Sophia is part of the reason their parents split. I can't imagine she'll ever be the cat's meow with the kids. Is that complicated?*

He changes the subject. "We've got a board meeting tonight. Can you hang around the office? I'm hoping to introduce you and get this general counsel thing off the ground."

"I owe my roommate my presence. She's been demolishing our entire house single-handedly, and besides, I promised to meet Seth's parents tonight and say good-bye to him."

He just nods. "You're a good girl, Ashley."

We get back to the office, complete with the dog we left with, and our appearance now gives new reasons for cubicle whispers. I rush into my office with Rhett, and make him lie down under my desk while I search databases for competing patents. Just as my eyes start to get fuzzy, the phone rings.

"Ashley Stockingdale."

"Ashley, it's Kevin."

My stomach twists like a churro. *That's not supposed to happen.* Engineering geek. Remember? *Bald is beautiful. Geeks are us. Bill Gates is a hottie.* Every woman would allow her stomach to turn at the sight of Kevin. How utterly cliché. I, Ashley Stockingdale, am beyond the obvious. "Hi, Kevin. What's up?"

"I'm coordinating my church team for the servers on Thursday. We're a person short on Thanksgiving at the mission. I know you probably have plans, but I thought I'd ask."

Okay. Mission work. Mission work isn't a date, and I get to see if Kevin thinks of me the same way when I'm not dressed to the nines, when I look like I could pass the Mensa test. Maybe I'll go without makeup even, so he can see the real me. *Um, no.*

I'm mulling this over when he continues. "You'll have time to get home to your family. We serve early."

Hmm. My family: all-day football, my mother showing me the "secret" to mashed potatoes once again, my pregnant sister-in-law who's still tinier than me. *Or,* down-and-out homeless people I've never met in this lifetime. No-brainer. "I'd love to help."

"Great, I'll pick you up at eight on Thanksgiving morning. Maybe if we have time we can swing by and see some of the kids at the hospital with Rhett."

"That sounds great." He visits his patients on his day off. He's a saint, a yummy saint, and I try not to focus on this. I am, after all, on the rebound. But the ride up is so much fun. It's that downward bounce that wipes you out.

20

Hans finally left the office at seven. I sneak out at seven-thirty. I'm late for dinner. I hate to be late, and I'm carting an oversized puppy with me. So much for first impressions. Oh well, Seth is my past. First impressions might also be called last impressions.

The happy news is that I haven't had time to worry about meeting Seth's parents, though I must admit I'm very curious. They've spent a lifetime in China preaching, they supplied their son with a Stanford education, and I wonder where the disconnect starts. Will they act like wealthy elite (like Kevin's parents) or godly missionaries? Perhaps a mixture of both?

I pull up in front of Seth's condo and let Rhett relieve himself on a growing sycamore, and then I knock. Seth's condominium is so typically bachelor. His walls are white, there's dirt in every corner, dust bunnies on the sixties-style linoleum, and the carpet lining the stairs is framed by darkened edges from a lack of vacuuming. On a happy note, I smell Lysol before the door even opens, so I know he cleaned today.

Seth opens the door, and his parents are peering out from behind him. They're tall, much taller than I imagined, and older. Probably in their late seventies. Seth's father has a full head of gray hair, a solid, stocky build, and the same piercing blue eyes as his son's. His mother is still beautiful, with a crown of silver hair up in a bun, gray-blue eyes, and skin aged by the sun. I hand Rhett's leash to Seth and bow like when I'm in Taiwan.

"Dr. and Mrs. Greenwood. It's such a pleasure to finally meet you."

Mrs. Greenwood envelops me in a hug and nods at her son in approval. Dr. Greenwood thrusts a weathered hand my way and shakes mine firmly.

"The pleasure is ours," Mrs. Greenwood says. "Seth tells us you have a beautiful voice from the Lord Himself, and you have a job as a patent attorney."

"Well, I'm a patent attorney, anyway. I'm sorry I'm late. See this gorgeous puppy your son gave me? He caused me a bit of trouble at work today. I had to stay a little late."

"You bought her a dog?" Seth's mother looks confused. *Yeah, join the club. I was thinking princess-cut diamond myself.*

"Ashley loves animals."

I smile, "Well, I love Rhett anyway. He's a great dog, and we're working on sitting. Rhett, sit!" I say, and my puppy jumps on my latest pair of nylons. I feel them unravel up my shin. I smile again. "Sit!" Rhett just looks at me, his puppy dog eyes not connecting. "Well, like I said, we're working on it."

"Let's go eat," Seth announces. "This is a late dinner for my parents."

Just help me out here. "Yes, I'm so sorry." I say again.

I see Mrs. Greenwood jab Seth in the back for being rude. Our ride in their rented Taurus is fairly quiet, but I'm sitting in the back with Seth's mother, and she's smiling at me. Finally she speaks. "So Seth tells me you spend time in Taiwan."

"I do. I'm not really supposed to, since most of my work is American law, but seeing the product firsthand helps me in the patent process, so I tend to spend time there."

"Do you like Taiwan?"

Hmm. How do I answer this tactfully? "I'm not really a fish person, so the eating is difficult. But I love the people." Which is true.

Mrs. Greenwood laughs. "When Cal and I first went to China, I'll never forget our first meals. I didn't know how to cook, and I'd burn the rice. I didn't know you could burn anything by boiling it, but apparently, if there's not enough water, you can burn anything. Cal didn't think going out to eat was a good example to set, so he hired an older Chinese woman who taught me everything I know. I think in those early days, the Chinese woman laughed at me."

"Now she cooks like a professional, of course," Dr. Greenwood says. "And she taught our daughter when she was still toddling, so when Sara came home for college, she fed some poor seminary student and now I have a son-in-law. They're based in Hawaii with the mission."

"You never told me you had a sister, Seth."

"You never asked."

Again, Mrs. Greenwood whacks the back of the driver's seat, and I have to stifle my laughter. "We always planned to leave China when our kids were grown, but now it's home. With Sara in Hawaii and Seth going to India, I suppose there is no place we really call home. We're a bunch of gypsies, this family."

I honestly think Seth's mother has the gentlest nature I've ever encountered. You just feel God's presence when you're around her, and his father, while stodgy and old-fashioned, still has that look in his eye when watching his wife. That John/Brea thing where you hold something very valuable. For all intents and purposes, Seth should covet marriage. He should be dying to get the same deal his dad has, but he's not. I long to tell Seth's mother how we breezed right through the Jeopardy phase and went straight into cut bait. I'm floating away as we speak.

"How long are you visiting for?" I ask.

"We'll be here a month. Dr. Greenwood has a heart doctor and we visit once every two years for medical care."

I look at Seth's dad who has the build of an old Marine, and I can't imagine him letting a heart issue get to him.

"We came to see Seth, too, Mother," Cal says.

"We did," Mrs. Greenwood says, "But of course, now that he'll be in India, it should be easier. Will you miss him?" she asks me. Seth looks at me in the rearview mirror. His intense blue eyes are lit by the headlights behind us.

"I will miss him, but Seth has to do what he has to do."

"I want Ashley to go with me, Mother," Seth explains.

"You don't want to marry Seth? You two seem so right for each other," Evelyn Greenwood says. And I feel the tears starting to sting. How do I explain he hasn't asked without making him look like a total loser?

"The subject hasn't come up," I finally say with a smile, and Mrs. Greenwood takes my hand.

She speaks again. "It's been so long since I had a pie from Marie Callendar's. I've been dreaming of it. I'm considering not ordering dinner and just getting pies to try. What do you think, Ashley?"

"I think if you came all the way from China, you should get whatever your heart desires."

"We've only been seeing each other for nine months," Seth blurts. I guess it's his late response to the question about commitment, but I'm just embarrassed for him.

"Your father and I knew each other six weeks." She turns back to me. "Lemon meringue and strawberry-rhubarb. That's where I'll start. What about you, Ashley? Will you join me?"

"German chocolate," I say trying to ignore the fact that Seth has just announced we're not getting married, and that all this had been decided before this fiasco called dinner.

The rest of "supper" as Evelyn called it, is a wash. Seth's mother and I bond and eat pie, while he talks to his dad about ministry possibilities in India. Mrs. Greenwood is so entirely normal. I wasn't expecting that. I think of people who spend their lives in the ministry on a higher plane, but she's probably the most down-to-earth woman I ever met.

At Seth's doorstep, I grab up Rhett and his water dish. "Evelyn, it was such a pleasure to meet you. You too, Cal. I hope you have a wonderful visit, and a safe trip home. If you need anything while you're here after Seth leaves, just call me." And I hand them each a business card. "Even if you just need more pie, you call me."

Seth walks me down to my car. "My mother likes you."

"I like her."

"She's a great lady."

Enough of the elephant in the room already. I didn't graduate with honors for this. "Look Seth, I know things are strained between us, but I do wish you the best with your future. With India and whatever else it holds."

"But you won't agree to go."

Not without a ring, no. I don't think I'd even go with a ring at this point. I'm failing to see what I ever saw in Seth Greenwood. He stands before me with a warm look in his perfectly incredible tanzanite eyes, and I feel nothing.

"If I went to a foreign country with a man who's not my husband, what would that say about my faith?" *Okay, besides my boss.* "I'm old-fashioned, I guess." I meet his gaze. "I'm not the one, Seth. If I was, it wouldn't be this hard." *Personally, I think you ought to look into a marble statue, but that's another day's conversation.*

He grabs my hands. Rhett whimpers. "I can't see myself marrying anyone else. I just don't think marriage is right for me, yet."

Suddenly, I don't see his strong moral convictions, or his piercing blue eyes. I see a wimp. A man who is so afraid of losing that he can't take a risk, and I'm momentarily disgusted by the sight of him: by his bald head, by his simpering expression, by his complete lack of guts. He's right. Marriage isn't right for him. And it's all about him. It always has been.

I pick up the Indian silk scarf that's in my car and hang it around his neck. "Good luck to you."

"I'm sorry, Ashley." His eyes carry the weight of the world in them. He hates to hurt me, but what can he do? He can't commit either.

You are sorry, I think to myself. *Sorrier than you know.* "Seth, I'm going back to the office. I didn't get anything done, and now I have Rhett to protect me."

"Will you come to the airport to see me off?"

I shake my head. "I don't think so."

"So this is it." He cups my cheeks in his hands. I pull away. Whatever I felt, it's like God just said, enough!

"Stay safe," I whisper.

"I'll miss you." He kisses me again on the lips, and there's nothing. No sweeping emotion, nothing. It's probably like kissing my brother, but Lord forbid I ever find out what that *really* feels like.

Rhett and I get into the car, and I watch Seth in my rearview mirror through the veiled view of the evening fog. Nine months and a heart full of love, wasted on a tin man.

21

I can't work. I go home and cuddle with Rhett on the sofa. I eat ice cream. Not that low-carb stuff, but full-on, bring-on-the-sugar-high Breyers. And I put it on top of a homemade apple pie that Kay made. I am on carb overload and I'm loving the endorphin response. Exercise helps endorphins. So what? Sugar is so much easier and *sans* the pain. Unless you count that thigh issue. And when you're in man-hating mode, does the thigh issue even come up?

I'm sitting in the kitchen, in the one little area that is still free of the combat construction zone. It's like I'm living in a campground. Our kitchen cabinet contents are strewn on one counter and covered with plastic in preparation for the contractor. Who of course, will arrive when he pleases. I'm letting Rhett lick my pie plate when Kay walks in from work at ten p.m. She's too tired to notice that I'm distraught, but hones right in on my food choice.

"What happened to the diet?" she asks, staring at the half-eaten pie in front of the dog.

"What diet?"

Kay lifts her eyebrows and plops down at the table. "Can I have a piece?"

I get a plate and serve her a heaping helping of starch and sugar. "So any word on when the construction will start?"

"I'm going to do it myself if I don't hear from them this week.

The demolition was a lot easier than I thought." Kay shakes her head. "You know, I think I'd really be good as a general contractor. Engineers and laborers seem to have the same issues with management. Not to mention actual work."

"You make more as an engineering director," I remind her. "And you can always reward a good job with a trip to Laser Quest. I think working men are brighter than that."

"Well, you're in a mood."

"Yeah. Seth's leaving for India for good tomorrow."

"Can't say I'm surprised. So what's going on with the dog? Are you keeping him?"

Rhett whimpers and lifts his head off the floor as though he knows who we're talking about. "Yeah, I'm keeping him." The dog relaxes again. "I know it's a hassle and I really have no place for him, but he's my baby now, and after watching Miles, maybe the only kind I can handle. Besides, I can't just get rid of him. He's the only male who understands me."

"How are you holding up?" Is a tear forming in Kay's eye? I'm beginning to see that she feels everything a woman should feel, but you think she doesn't, because she's so capable, so above common emotions. She must have had her heart broken at least once. I can see it in her eyes now.

"I'm okay." I shrug. "I think when he said 'India,' I started to brace for this. When you love someone, you want so badly to make it work, to be the person he wants, and then one day he says the name of a foreign country, and it strikes you . . . *I* don't want this. I don't think I want *him*."

As a woman, it's easy to forget your own dreams. And it's so very dangerous.

"You do seem to be taking it well. I guess that has me a little nervous. You aren't known as the drama queen for nothing. Did you call Brea?"

"Brea's got enough to worry about." I pick up the plate off the floor and head to the sink, moving plastic sheeting as I go. I put the plate in the sink with a clunk. "I just wish I hadn't wasted so much time, you know? And so much of my heart." I turn around and face Kay. "When he didn't want to marry me, why did I think I could change that? Arin, Kevin, the dog . . . why didn't I read any of those clues, Kay?"

"Because, quite simply, the clues stink. Who wants to think your fears are realized? That you're ticking away your biological clock on a man who doesn't care about the impending explosion." Kay's got tears running down her cheeks now, and she shoves a heaping spoonful of pie in her mouth.

"If it had been a patent, I would have reworked everything immediately." I drop my head. "I waited around thinking I could control my destiny. I can't even control my dog."

"When it happened to me, it shook my faith to its foundation," Kay admits, and suddenly I see that she is not made of stone. She loved a man once, and he didn't love her back.

"I believe that's because the Bible says beauty is fleeting, and Christian men used to understand this. The truth is, Christian or not, today's men live in a Victoria's Secret state of mind, Ashley."

I shake my head while I rinse the plate off methodically. "I'm sorry, Kay."

She waves a hand. "It's ancient history."

"Look at this gorgeous house, Kay. And think about our great jobs. I was never thankful for anything. I was always just thinking I deserved something more. I thought when Seth *rescued* me at my brother's wedding, my life was beginning. It's pathetic really."

Kay is sniffling now as she nods in agreement. I feel like I'm in an earthquake. Kay is a rock. She's always a solid foundation beneath me, and seeing her so shaken up rattles me to the core. It's like a 7.2 on the Richter. "I'll be in my room," she says. "God has something better, Ash."

"Thanks. That seems to be the consensus of the day, and I think

I'm going to believe it." I pick up Rhett after Kay shuffles down the hallway.

"I'm a downer, Rhett. Are you prepared for that?" Rhett licks my face with a big, loud slurp.

It's past eight a.m. when I wake up. I have a major headache from the sugar OD last night. Still, I feel refreshed and ready to turn over a new leaf. It's like the Seth part of my life needs to be purged so I can move on to health. Maybe that's a bit dramatic, but I feel relief that he's leaving today. I'll mourn. He'll always have a piece of my heart, but I praise God that he'll have nothing else. I'm worth more than that.

I notice that Kay has fixed the back fence, and I leave Rhett in the yard with a hope and a prayer, not to mention a few chew toys. I zip up a pair of Franco Sarto boots, and I'm on my way. This is the first day of the rest of my life. Wait. I think that's for alcoholics, not emancipated girlfriends. Whatever.

I stop for a breve latte, and decide to start fresh with Mr. Atkins after my sugar-filled binge, which has left me with what, I think, feels like a hangover. My mouth is cotton-ball dry, and my skin looks like wedding parchment paper—a sad irony—and I can feel my heart beating. I'm made aware of each thump pulsing through my thin, pasty skin. This can't be good. I grab a bottle of water too and suck down my breve latte like I'm in a decaf desert. Pulling into the parking lot, I see by his Jaguar that Hans has already arrived.

Straightening my shoulders, I head for his office. He's on the phone, and holds up a lanky hand, motioning me in. He covers the phone. "Shut the door." I shut it and wait while he yells at someone in a foreign language. Without so much as a good-bye, I think, he hangs up the phone. "I did it."

"Did what?" I ask, thinking I'm going to hear about a fabulous new deal, or even better, my impending promotion.

"I am sending Sophia home. Made the arrangements early this morning."

"Does she know?"

"I'll tell her tonight."

"She's not a dog, Hans. You just can't decide to ship her home like Italy is the pound." My hands are flailing as I pace the office. Is this what men think? "This is not King Henry's times. You can't rule with an iron fist."

He leans back in his chair, oozing confidence. "She has no green card. She doesn't have a choice."

"You've got to be kidding me! She lives with you, takes care of your house among . . . other things." *Like your marriage.* "So you just send her home without a word?" I bite down on my lip. I've just accused my boss of shacking up. I'm thinking this doesn't bode well for a promotion, and I finger my ear, like maybe what I said can go away. "I'm sorry. This is none of my business. I've had a bad couple of days. I'll be in my office when you're ready to discuss the latest contracts."

"Wait."

I turn around and face Hans, and I feel a tear escape from my left eye, followed by another from my right eye. As sure as I stand here, I know that Sophia is no different from me. She must move on without an option. At least I still have my self-respect.

Hans's palms are open to the ceiling. "You were telling me to send her home, were you not?"

I stare at him. "I didn't think you'd listen. Why would you listen to me? Besides, she's a person, Hans. What I meant was, tell her that you don't plan to marry her. Let her start over again and not waste her time. I didn't mean for you to book passage on the *Titanic.*"

"That's what I plan to do. Be honest with her. That's what you said and being honest is sending her home."

"Being honest takes on a different meaning when she's staring at some airline ticket you just handed her. That doesn't give her a whole lot of options. Your plan is to tell her it's over, just like that, and send her on her way?"

Hans sits back in his chair, tosses his feet on the desk, and studies me like a psychologist. He can see my tears, but doesn't want to address them. And why would he? "Your promotion came through last night at the board meeting. Congratulations." He stands up to shake my hand.

I'm just numb. I don't know how to react, but I know my mind isn't on this supposed promotion.

"Men stink," I hear myself say.

"Did you hear me? About the promotion, I mean."

I nod. "Doesn't it matter at all that Sophia loves you?"

"I don't love her. She's always known that." He straightens some files on his desk. "She needed a place to stay, and I got a girlfriend. But it's over. My wife has moved on, and now I can too."

I shake my head and lean against the wall for support. People really are cold. That's a stark realization. "I saw Sophia's face at the airport that day, Hans. I don't think she was nearly as enlightened as you think."

"Do you need some time off, Ashley? You seem quite concerned about my love life when you've just gotten the promotion you dreamed about."

I feel my head bob up and down. "I think I do need time off. I have a sugar hangover."

"A what?"

I fling my hand. "Oh, never mind. You wouldn't understand." And then I jump off the pathetic precipice I've been straddling so carefully. "Sophia deserves better. I deserve better."

"Take the afternoon off. You're useless to me like this, anyway." He points his lanky finger at me. "But don't give me that glass ceiling business, Christopher Henway is never in my office in a mental state. It's a way of life for you."

I nod. I go back to my office, grab the work I need to accomplish, and stuff it into my briefcase. The gift certificate Brea bought me tumbles out, and suddenly rain-forest therapy doesn't sound nearly so ridiculous. I call the spa's number. Incredibly, they have time for me.

Yea for a slow economy! It's been ages since I had a spa treatment, and I just feel haggard. There's nothing like slothlike lounging and being slathered in natural creams and potions to make me forget that I am a loser. With a capital *L*.

22

Taking stock of my life is like counting up negative numbers, and I never was very good at math. I bought a house, but it's in several pieces and missing a bathroom, which happens to be the very bathroom I purchased. Yes, I got promoted, but I'm really more my boss's shrink than his employee. Far worse, he's turning into mine. I had a boyfriend, but the lure of a squalid, poverty-stricken third-world country beckoned him away from me. At least my dog loves me, and I'm still a full-fledged member of the Reasons singles group.

I stare at my steering wheel, contemplating my destination when my cell phone rings. I see it's my mother. I look up at the sky. *You know, just kick me when I'm down.*

"Hello, Mom."

"Ashley, where have you been? It's like you live in another country with how much we hear from you."

I'll admit, I don't see my parents nearly as much as a good daughter should. My mother is like June Cleaver brought back from the vaults. She's like Nick-at-Nite live. I love her dearly, but success to her is a man in the house and a bun in the oven. I'm afraid my advanced degrees and job title will never impress her. She just wants more than that for me.

"I've been in Taiwan and working as usual. But I got a puppy," I add cheerfully.

"When do you have time for a puppy? Does Seth like animals?" My poor mom, ever worried about the elusive husband who slips through my fingers like tiny sand pebbles.

"I guess he does because he bought Rhett for me. But Seth is in India." I look at my watch. "Well, he will be by this time tomorrow."

"I'll never understand you young people, Honey. Why can't you just settle down? You spend more time on planes than in your own home. In your grandfather's day, they had no choice; there was a war. But you kids do have choices. I know your father and I are old-fashioned, but it's just no way to live. I want you to have more than this, Honey."

"Amen to that. How's Mei Ling, Mom?" My sister-in-law is expecting. How green is my valley.

"She's doing well. She's got that little basketball tummy like Brea. She's happier than a clam and eating like a warthog. I told her she must be having a boy." My mom laughs in her giddy way. Her grandmotherly days are about to begin. "When will Seth be back? I'd like to have you both for Thanksgiving."

And here it comes. "He's not coming back, Mom."

She's quiet as she assimilates this information. "Before Thanksgiving? He's not coming back before Thanksgiving?" Ever the optimist.

"He's not coming back at all, Mom. It's over between us."

She gasps. "I don't believe that. At your brother's wedding, you two were the talk of the casino."

"Denial only works for awhile. Trust me on that one."

"Ashley, Honey, I'm sorry."

"Thanks, Mom." And suddenly I'm overwhelmed with the desire to call Seth. Call it a setback, but my dialing finger is itchy. "You know Mom, I'd like to call him before he goes. Just to wish him luck and all."

"Sure. Sure, honey. We love you. Dinner's at four on Thanksgiving."

"Can I bring a friend?"

"Of course. Kay's always welcome."

I open my mouth to explain about Kevin and the food kitchen, but decide it best just to leave that for another day. Telling my mother I'm bringing a Stanford surgeon to dinner is a bit like telling her the wedding's on. And then there's the whole Mensa issue. My parents would probably think that's a monthly visitor.

I say good-bye and dial Seth's number. His sweet mother answers and I'm just about to snap the phone shut . . .

"Ashley?" *Grr. Caller ID.*

"Mrs. Greenwood?"

"Seth's gone, honey. Are you looking for him?"

I try to hide my pathetic disappointment. "Of course, he's gone. I guess I just wanted to make sure."

"He left about an hour ago."

"I wanted to tell him I made general counsel." *Not that I ever work currently.*

"That's wonderful, darling. He'd be so happy for you." Mrs. Greenwood's tone changes. "I'm sorry about Seth, Ashley. I don't know what we did to scare him on marriage, but I'm afraid he might never settle down."

I try to laugh her comment off. "Maybe he'll find a nice Indian girl." Or perhaps Arin.

"He's missing the chance of a lifetime with you. His father and I know that, dear, but God's will be done."

"Thank you." There's such peace in knowing you impressed the parents. That, given the opportunity, they might embrace you into their family. I take solace in the fact that this gentle-hearted woman thinks I'm good enough to marry her son. And I didn't even have to take the IQ test. We say good-bye, and I dial Brea.

"Hello?" Brea's tone is desperate.

"Are you bored?"

"You have no idea. Did you know the same people are on *All My*

Children that were on it when we were in high school? I thought *we* were in a rut. But Erica still looks as gorgeous as ever."

"I feel for her. But she is married in real life. And she runs like this billion-dollar company on the Home Shopping Network. So I guess I don't really feel for her."

"Remember Edmund?" Brea sighs wistfully. *Every man she ever mentions looks exactly like John.* "Ooh! Ooh, wait a minute. You know, Ash, if I could have this kind of plastic surgery, I would *so* be there. They look fabulous. Where are you? Turn on the TV a minute. Channel 7."

"I'm in the car."

She's quiet for a minute. "Did you want to tell me something?"

"And miss the recap of the morning soaps, you mean? Fill me in. My life has nothing on soap operas."

"I don't know about that. How's the boss?"

"Funny you should ask. He's sending his girlfriend home to Italy. The international affair has ended."

"Did you have something to do with that?" *Hmm. How would a politician answer this question?*

"I'd like to think not." I slink back against the leather driver's seat. "Why do people listen to me, anyway? I can't even get my own life together, and people are taking my advice like I'm Dr. Laura. Would you take advice from someone overwhelmed by a puppy?"

"Yes. You're very good at looking at the big picture, Ash. That's why people trust you."

"I'm good at looking at the big picture." I start to laugh. "Brea, if it was paint-by-number on a four-inch canvas, I couldn't see the whole picture. And I'll prove it." I clear my throat. "Seth left for India today. For good. Without me."

I hear the TV click off. "You knew he would."

"Yeah, I did."

"So, Kevin was here earlier. Brought me some more ice cream. So we're mourning Seth, why?"

"I'm a glass-completely-empty-with-a-hole-in-the-bottom kinda girl. Give me a chance to wallow, okay?"

"Maybe you make negative things happen with that attitude."

"Fair enough. Maybe I do." I look at my watch and speed through a yellow light. My Rainforest sprinkling awaits. "I'm taking the day off and going to get that treatment you bought me. Hans got me promoted to general counsel."

"In return for what?"

"And you talk about *me* being negative? What do you think? I've suddenly turned into a wanton ambitious vixen?"

"No, I just think it was hard work those first couple weeks, when you never had a day off," Brea says enthusiastically. "Hard work and solid commitment and rock-hard patents. When all others failed, you were there. You were in Taiwan. You were in Seattle. You were—"

"Are you through?" I ask.

"I'm sorry. I'm sure that's what the secretaries think. I'm happy for you, but not really, because I hate that you keep getting these promotions, and you keep working so hard that you don't have time to meet anybody decent. It's kind of a treadmill, only not the kind that makes you thinner. I thought you and Seth stood a chance because he's just as big a slave as you are."

"I'm here at the spa." I find parking right in front. Again, loving the down economy. "It was a perfect gift. Thank you for that."

"You're welcome. Do me a favor, don't get in there and start thinking about all the patents you left on your desk, or what you should have said to Seth, or that you've stressed me out with your news. Just relax. Can you do that for me?"

I look down at my empty double latte cup. "I can try."

"He's not wer-thee, Ash."

We both laugh at the reference to our youth, and Wayne and Garth from *Saturday Night Live*. "I'll call you tonight."

It's early and I park my TT right in front of Provence in Saratoga. Saratoga is a small, wealthy town surrounded by the mountains that separate Silicon Valley from the Pacific Ocean. I should say wealthier because the Valley is a place where money is entirely taken for granted. If you live here, you just have it. You might not have friends, or time, or serious relationships, but money is the least of your worries. Unless you're looking for a place to live.

The soothing scents of Saratoga reach my nose: heady redwood and eucalyptus mingle with fresh-roasted coffee and the various aromas of the culturally elite restaurants preparing for the lunch rush. I was born to live here.

I enter the spa's courtyard and the little dripping sounds begin. What is that? Is it supposed to be relaxing? Because I'm thinking Chinese water torture, and what's the difference? Once inside Provence, I'm met with a whole new realm of sensations. There's the soft continual splash of the fountain, and the soothing scents of lavender and almond oil with ylang-ylang. Combined with the subtle mural of the French countryside, I feel like I've been transported to Europe, and hope for serious change starts rising inside me.

"Good morning. Velcome to Provence. How may I help you?"

"I'm here for a rain-forest therapy." That sounds so stupid, I feel like I'm ordering McNuggets. "The reservation is under Ashley Stockingdale."

"Ah yes, you'll find a robe and slippers in the dressing room. Vould you like some tea or water perhaps?"

"No, no, thank you." I make my way to the dressing room, which is draped in rich taupe brocade, and looks like something out of a Gold Rush brothel, but I try to dispel such thoughts. There's a younger, more refreshed Ashley waiting to burst forth onto the scene, and this overly decorated spa holds the key.

A teenager, at least I think so, meets me in the waiting area. "Hello, Ashley. I'm Isabella, and I'll be doing your rain-forest therapy today." She sits me down in front of a mirror and begins to finger my hair, feeling the texture like it's a piece of modern art. "Your hair is natural, no?"

"Naturally curly, yes."

"Such a beautiful auburn. But you are stressed, no? I see in your skin the toll of your life."

Now there's a comment I could do without. Let's get this over with. I stand up. "I was given this therapy as a gift. I'm not sure what it is, or if—"

"You vill love it." She moves her arms around like she's doing some intense foreign dance. "It vill take zee impurities from your skin and your body, and zee therapy vill vork for days after your visit. You vill be a new voman."

A new vermin. There ya go. The sum total of my life. I can be transformed into a new rat. She leaves me alone, I undress, climb onto the terry-cloth table that looks like some kind of torture device, and wait for an eternity until Isabella decides to return. So passive-aggressive the way they leave you waiting naked under a blanket like a slab of meat waiting for marinade.

After what feels like an eternity listening to creepy nature sounds, Isabella returns. "The temperature is okay, no?"

"It's fine, thanks."

She starts to massage my back, then says, "Now I vill add zee marjoram oil." As she drips it on my back, she explains further. Like I need a narrative on this. I don't want to know any more about what's happening than I want to know the contents of a McNugget. "It helps to lower the blood pressure and vorks as a laxative," she rambles, "and to help calm the nervous system." *Ah, well slather it on then!*

She rubs that on, then I feel another dribble. "This is oil of rosemary." I smell like a chicken. "It is used to aid the immune system and support hair growth." *Where was this stuff after my last haircut?*

My back starts to sting just a tad. "Can you wipe some of that off? It's stinging a little."

She just keeps rubbing. Apparently, her English is not as good as her aromatherapy. "This should help," she finally says. "This is oil of oregano." Now I smell like an Italian chicken. And I'm getting hungry. "It promotes balance and clears the bronchial tubes."

"You know, this is really starting to hurt. Do you have anything gentler?"

"Oil of eucalyptus. It is help to deepen concentration and to increase awareness."

I turn around and see she's reading this garbage off the bottles. *Aromatherapy for Dummies,* it probably says. My back is now feeling quite raw, like a really bad sunburn.

"Ouch, that stings!" I hop up in my towel and my voice sounds unusually high pitched. "Get it off me!"

But there stands Isabella with even more bottles, more soothing jars of mystery potions to scald the skin from my body.

"Where's a shower?"

"A shower might cause the oils to react with your skin." How strange. Her accent is now completely gone.

"How do I get this off me?" I say, hopping like a fish on a hook. I rub against the towel, but the more I move, the more I hurt. "Please. Please get this off me."

"Lie down," she says. "You must have sensitive skin. Why didn't you tell me?"

"Oh yeah, this is my fault. Because I didn't know you were going to slather me up and sauté me in pain, that's why!"

Okay, Christian reaction not good, but I hurt! This is so *not* suffering for Jesus. I look at the pots and jars of stuff on the counter, praying for something soothing-looking. I find a green cucumber medley that looks souffléish and slap it on my back. "Oh," I gasp, feeling like I've just hit ice after being on fire. "Put that on, please!"

Isabella rubs it on and then takes a towel to my back. I don't even care that my backside is completely flailing in the wind. I pull my clothes on as soon as the piercing irritation stops. I pick up the eucalyptus oil. "Look, it says right here to be used sparingly or in a bath."

"It's pure oil. It cleanses the system."

"It *strips* the skin, Isabella. Like a deer tick." Poor Isabella's face is stricken, and I realize I'll be terrible in labor. I can't even handle massage therapy. "I'm sorry. I just wasn't expecting that. I guess my skin *is* sensitive."

"Please don't tell my boss. I need this job," she says again, in perfect English.

I look at her and start to laugh. "Please don't tell my best friend that I couldn't relax." I look over my shoulder at my back, and it's red like fresh-cooked lobster. "Anyway, I do feel purged. We've just eliminated the essential oil of Seth and that's a good thing."

She looks at me like I'm crazy. But I suppose it's not every day she sees a customer do the hokey-pokey during rain-forest therapy.

23

Thanksgiving, and I have a million things to be thankful for: I made general counsel by the age of thirty-one. I have a best friend from heaven, a church that I love, a great family. Well, okay. A really nice family, anyway. I'm going to be an auntie. (Three times over if you count Brea's babies.) And of course, most importantly, I'm loved by Jesus. There, that's the positive view. Now I can whine.

It's another year where I'm technically alone on Thanksgiving: lost between a legitimate spot at the adult dinette and the folding table beside my ten-year-old second cousin. It's a year when the draw of a foreign culture was stronger than my boyfriend's love for me, and being dumped is fresh and raw—right before the Christmas season. Remember how in high school, guys would break up right before Valentine's Day so they didn't have to buy a gift? Well, bingo. Here I am, only worse than that.

Once, I read the story of Mumtaz, an Indian princess so loved by her emperor husband that when she died giving birth to their four-teenth child, Shah Jahan built the Taj Mahal for her mausoleum. Mumtaz inspires love. I apparently inspire fear, and Seth's escape to India, Mumtaz's final resting place, is as close as I get to true devotion.

And yet there are all these men in my life that don't run. All these possibilities that aren't really possibilities. Like my boss. The way he looks at me makes me feel desirable. But then reality sets in. This is a man who hangs women on a tree like ornaments. Call me: *Christmas 2003*. And then there's Kevin, who is clearly impossible. And then there are the Reasons.

Kay is organizing Thanksgiving dinner for the entire abandoned singles' group. Their parents are somewhere across the country, and they're here. Generally, the Reasons eat out, but there's a paltry selection on Thanksgiving Day, and it gives Kay an excuse to use the fine china. So everybody's happy.

"Everything looks great, Kay." There's a harvest-colored, plaid tablecloth with rust candles, and a huge bouquet of fall flowers adorning her antique table.

"You don't think it's too much?"

"Kay, you know everything you do is perfectly incredible, and you'll be the talk of the Reasons for a month."

She pouts at me. "That doesn't make me feel any better. I want things to be nice, Ashley. None of these people have anywhere to be today. Our house is such a wreck right now. I hope everyone's okay with that."

"They could all be with me at the food kitchen. They need servers, Kevin says."

"That's not fair. You're going to your mother's for dinner later. The guys are going to watch football here. It's so anti-Silicon Valley, there might actually be conversation. I would think you'd like us getting together. You're always saying that we need to get a social life."

I said that? "Forgive me, I'm Scrooge today, okay?"

"Seth hasn't called?"

I toss my hand. "Oh, who cares about Seth? I'm loyal to the wrong people." Rhett whines at my feet and I scrunch his face in my hands. "Not you, Sweetie. You are worthy of being loyal to."

"Did you invite Kevin to your mother's?"

"I'm just going to tell him he can come if he wants once we're done." I shrug. "I don't want him to think I'm making any kind of move. I'm very leery of his attention, especially when I met this sweet little nurse the other day, who seemed enamored of him." I crinkle my face. "Actually, she was a complete shrew, but I imagine Kevin needs a strong woman to put up with his mother."

"You're hopeless, Ashley. Just because a guy resembles Bill Gates, it does not make him good husband material. Sheesh, talk about judging someone by their looks. I honestly think you're prejudiced against good-looking men."

I laugh out loud. "I'm so not prejudiced against good-looking men. But come on, a doctor and a lawyer? That's not exactly a match made in heaven." I sigh. "Kevin's under this delusion that I'd be a fun date."

"And you're refusing to check that out. Why?"

I shake my hands. "I'm not into that whole Mensa thing, the country club thing, the handsome-like-Hugh-Jackman thing. We're from different worlds and that never works." I puff out my chest. "I'm going to find myself a nice, middle-class guy and work from there. Move up in baby steps, you know, maybe a little more hair than Seth. Not a full, luscious crop like Kevin's." But thinking about his warm brown locks gets my fingers itching. I'd love to know what it felt like to run my fingers through. *No, no, no. Don't go there. So not healthy.*

"Are you saying you're looking for ugly? Because I can get you ugly. I have the nicest guy that works for me, but he's hairy like a gorilla. It sticks out of the back of the golf shirts he wears every day and covers the back of his arms. You interested?"

"Okay, ick. I don't want to talk about this. I'm just not interested in Kevin that way, and you can't force that feeling if it isn't there." Instantly I remember that stolen kiss in the parking lot. I know too well that the possibility is there, but I don't want to explore it anymore than I want to explore the Taj Mahal.

The doorbell rings, and Rhett barks.

"That's gotta be Kevin now. Stay out of it, okay? I'm begging you."

Kay shrugs. "No skin off my nose. But you wouldn't know a good man if he brought you flowers and introduced you to fine dining. Isn't that what Kevin did?" Kay winks, takes off for the kitchen, and calls back out at me. "If you want to meet Bigfoot, let me know. I imagine he's free."

I open the door and Kevin is standing there with huge yellow sunflowers. I have a picture of a hairy Neanderthal engineer in my head. "Hi, Kevin," I say through my giggles. "The flowers are gorgeous."

"Gorgeous like you." It sounds cheesy, but not the way he says it. Kevin is just suave, like there's a soap opera writer behind him, feeding him the words. Taking his jacket, I twist him around and study his arms, which sport the perfect amount of hair. Enough to be manly, not enough to resemble my local primate.

"Are you ready to go?"

"Yeah, let me get my coat." I put on my new Ralph Lauren navy peacoat, and maybe I do a little spin to get into it waiting for the forthcoming compliment.

"Is that new? It's beautiful."

I smile. "Got it on sale. Do you like it? Just my part to support the troops. Isn't it patriotic?"

He breathes deeply, then speaks. "It's a little fancy for the food kitchen. I wouldn't want you to get it dirty."

I sigh audibly. *Duh. Like the food kitchen is fashion week in New York.* "Right. You're right." I put the peacoat back on its hanger and get out my balled-up Lilly Pulitzer sweater. It doesn't match what I'm wearing, but what do I care? "Let's go."

His eyebrows lift, and I think he's about to point out my lack of color coordination, but he quickly sizes up my response and says nothing. Then his beeper goes off just as he opens the door. He looks at the phone, then at me. "Can you wait just a second?"

"Go for it." I plop back on the couch and sniff deeply to get the turkey aroma and to try to get into this day. Maybe matching clothes would help. I go to the closet and get out a red cardigan I bought at Bon-Macy's when I traveled to Seattle for work. It has seen better days, and I would have given it to Goodwill long ago if I didn't love it so much. There are those pieces that just define an era and make you feel good when you wear them.

The doorbell chimes again, and I open the door to Seth's leech, I mean, roommate, Sam. "Hi, Ashley, you staying?" He's carrying a pint of mashed potatoes from Boston Market. *Now I remember who did that the last time.*

"I'm going to serve at the Food Kitchen. Want to come?"

Rhett gets so excited by Sam's presence, he whizzes all over the entryway. Sam laughs like a little boy in a movie's obligatory burp scene. "Nah, I don't want to come." He says through his laughter.

I shove a rag and some Pine Sol into his hands. "Good, then you have time to clean up." I walk onto the porch into the crisp fall air and breathe the heady scent of sycamores. *Reset. Lord, I need a reset. Tell me what to do with my life. I need more than a map. I need GPS like Kay has in her Lexus. Tell me where to turn!*

The door opens and Kevin appears. "You ready, Ashley?"

"Don't you need to go to the hospital?"

"No, I just needed to consult with someone on duty. Let's go. We're going to have such a great day."

He leads me down the pathway, which Kay has lit with little turkey luminaries.

I look up the street. "Where's your Porsche?"

"I got rid of it. I felt like a jerk driving into the hospital. There's all these sick children, and I'm driving a sports car. It's like a bad joke. I worried I'd run into one of their parents in the lot."

I swallow my obvious response, like that I drive an Audi convertible, but maybe I *am* heartless. Kevin looks at me as if he reads my mind and lifts my chin.

"Because I make my money curing sick children, Ashley, not because I'm suddenly pious. I know you love your car, and it wasn't any kind of judgment."

I'm so transparent.

Sam comes out onto the porch and shouts at me to the sidewalk. "Ashley," he says, holding up the phone. "Seth's on the line. From India."

I look at Kevin and his smile disintegrates. I'm having a rotten holiday. No reason to ruin his, too. "Tell him I left already."

I take Kevin's arm and we walk to his new Dodge Stratus. He opens the door for me and kisses me on the cheek as I get in. "I can't wait to serve beside you."

Something about that comment feels so intimate that it makes me tingle. I shake it off, and look straight ahead as we drive. *Mensa. Mensa. Mensa,* I remind myself. Different kind of freak altogether. And the country club set?

I'd like to say that I'm so into serving at the food kitchen that I don't think about Seth and his phone call, but I do. I wonder why he called. What, if anything, he had to say about India. I wonder if he's seen Arin, and secretly, I hope he hates life without Thai food and Mexican cuisine. I plop a pile of mashed potatoes on a child's plate, and he smiles up at me from his five-year-old height. He has the bluest eyes I've ever seen next to Seth's.

"Thank you for the potatoes. They're my favorite!" He smiles and it lights up the room. "You're very pretty." He looks up at his mother for approval.

"You're going to have to watch out for this one," I say to his mother and she nods back to me.

Kevin leans over to the boy. "You have a good eye."

The little boy bobs his head up and down. Kevin drops the end of his spoon into the stuffing and gazes at me like I'm the whipped cream on the pumpkin pie. He opens his mouth to speak, but says nothing. The action leaves me breathless, like the time I macked this poor man in a San Francisco parking garage. I focus on the mashed potatoes in front of me.

"So . . . Ashley, where should we go so you can show off that new peacoat?"

"I have dinner at my mother's. You know it's Thanksgiving, right?"

"Are you inviting me?"

I nod. He notices the line is getting backed up and goes back to putting stuffing next to the turkey. I watch him momentarily, and decide he won't last an hour at my parents' house. With Dave there? Maybe ten minutes. All those country club manners he learned in Atlanta are useless against the Stockingdale clan.

24

As we get into Kevin's new car, we smell a bit rancid from all the cleanup work. Kind of a mixture of poultry innards and Ajax. "Do you think we should stop by home and clean up?" *Which is a nice way of saying, you smell like turkey guts soaked in sweat and I'm having trouble inhaling.*

"That'd be good. I don't want to meet your parents like this." Kevin looks down at his physique, and I admit the sight stops me cold. *Is it hot in here?*

I love Kevin's optimism. He doesn't want to meet my parents wearing Thanksgiving dinner, but will my dad even bother to zip his pants up for Kevin? That's the question of the day. Football and unencumbered eating go together like a Big Mac and Diet Coke.

Kevin drops me at home and says he'll be back in thirty minutes. I rush into the house, wave at all the Reasons, but hurry out of the living room. Currently, there's only one bathroom and someone's in it. Rhett comes bounding in the house to meet me and starts licking off the remnants of my morning. Rhett is followed by Kay, who comes down the hallway obviously miffed at my presence.

"What are you doing here?" Kay asks, a tray of puff pastry in one hand.

"I want to get cleaned up. Look at me. I'm filthy."

"We've got only one bathroom for the guests. Go to your mom's house."

"I can't go to my mom's. Kevin's picking me up in a half an hour."

"Well, do your best without a shower. *Please.* I've got twelve engineers here drinking apple cider and eggnog. Do you mind?"

The door opens to the bathroom, and poor Steve Welby comes out with a guilty grin. "Sorry."

"Ashley, please." Kay says again.

"Fine. Come on, Rhett." I grab my makeup bag and head to my room. I pull back the Sheridan quilt, take out some makeup remover with a cotton ball, and start the process. My hair is stringy from the steam in the serving trays, and I try to fluff it up with gel, but now my pasty face looks like it's crowned with a full mop of straight brown clumped-together straw. Well, I wanted to get into the Thanksgiving spirit. What better way than to look like a scarecrow?

I yank a brush through my hair and decide a ponytail is my best option. Grabbing a tortoise-shell barrette, I clip it up, and make the straight work for me. Oh yeah, now I got that '80s punk thing going on where it sticks out around the clip. Enough with the hair. Next.

I start to apply foundation and it's sticking to the still-wet makeup remover, so I have these streaks of pinkish-brown lines making me look like I have some kind of rare disease. Let's hope Kevin doesn't diagnose me. I go for the makeup remover again, and grab my blow-dryer and flip it on, letting the soothing heat breeze over my skin. There. My skin is officially dry.

I grab for the moisturizer (my mistake last time) and pat it on evenly and thoroughly and once again invite the desert breeze of the hair dryer to blow across my skin.

Layering. It's all about layering. Smooth layer of foundation this time, don't look like I'm developing leprosy. Now I go for the blush, and it's one of those new crème versions that's supposed to go on evenly, but I look a bit like my Great Aunt Babe. A pink splotch of rouge without reference points on the cheekbones. I try to rub it in, and it's better, but I still look like a Bratz doll without the dramatic eyes. Those are next.

I take out a brown eyeliner and try to hold my hand steady, but I'm just too nervous that I won't finish on time. "Forget it!" I brush on some mascara and call it a day, just as the doorbell rings.

"Clothes. Ack, I forgot clothes!" I slither out of my turkey jeans, and pull on an autumn-yellow Juicy hoodie and pants. It sounds too casual, but in velour and the fall color, it's perfect for an afternoon at my parents'. Quite couture and all, but I still smell like poultry.

I take a deep breath and see that Kay is greeting Kevin at the door, and I panic as I see his society parents standing behind him. I look down at my sweatpants, feel my pixie stick hairstyle, and start to hyperventilate. I am about to head back into the bedroom when Kevin sees me.

"Ashley, are you ready to go? Guess who showed up at my house?" He smiles at me, and my mongrel dog goes straight for the mother's nylons. I run after the dog, but he wants those pantyhose, and knocks over a table with a silver bowl of nuts on his way. All of them fly onto the hardwood floors in a torrent of hail-like bullets.

Mrs. Novak is horrified. Her first instinct is to run, which of course Rhett sees as an invitation to play tag, so he takes off after her.

"Ashley!" Kay yells at me and then bends over to start cleaning up the nuts.

I jump over the table and take off down the street. "Rhett! Rhett! Stop right now!"

Mrs. Novak is running, and she's pretty spry for an older woman. She's at the corner before Rhett even slows. He turns around, disappointed that the chase wasn't nearly as fun as he'd planned. His lowered head implies that he's sorry, and I take his face in my hands.

"What are you doing? No running!" I'm like one of those ineffective parents who's screaming at her child, "Stop hitting Mommy!" I grab a hold of Rhett's collar and drag him into the backyard. "Kevin! Tell your Mom it's okay to come back now. Rhett's put away."

Mrs. Novak is smoothing her St. John jacket, trying to walk back up the street with dignity. Oh, how I feel for her. I remember what it was like when I thought I had dignity. No one really has dignity; it's all an elaborate façade for the sake of others, and you just have to see how long you can go before the others figure it out. I bet Mrs. Novak generally makes it last beyond the first five minutes. But then, she hasn't spent much time around me.

I'm thinking Mrs. Novak knows now why I'm not a member of the IQ elite. My false image has dissipated into oblivion like a drop of water on the skillet. I walk back up to the porch and hold my hand out to greet Dr. Novak senior.

"Dr. Novak, I'm so sorry about the dog. What brings you into town?"

"We played in a charity golf tournament in Palm Springs. Thought we'd fly up and see what our son was up to." He pats Kevin on the back with vigor. Mrs. Novak squares her shoulders and walks up the steps to the porch. "Well, it seems dog training school might be in order."

"I'm sorry, Mrs. Novak. Rhett has a thing for nylons. It's like he has radar when he sees them."

Kevin's mother rolls her eyes and says, "A good obedience school would train that right out of him."

"Absolutely," I say. *So how did Seth turn out so warped with his kindhearted parents, and how did Kevin get to be normal? Genetics are a funny thing.* "Kevin, are you and your parents going out for dinner now? Because I'll just drive to my parents' alone."

"We were hoping we could take you by your parents, say hello, and that you'd have dinner with us afterwards." *Oh yeah, sign me up for that invitation.*

I smile, albeit condescendingly. "That's sweet, but it's been nearly a month since I've seen my parents and they only live across town. Besides, no one makes stuffing quite like my mother, and I want to see how Mei Ling, my sister-in-law, is progressing."

All righty then. Good to see you all. Don't let the door hit you in the rear on the way out.

I start to back up into the house, but Kevin stops me. His eyes are pleading as though he's looking forward to an afternoon with his parents about as much as I am. "We're going to eat at the Acorn. I know it's one of your favorites."

But of course, we've never discussed my meal preferences. Kevin is searching here, and I throw him a bone. "Will you have time to make your reservation if you drop me off?"

"We're Novaks, dear," the missus reminds me. "They'll hold us a table." Mrs. Novak throws her head back and laughs. I'm swearing I've seen her on a soap opera before (great plastic surgery notwithstanding). "Now darling, we'd really love to meet your family. Clearly for you to have made general counsel at your corporation by now must have made them quite proud."

"It's just . . . my mom will want to feed you. She can't stand someone coming to her house and not eating. It gives her physical pain, I think." I smile at Kevin, and he warmly winks at me. "She'll be quite offended if you just come in and run off, so maybe it's best if—"

"Mom, I think it's best if we just head to the restaurant. It's a family day at Ashley's. We've got no right to barge in."

"No, no, you wouldn't be barging in," I say, even though, yeah, they would. "Let me just call my mother so she knows what's happening. She'd love to have you." I dial the too-familiar number. "Mom? It's me, Ashley. You know how I wanted to bring a friend?"

"Yes, dear. We're waiting supper for you. Are you coming soon?"

"Can I bring three friends?"

"They're not friends of Seth's are they?" So I guess Seth has been officially crossed off my mother's Christmas list.

"No, Mom. I'm sorta seeing this doctor, and his parents are in town from Atlanta." I have to cover the phone from the squeal. "Mom, it's nothing serious. Just a friend that I served Thanksgiving with at the food kitchen with today." *A man that makes me look like yesterday's lettuce.*

"Oh dear, I look awful!" There's a muffled sound like my mother is fighting with the phone. "David, your sister is bringing a man home. Get this place cleaned up."

"Ashley found a guy? It's not the dog, is it?" Dave yells.

If there is any thought that I might be the right one for their son, and if Rhett hasn't taken care of any lingering doubts, my family is about to do the rest. I look toward Kevin, and he really does make me feel like a princess. It's a pity that his parents are straight from the inner sanctum of the country club on the lake of fire.

Kevin is in my living room, introducing his parents to the Silicon Valley geeks that are, for better or worse, my people. The expression on his mother's face tells me that she is seriously concerned about her son living amid a herd of walking robots. But there's little she can do about it at the moment, and she's all graciousness. She'll rise to fight a different day, just like the *Terminator.*

"Mom, we'll be there soon. Okay?" I say into the phone.

"Okay, Sweetie. I put the good Avon wine decanter on the table. Do they drink white or red?"

Safeway Chablis or Vinegar Chianti. Hmm. "I'm not sure, Mom. I doubt that they're drinkers, so don't worry about it or do anything special. I'm sure soda will be fine. They're from the South. Maybe they like tea."

There's this evil streak within me, where I can't wait to show off my parents. Not because I'm embarrassed by their complete lack of society rules, but because I'm proud of them. My parents, while they may lack in ritzy manners, are good solid people. Salt of the earth, as they say. My mother would give you the apron off her back. My father would build a patio for you for free and think nothing of it. I think Dr. and Mrs. Novak could use a lesson in the art of decency. And they're about to get it, Stockingdale-style.

I walk out into the living room. "Well, my mother says come ahead. She's looking forward to it."

"It simply isn't done, Dear." Mrs. Novak gathers up her purse. "I feel quite common for disrupting your mother's party." *Clearly, she doesn't feel common enough to not come.*

Kay follows me out the door, obviously hoping I don't ruin anything else about her special day as I go. Martha Stewart never had a roommate like me. There's a bouquet of dead black roses on the porch and a card addressed to me.

Gingerly, I bend down, open the card, and it reads: "Ciao, Bella, take good care of Hans. You seem to have taken good care of me. Sophia."

I crumple the card and shove it into my sweatshirt pocket. "What a sense of humor." I try to laugh it off, but I know all too well that my advice sent someone back to her country of origin. Guilt prickles down my spine, and the evil vision of black roses is doing nothing for my peace of mind.

Kevin comes up behind me and puts his arm around me. His parents start down the walk. "You all right? I'm sorry."

"I'm fine."

"My mother doesn't fool you, does she?"

The corner of my mouth lifts. "She doesn't *bother* me if that's what you mean." *Those roses on the other hand . . . now that's a little creepy.*

"That's how I knew you were special, Ashley. I knew the very first day you met them in San Francisco."

He jumps down the steps, and turns back toward me with a smile that makes me wonder if I don't have things all wrong. Kevin opens the door for his mother and me and slides into the driver's seat.

"I cannot believe you bought a domestic car, Kevin." Mrs. Novak is acting as though sitting in the vehicle might somehow infect her, and next thing you know, she'll be shopping at Wal-Mart.

Kevin turns around and winks at me. "A resident can't be too careful with finances, you know."

It dawns on me now that Kevin is not the man he was a year ago. He never talks about Mensa, he's traded in the Porsche, and he puts more time into ministry than the combined total of engineers at Kay's house for dinner. Maybe Brea is right. Maybe instead of Mensa I belong in the "special" class when it comes to romance.

25

We pull up to my parents' small bungalow. I instantly notice that it is not surrounded with the luxury of a manicured lawn, or, in certain parts, with any lawn at all. I see Mrs. Novak's eyes widen. Dr. Novak is talking patents with me, and Kevin is simply following my sporadic directions while his mother offers up a litany about golf swings.

Kevin parks on the street, behind my brother's 1984 Jeep Cherokee and in front of my Aunt Babe's Cadillac Seville. And suddenly, this really doesn't seem like a good idea. Mrs. Novak sits, ankles crossed, and waits for Kevin to open her door like she's Princess Di. Rather than appear to be equally high-maintenance, I clamber out of the car, only a little disappointed that I didn't get to see some chivalry in action. I charge up the walk, hoping to run interference, but my mother opens the door before I reach the porch.

"Ashley!" Mother cries out, as though I've just spent the last three years on a foreign mission trip. "Oh Sweetheart, it's so good to see you! And this must be . . ." She moves toward Kevin and kisses his cheek. In her mind, she's bowing at his feet. *Thank you. Thank you for dating our daughter! Where do we send the dowry?*

"His name is Kevin, Mom. Kevin Novak."

She looks at me expectantly.

"*Dr.* Kevin Novak," I clarify before my mother needs the heart paddles.

Now my brother Dave is in the doorway. Smiling. And my stomach plummets. Dave enjoys the oddest things in life, and I can picture him making up a fake disease for himself just to check Kevin's credentials. Anything that offers Dave a little humor gives him the utmost satisfaction. Hence, I don't usually bring guys home unless I'm either trying to get rid of them or am quite serious. At the moment, Kevin doesn't fall into either of those categories.

"Ashley!" Dave hops down the steps, taking them two at a time. He comes by my ear, whispering. "Not too bad. What's he got? Six months left to live or something?"

I clear my throat and make the proper introductions, trying my best to ignore my brother, who, by his very nature, relishes my misery.

My Great Aunt Babe comes out of the house, smoking her trademark ultrathin cigarette with her pinkie in the air, and just watches the whole exchange as though she's invisible. "I'll meet everyone when I've had my smoke," she rasps.

Dad's gardening skills give the impression that the house is a dump, but my mother is the world's most sanitized house cleaner in all of Palo Alto. She makes Kay look slovenly. And me? Well, she makes me look like the reincarnation of my father.

Mrs. Novak walks into the house, what little there is of it, and tries to find a proper place to sit. My mother takes her coat and welcomes her into the kitchen with the ladies. I'm sure entertaining in the kitchen is something the "help" normally does, but Mrs. Novak seems all right with it. Maybe to prove that, on this special day, she's thankful for servants.

My dad and Dr. Novak find their rightful place in front of the television with Dave. Immediately they are absorbed in football and start talking plays and injuries. Dr. Novak seems to have some disgusting tales about putting bones back in place, and my dad is listening with eager, shining eyes. When I hear his "snapping bone" impression, I have to move on into the kitchen with the domestics.

I turn around at the doorway. "Do you want anything to drink, Dr. Novak?" Kevin and his father look up. "Either of you Dr. Novaks?"

"A soda would be great, Ashley." Kevin looks up at me warmly, as though there isn't a place on earth he'd rather be, and I think, *Oh, honey, I'd get you a soda every day of my life.* I feel guilty of course, since it wasn't but earlier in the week that I was dumped like yesterday's trash. I can only imagine that my romantic meter is way off kilter. Like a pound puppy lacking attention, I don't want to go wagging my tail at every pair of Nikes that walk my way. Even if they are Cole Haan's like the enigmatic Greg Wilson from high school.

"Kevin," his mother says from the kitchen doorway, "call the restaurant and let them know we won't be coming."

Won't be coming! I run into the kitchen without taking Kevin's dad's order and notice that my Aunt Babe has finished her cigarette, and she, Mrs. Novak, and my mother are sitting around the kitchen table dishing. Mrs. Novak seems perfectly at ease and there's not a word about golf. Everyone, in my opinion, appears a bit too comfortable.

"So I said to my husband, let's go see Kevin, and so here we are." Mrs. Novak laughs, while my mother mashes potatoes across from the native Atlantan's couture jacket.

"Oh, Ashley, I'm so grateful you brought these wonderful people here. The Novaks are staying for dinner. Can you set them some places at the table? Mei Ling will be here a bit later."

"Where is Mei Ling?" I ask my mother, just now noticing that my sister-in-law is absent.

"She wasn't feeling well, poor dear."

Poor dear indeed. I feel a little stomach cramp coming on myself. Mei Ling did the time, though, living for six months with my parents because her husband was "saving" for a rental deposit, so I see that she deserves to be late. She probably deserves a month at a spa, but Mei Ling isn't me. She has the patience of Job.

I'm standing in the doorway a bit torn. Do I leave my mother alone with Mrs. Novak, terrified that she'll tell her those stories from my youth, like the time I was dancing with a skirt on my head pretending I was Madonna? Or about knocking myself out on the podium during my valedictory speech?

"Ashley, go set the table," my mother says again.

"I just need to get the Novak men some drinks." I go to the fridge and rummage around extensively, waiting to hear anything of interest.

My mother and Mrs. Novak are back to discussing parenting—the universal discussion of mothers everywhere. And they sound like they're comparing résumés: law school, medical school, valedictorian, college honors, and parenting two different personalities.

Kevin apparently has a sister. From the sound of what's *not* said about her, I can only assume that she and my brother Dave have something in common: namely, they're not really the résumé material a mother hopes for, but wonderful people. Presently, I'm moving the yams and the cranberry sauce back and forth in the fridge, anticipating more information. I mean, how long did it take me to learn Seth had a commitment issue? By the time I knew, I'd been put in the classification of pathetic. Spying might be something I should add to my résumé.

Mrs. Novak takes a sip of her Folgers, my mother's house blend for thirty years. "This is such wonderful coffee. We can't get coffee like that in Atlanta. Let me tell you, Mary, I'm so glad to meet you and your husband. I was a bit worried when Kevin started spouting all that religious stuff that Ashley here would be a bit of an odd duck."

Oh, I'm an odd duck all right. I pull my head out of the fridge and look at Kevin's mother. She smiles.

"You're not an odd duck at all, Dear."

Oh, trust me on this one. You know what they say, if it walks like a duck, and quacks like a duck . . .

"We hadn't even heard about Kevin, Elaine!" my mother bellows. *Elaine? Kevin's mother has a first name, go figure.* "Ashley never tells us a thing. We thought she was nearly engaged to another man, then boom, here's this doctor appearing on Thanksgiving. But Kevin seems like a nice boy. That last guy of hers, Seth, was the pocket-protector type, and bald. My grandchildren would have been bald in their twenties. Young women just never think long-term."

Mom, I am standing right here." *And bald men? Bring 'em on.*

"I know, Honey. I just never did like that Seth character." *Since, um, five minutes ago?*

"Ashley, what are you doing in that refrigerator? Go get the men their drinks and set the table."

"Kevin is the epitome of a southern gentleman," Elaine says. "He was just born that way, full of affection and concern for others. When he was only a small child, the first thing he would do is bypass the nanny and come say good morning to me. When he became a doctor, I thought, *Oh, how wonderful! He's following in his father's footsteps.* But he's nothing like his father. His father is like most surgeons, very straightforward, very hard-thinking. Kevin was never like that. He was always warm, and I wondered how he'd manage as a doctor. I guess he's found religion for that now."

I watch my mother listen with intensity to Kevin's mother, and suddenly realize that I never had anything to be worried about. Mary Stockingdale is the epitome of manners and hospitality. Oh sure, it may not be what Mrs. Novak is used to, but my mother could hold her own with Queen Elizabeth.

I'm the one with the issues and I worry about my mother. I laugh out loud, and the two mothers look at me.

"I'll just go set the table now."

Everyone looks so cozy as I walk into the living room. The guys are all laughing, eating dip and waiting patiently for their sodas. Kevin grabs for my hand as he takes his soda, and I have an epiphany.

Affection—that's what was missing! I was so busy searching for a commitment that I never bothered to notice that Seth possessed not an ounce of affection for me, or possibly for anyone. When Rhett acted like a puppy, or got in the way, Seth's answer was to take it back to the pound. And when our relationship got out of control, or as I like to say, in the double Jeopardy phase, Seth threw the playing pieces off the board and stalked away.

Kevin offers affection so readily that it makes me wonder. Maybe Hans and Seth have more in common than I want to admit. Maybe they both suffer from hardness of heart. Maybe I didn't want to face that because I was waiting for commitment, but I needed to face it as a practical woman in search of a godly husband. I so hate learning these lessons. I'm an A student in the classroom, but once I leave the hallowed halls of the academy and get into relationships, the word *flunk* takes on a whole new meaning.

Kevin is still holding my wrist. His smile starts with a simple grin, then spreads to his eyes and soon, his entire expression. While Seth could hide everything, Kevin is so transparent in his emotions that I have to admit he scares the daylights out of me. Dysfunctional and robotic I understand. After all, the Reasons are my people. But open and genuine? That is not my expertise.

"Ashley?" Kevin puts his drink down, takes my hand in his, and leads me to the porch.

"Kevin, I'm sorry I'm taking too long with your drink. I'm not my mother when it comes to hospitality." I'm just talking, trying to avoid my inner turmoil.

"You're wonderful, and you can take forever with my drink." He looks down at his pager and holds it up. "I need to go back to the hospital. It buzzed while you were in the kitchen. I've got a transplant patient, and he's not doing well. He's waiting for a liver, and his spirits are down today. I want to go back and assure him that liver is coming. I want to pray with him."

"Will his parents mind?"

"He's a transfer patient from Chile; his parents are there. My

Spanish is rusty, but I imagine God understands the prayers. He's here with a cousin who speaks English, and the little boy and I seem to communicate on a different level."

I look back in the house. "Can I come with you?"

"Este is in isolation to keep him healthy for the operation, but I'd love to have you keep me company on the way there."

"Oh, I don't want to interfere, but it will give me a chance to visit with Brea." *And get out of here.* "Do you think I should stay with our parents, or is all right to leave them?"

"Look at our parents. They're practically planning our wedding. I think your mother just told my mother your SAT score. You're in." Kevin laughs and I can't help my rapid blinking. He said wedding in a sentence, and he did not explode. He reaches for my other hand and takes both of them into his own. "I know Seth just left. I know all about your transition girl/guy theory. Arin explained it to me. But Ashley, what we shared in the parking lot that day was not just a wild moment."

Still, as far as wild moments go, it was a pretty good one. Strangely, my stomach feels this incredible surge as I remember his kiss, and I'm seeing that familiar look in his eyes. I look to my feet immediately. "I have other theories, you know, not just the transition theory."

"Are they all as completely ludicrous as your transition guy theory?"

"Once I thought you had Kohlitis."

"The disease?"

"No, the lack of personality. It's when people are good-looking their entire life, like Kohli Cahners, and so they don't develop a personality."

"Wait a minute. You thought I didn't have a personality? Ashley, need I remind you that you were dating Seth Greenwood!"

"I didn't say I was right. It's just that I thought you might have it. Besides, the transition theory is quite respectable. I don't even think it's mine." I stand up straighter, ready to defend my ideas.

"Fair enough. But technically, Seth was the transition guy because remember, we were seeing each other first. We went out before I became a Christian, before the engineer was even officially in the picture. But I have a proposition for you."

"What kind of proposition?"

"I work with this great surgeon named David. He's single, not a Christian, but not looking for a serious romance either. He's perfect."

"And this relates to me how?"

"I'm volunteering him to be your transition man. You can go on a couple of dates. He can even use the jalopy I used on our first date. I'm confident you'll come to the realization that Kevin Novak is irresistible by comparison."

"You're a bit full of yourself, wouldn't you say? What if I fall madly for David? What if he becomes a Christian like you did?" I cross my arms. "What if he's bald?"

Kevin laughs out loud. "You like your men bald? I can shave my head." He lifts his eyebrows, and looks at me from a down-turned face. "Let's go have dinner on our own."

"We can't just leave. It's Thanksgiving. What will they say?"

"Who? Our parents?" Kevin looks into the window. "They won't miss us. It will give them a better chance to sell us on each other. If we were real estate, we'd be as good as in escrow."

For some strange reason Kevin is under the impression that I'm Boardwalk. I'm not in a hurry to get married like I was a month ago. All at once it occurs to me that jumping from the frying pan to the fire can cause serious burns.

As we discuss our options, my sister-in-law, Mei Ling, gets out of the car. Mei Ling is from China originally, but she has that American-Asian model look. With the perfectly shaped nose for profile shots, and the skin that glows like J Lo's does without the help of a bronzer. My life is like an international runway between Sophia's exotic Italian looks and Mei Ling's sophisticated appearance.

"Ashley!" Mei Ling pulls me into a hug, and we're separated by the tiny ball that is my niece or nephew. "Where in heaven's name have you been? I thought I might not see you before the appointed day."

Mei Ling wants me to be in the room when the baby's born. Brea asked the same thing, but Brea I know well enough to say, *Not in this lifetime.* With Mei Ling, I'm just hoping a legal emergency comes up.

"Kevin, this is Mei Ling, my sister-in-law." I smile. "Believe it or not, she's married to Dave."

Kevin slaps my arm gently. "Mei Ling, it's a pleasure." Then he leans in as though sharing a great secret. "If Ashley and I escape this event, will you cover for us?" He holds up his pager. "I have to run to the hospital and I want some company."

Mei Ling looks at Kevin, then to me. Her estimation is immediate. "You're the doctor at Stanford?"

"I am."

"Can you make sure the epidural flows freely when I need it?"

"Consider yourself numbed."

"Then she's all yours." Mei Ling laughs and opens the front door.

"Can you really do that?" I ask Kevin.

"I can do anything. Fly with me, Ashley Stockingdale." He clutches my hand and leads me into his car. And I just close my eyes. *Prepare for takeoff.*

26

There are some men who never learn to overcome their fear of commitment. According to statistics, they live nine years less than men who do get married. So I take heart that it's Seth loss. I may have wasted nine full months, but he might be up to wasting nine years, so let's call it even. On another interesting note, women who are married happily live longer. Not married happily, they die younger. That gives me pause on the whole commitment issue. Before you race toward that goal, be sure it's the right finish line, you know?

As I look over at Kevin's handsome profile, it disturbs me that my mind is elsewhere and not in the present. Life is precious. I'm going to make a commitment to be more upbeat. I'll make that list tonight.

My cell phone rings as we're on our way to the hospital. "Happy Thanksgiving, Ashley Stockingdale here."

Kevin smiles at my creative greeting.

"Ash, your dog got out. He's wandering the streets of Palo Alto as we speak, and I'm not chasing him." Kay's used up her last nerve and hangs up after delivering her message. Short and to the point, gotta love that. I know it's not entirely Rhett's fault. Serving dinner to the Reasons could do that to anyone, but Rhett is certainly not helping matters.

"I'm on my way," I say into the dead phone.

Kevin wears a look of disappointment. "What?"

"My dog. He's out."

Kevin doesn't even ask. He flips the car around. "I tell you, between you and me and our combined total of communication gadgets, the chance of us actually making it out on a date are slim."

"I'll come to the hospital after I find him. I promise." *I might not be welcomed at home otherwise.*

Meanwhile, I'm praying silently for Rhett. He's the sweetest dog in the world, and if it weren't for his fetish for nylons, he'd probably be content in the backyard permanently. But it's Thanksgiving, it's practically a hosiery lover's holiday out there on the streets of Palo Alto. Rhett is a victim of poor self-control tendencies.

When I pull up to the house, I see that Kay's luminaries have been trashed and there's sand lining the walkway from the bags. Kay is at the doorway, and in escrow or not, I think my days here are numbered.

"Ashley, that dog has to go. He ruined my party!"

Well, I'm sure the guests didn't help.

Kevin looks at me, anxious to avoid the wrath of Kay. And who can blame him? "I'll see you later, okay?"

I nod. "At the hospital. I'll page you when I get there. And I will get there. I promise."

"I've got plenty of work to do until you do. Take your time." Kevin waits for me to close the door and drives off.

I stalk up the walkway, noting that my black roses are strewn about the porch in some kind of freaky indication that my day is not looking up.

"Come in here. We need to talk," Kay says, sounding remarkably like my mother. Actually, worse than that, she sounds more like Brea's mother.

I march into the house, and it's a complete disaster. Which has nothing to do with my dog. The Reasons didn't even clear the plates. The turkey carcass sits as a trophy in the middle of Kay's table, wadded-up napkins are strewn across the floor, and a broken water glass gleams under the coffee table. Kay falls onto her sofa and starts to cry. I'm not talking a sign of simple emotion like a random tear, but these racking sobs.

"Kay, I'm so sorry. I never should have left Rhett here. I thought only of myself. Really, I'm so sorry." I'd do anything to make her stop crying. Kay is the kind of woman you wouldn't want to meet in a dark alley, and this is absolutely unnerving to see her performing an Ashley imitation. Maybe I should call Hans.

"It's not Rhett, Ashley. He came back," Kay sniffles. "He's in the yard."

"What is it then? Are you all right?"

"Look at this place, Ash! They left here as soon as the game was over. They didn't offer to help clean up. They didn't even say thank you." She drops her face into her hands and continues to sob.

"It's the expectation thing again. Kay, you need a good chick flick. I'm going to clean everything up. You sit here, and I'll get one of my fluffy films, and you can pretend you're me. Simple and care-free and entertained by sophomoric humor." I smile at her, and she starts to laugh through her tears.

"I'm not going to leave you with this mess. Just give me a second to regroup."

"I insist." I run into my bedroom and grab *So I Married an Axe Murderer*. It doesn't get any fluffier than Mike Myers, and when life is this depressing, only stupid humor will do. I flick on the movie, and start for the kitchen.

Kay is very neat when she cooks, cleaning as she goes. There's hardly a mark that she's just cooked for thirteen people, but the dining room is a disaster. Aluminum cans all over her antique table. Spilled soda everywhere, like a bunch of three-year-olds ate here.

"That's it!" I slam my hand on the counter.

"Ashley?" Kay says from the other room.

I push through the swinging kitchen door. "No more of this!" I've got my fists clenched around a dish towel. "No more of these excuses for these people. They are not infants. Pastor Max is going to preach about decency or I'm doing it for him. Look at this crew, Kay. Kevin becomes a Christian and he can't even be a part of the group because he's not a lump. We are more than conquerors!"

"Sit down, Ashley. You're getting flushed. I'll clean up later."

"No, no! This has nothing to do with cleaning. This is epidemic. Christians should act better than the average person. Seriously, with the Holy Spirit within, we have no excuse not to, and look at this mess. Do you think this lifestyle would attract anyone?"

"Flies?" Kay shrugs.

"I realize faith isn't about the law, or doing, but this is ridiculous. How did these sloths ever become Christians in the first place? Most of them are still living off their parents' faith, still living off their parents' tithes. No more, Kay. We're not enabling them anymore."

"You're pretty worked up over this."

"I am! This culture enables these adults to remain children. I for one am through aiding in their destruction. You know that verse? Crave pure spiritual milk so that you can grow up in your salvation?"

"Yeah, it's 1 Peter, I think."

"Well, they can't crave spiritual milk when we're feeding them the regular stuff. Promise me. You're done with this." I run into the kitchen, grab Kay's clipboard, and come back out.

"What are you doing with that?"

"I want you to give up the clipboard, Kay. I want you to let these babies handle their own Saturday night schedule."

"Ashley, give that to me."

I pull it away. "No, I'm not allowing you to enable them anymore." I stop the DVD.

"Give me the clipboard." She gets up and comes toward me, and I see the fire crackling in the fireplace.

"Don't come any closer or the clipboard gets it."

"You wouldn't dare! I've got everyone signed up for the Christmas dinner at MacArthur Park. I won't know how many to make reservations for!"

I hold the clipboard closer to the fire. "Tell me you're going to make them call for themselves, or it's history."

"Ashley, no, I have everything on that clipboard." I take off the pages of Reason-related stuff and throw the clipboard at her.

"Promise me. And promise me you'll erase this from your hard drive." I wave the papers in the air.

"I like organizing. I have the gift of administration. That's biblical."

"You're babying them! You're aiding in the ruination of adult men in the Silicon Valley. For the sake of single Christian women everywhere, will you quit?"

She sits back down on the sofa and calmly crosses her legs. "I'll quit."

And just as I turn my back to head for the kitchen, she starts after me. I run to the fire, and she's grabbing the pages when I pull them away and thrust them into the flames. The edges slowly burn to a crisp black, and soon the type changes color. Then it is gone.

"You had no right to do that!" Kay screams.

"Look at this dining room and tell me you did a good thing today."

"I served dinner to people who had nowhere else to go!" she yells.

"You served them fish instead of teaching them how to cast their line!"

I continue to pick up the dishes, and Kay sinks back down into the sofa, staring blankly into space.

"You're just bitter because Seth left you."

"I left Seth. And, if you want anything to change in your life, you'll leave them."

I flip the DVD back on, right to the infamous "head" scene that is such a true classic, and head to the kitchen. I start to run the warm water and find myself mesmerized by the translucent bubbles. It isn't long before I hear Kay laughing at the scene in the movie, and it's contagious and I laugh too. It's comical, thinking I have the power to change anything. But I'm going to try anyway.

Rhett comes in and sits at my feet while I do the dishes amid the plastic sheeting of the kitchen, and I sigh deeply. Maybe a woman and her dog are the key to longevity. "I wonder, how many extra years will I get out of you, Rhett?"

27

Ashley, I'm back. Did you miss me?" Seth smoothes his head and tips Ashley's chin up.

"No," she says reliving The Thorn Birds *beach scene. "No more!"*

"I didn't know what we had. I didn't know how much I loved you."

Ashley shakes her head frantically. "I loved you once, but not any longer. It's over. You chose India. I choose Rhett."

"You're sure it's not Kevin that you choose?"

Ashley gasps. "How did you know about Kevin?"

"Arin told me all about Kevin. My going to India was her elaborate plan to keep us apart, but we can't be apart, Ashley. We were meant to be. Our lives are forever woven together like an intricately made Indian carpet."

Perhaps more like a handmade toupee. However finely woven, a toupee still sits on the head like a bad baseball cap. Kevin doesn't answer his page, so I head to the hospital in my own car, and leave Rhett and Kay laughing over one of my favorite cult classics. Kay's not talking to me, but that's to be expected. I figure I deserve some credit for not destroying the entire clipboard, but her expression doesn't seem to imply gratitude as I leave the house. Hopefully *Axe Murderer* will have her in a better mood when I return.

The hospital parking lot is nearly empty, a virtual ghost town on the holiday, and I park my car right toward the front. I can see Kevin's car in the doctor's lot nearby so I know I've done well.

I flick my cell phone off, as I'm warned to do at the entrance, and head to Brea's room. Again, I can hear her laughing. As I come in, she's chowing down some turkey that her mother, who is scowling at me from a chair beside the bed, must have brought from home. Miles is beside Brea, gumming his fist.

"Ashley! Just what the day needed. Cute Juicy sweats! You got some kind of hair going on, though." Brea puts her plate in her lap and claps her hands. Seeing the turkey reminds me that I've witnessed a lot of good food today, but I haven't touched a bite of it. My stomach growls. "Are you hungry, Ash?"

"It's okay. I'm going out to eat after this."

Mrs. Browning folds her arms across her chest. "You're not eating at your mother's house?"

"She's full up at the inn. Kevin's parents are there."

"What on earth?" Brea eyes widen. She's ready for the story.

"Who's Kevin?" Mrs. Browning shakes her head. "You go through men faster than a badly run coal mine."

"Mother!" Brea chastises. "Ashley dated Seth forever. She does not go through men. They just don't stick around."

This is helping.

"Kevin's parents came to town," I explain. "They're having dinner at my folks'. Kevin is here working, and then we're going to grab a bite. We worked at the shelter this morning."

"It's time you both cooked for your own families." Mrs. Browning is picking at baby Miles, smoothing his hair and wiping his face until I want to slap her hand away. *Leave that baby alone!*

"Brea, is your cousin Roy still single?" Brea's cousin is trying to be an actor. As in, he's been in L.A. waiting tables for nearly a decade, but because he's part of the elite Browning clan, Brea's mom would rather see him bus the counter for an eternity than my marry into the family.

"He is still single!" Brea says with too much enthusiasm.

"I'm leaving." Mrs. Browning says. "Brea, I'll come take care of Miles on Monday when John goes back to work."

"I'm coming home tomorrow, Ash. Me and my little friend here." Brea grabs the IV rack.

"Well that's great! At least home has cable."

"And Tivo. John's been recording for me for the last week. Every reality show known to man is there waiting for me."

"You girls would be better off to get your head into the Bible."

"How utterly true, Mother. Thanks for the tip of the day. Get it, Ashley? Like on *Queer Eye?*"

"You two speak an entirely different language." Mrs. Browning reaches down and kisses Brea's forehead. "Take care of yourself. And don't fool around too long. You need your rest."

Once Mrs. Browning disappears, I go straight for Miles. "Can I have him now?"

"I personally thought you showed great restraint while my mother was here. Did you want to strangle her while she was doing that spit-and-polish thing on his face?"

"I'm that obvious, huh?"

"How's your puppy?"

"Huge. He's not part terrier after all. I bought this darling bag for him in Taiwan, but you can have it now. I thought I could carry him around in it, but he going to be so gigantic it won't even hold his future chew toys."

"Cool! Ashley castoffs. Much better than my TJ Maxx finds. So you don't tell your best friend when there's a new man in your life? Or an old one as the case may be? Kevin came here looking for you, so I knew to expect you."

"I told him I'd page him, but he didn't return my call. Story of my life."

"He didn't think you'd last long with Kay. Said she looked hot enough to spit fire."

"You should have seen her after I burned the clipboard contents."

"You did not!"

"Long story. I have washed more dishes today between the shelter and my house than I've ever done in my whole lifetime. Even that time we whipped cream all over the open cabinets at your mother's house and she made us clean up. Look," I say, holding out my hands. "I even have dishpan hands and not a manicurist open on the entire peninsula. Tragic. Utterly tragic."

Just then Kevin walks into the room and his smile just completely charms me. "Ashley, you are a sight for sore eyes." And I must say, his voice is like heaven. I can't believe how his smooth baritone instantly relaxes me. Kevin is like aromatherapy, only for the ears. What's that called, audiotherapy?

Brea has a huge grin on her face, saying, yeah, she approves. That alone makes me want to forget that Seth ever existed.

"I'm starving! Quick! Let's turn off our cell phones."

Kevin rubs his stomach while he looks at Brea's turkey dinner. "No emergencies during dinner. I prayed. Let's go eat, I'm starving too. But no turkey. I don't want to see another lump of stuffing as long as I live."

"No turkey," I agree. "I should have changed before I came. It never dawned on me after I finished all those dishes. I felt so sudsy and clean."

"You did dishes again?"

"See?" I say, holding up my hands, looking for sympathy. He takes my palm and gently kisses it. *What's it like to breathe again?*

He shakes his head. "No more dishpan hands for you! Come here." He takes me to a long hallway, populated only by the rare sighting of a nurse. We duck into a room, and Kevin pulls out a tube of Nivea. He pours a bit out into my palm and starts to rub it in while occasionally planting a kiss on my wrist. It's entirely too intimate for my comfort, and I yank my hand away while continuing to rub the moisturizer.

"Thank you," I say quietly.

He grabs my hand, and we walk toward the exit when I see the lithe little nurse with the Bible, Kendra, I think her name was. She has no Bible this time, and Kendra stops in front of us.

"Going to dinner?" Kendra asks.

"I'm not on call today. Do you remember Ashley?" Kevin asks.

Kendra only nods, still apparently not willing to address my presence. I suppose this is what it's like dating a human Adonis. And it doesn't feel fun. At least with Seth, you knew the women weren't exactly gathering around to garner his attention. Maybe that's not exactly true, Arin had her own attention-getting tricks. I never will understand women who go after other women's men. I mean; if you "win," don't you have to live with the fear that someone younger and perkier is coming along?

"Kendra, right?" I say, and thrust my freshly moisturized hand forward.

"Have fun at dinner," Kendra says without taking my hand and walks down the hallway away from us.

"If there's something I'm getting in the middle of, because with where I've been lately, I'm not really interested in—"

"You're not in the middle of anything. Kendra wants a doctor for a husband. Every hospital has lots of women like that. I'm just the freshest cut of beef at the moment."

I laugh out loud. "Freshest cut of beef?"

"Filet mignon," he says with a wink. "Not that hamburger you're used to."

"Where do men get their egos? Can I buy one?"

"An ego for a lawyer? Now, there's a novel idea."

I cross my arms. "Are you giving me lawyer grief?"

"I could comment that you found the hospital by chasing an ambulance here, but I won't."

"You're terrible. I mean, really terrible. Don't quit your day job because, as a stand-up comedian, you haven't got a chance."

"Oh really? You, who watches *So I Married an Axe Murderer* over and over again, are going to tell me about humor?"

"Who told you that?"

"Kay. I called there looking for you."

"Don't be picking on my movie, or we're going to have to call it quits. I can't trust anyone that doesn't know at least two lines from that movie."

"I can quote from both the Harriet poem, and the 'orange on a toothpick cranium' scene."

I fall into Kevin's arms. "Then you have distinct possibilities."

His arms close around me and his eyes meet mine. It's never good to feel this strongly. *This* lacks control, and I don't ever want to lack control. But as Kevin bends down to kiss me, I can't feel my feet and so I know to fight it is futile.

He's too good to be true, I tell myself. *Too good to be true. Think dogs. Think longevity.* But I'm lost in his kiss, and I don't care about the *facts*. Which makes me start to giggle, and Kevin pulls away. "Remember that scene where his mother says the Weekly World News is full of facts? These are facts," I say in my best Scottish accent.

"You know they'll be hauling you away one of these days? And that my family has never heard of Mike Myers?"

I'm still giggling. "So which will you choose, Kevin? Mensa? The country club? Or the sophomoric humor and never-ending statistical facts of Ashley Wilkes Stockingdale?"

"You drive a hard bargain, and I'll let Mensa go, but I think I might run a check on that SAT score of yours."

"SATs are just memorization," I say through my laughter. "I have a memory as long as this hallway." I point to my temple. "It's full of legal cases, patents, several thousand quotes from *People* magazine, and George Michael songs."

"Now that is a combination I cannot refuse."

He kisses me again, and I have to admit, my appetite has long since gone away. On the other hand, if I don't get to a restaurant soon, I'm in danger of playing with fire.

"You can refuse. Seth refused. I think it was my lack of initiative to learn *Matrix* lines." There I go again, bringing up the ex's name. I lack tact.

"Seth is history. I knew he would be the minute I laid eyes on you singing that hymn."

I'm hearing Ariel's aria from the *Little Mermaid* in my head, wondering if my voice has that much power. Do you think?

"Back to earth, Kevin. Your head is like Sputnik."

Kevin throws back his head in laughter. "And you love me anyway."

I draw in a deep breath. Kevin presses his lips to mine once again. I pull away and look down the hallway. "We have a really bad habit of kissing in inappropriate spots. Did you ever notice that?"

"Must you narrate everything?"

"I narrate when I'm nervous."

"I thought you shopped when you were nervous."

"I shop and I talk."

"Then let's feed you since the mall is closed." Kevin takes my hand and leads me to his car. I keep my lower lip between my teeth for fear I might narrate myself right out of dinner.

28

The restaurant is dark, and live classical piano music makes me feel like I'm in a very expensive elevator. It smells like a mixture of wine and several designer perfumes vying for attention—not the most appetizing scent, I must say. We are the only people under the age of sixty, and I'm the only woman not dripping in carats of diamonds as if a QVC cubic zirconia event was taking place. *So this is what the other half does on Thanksgiving, when their cooks are home cooking for their own families, and the well-appointed kitchens become just more quality furniture.*

I look at Kevin, and he doesn't just go straight to the maître d' like I expect a confident surgeon to do. He stands back, as if waiting for me to take control. Well, I'm not shy. I step forward when I notice he's halted on purpose.

"What?" I say, like his mother. "Is it my sweatpants?"

He pulls me outside into the parking lot and lets out a laugh as though he's been holding his breath. "I can't eat in there," he says.

"Why not?"

"I didn't want to have dinner with my parents. I don't want to have dinner with forty of their closest clones."

"I thought you were hungry."

He stares down at me, and I notice, not for the first time, how totally perfect his jawline is. You know how Johnny Depp has that incredible profile, that smoldering look that would inspire his face in marble? Well, I'm serious, Kevin is a major contender for his bust being cast in stone. He's talking and I must say I got lost for a minute.

"What?" I ask.

"Those people were wearing bibs, Ash. I don't want lobster for Thanksgiving. It's like their way of justifying their lives aren't total garbage. That they can't admit that there's no one who wants to cook them a meal, or a place to go. I don't want to end up like that, so I don't think we should start like that."

"Lobster on Thanksgiving isn't exactly roughing it, Kevin." As if I need to explain this.

"Did you notice how thrilled my parents were to have an invitation at your parents' house?"

"I assumed they did it for you."

"My parents were at a golf tournament for Thanksgiving week, Ashley. Don't you find that slightly sad?"

I shrug. *Doesn't sound so bad to me, actually. Palm Springs and a golf course and spa? My life should be such garbage.*

"They had nowhere to go, so they came here not even knowing if I'd be around. I think they hope I'll bring some warmth into their week."

"They seem happy enough. I mean, for people without God in their lives." I shrug. "When you're not a believer, what is life but one big way to avoid Him? Your mother was telling me that she came in second in the ladies' tournament. From what I know about golf, that has to feel pretty good."

"Far be it from me to judge them, Ashley. I'm happy they have something more to do than the IQ conventions, but I left my Georgia roots for a reason." He sniffs away the remainder of his laughter. "I'm sorry. I know what you're thinking. Poor little rich boy. Huh?"

"No, actually, I wasn't thinking that at all. I was thinking it makes me want to learn to cook. So I could make you feel like *you* had somewhere to go on Thanksgiving."

"I think that's the nicest thing anyone ever said to me."

He stares down at me, his green eyes gazing into mine, and I feel his smooth hand come to my cheek. "I don't know how I knew about you, Ashley, but I saw it the very first time I laid eyes on you. That day you were singing. It was like a sign that you were just who you appeared to be. You don't really care to marry a doctor, do you?"

Did he just say the word marry? I'll be. "I like someone around. And you're never around and that beeper is always attached. Besides, I've been waiting for Prince Charming for a long time. I want to be content with my life just the way it is. I have a great life."

"I'll be here, Ashley."

I swallow the lump in my throat. No one has ever spoken to me like Kevin. He's straightforward-honest. I'm so used to playing verbal poker with the men of Silicon Valley. There's no reason for that with Kevin. He says what he means, and means what he says. Without fear or trepidation. Which, of course, makes him completely suspect.

I'm fiddling with my hands, and he keeps pulling my chin up to look him in the eye.

"I know you'd want to be there, Kevin. But I'm high-maintenance. At least that's what Seth tells me." I laugh and start to walk toward the car.

"Seth doesn't know a thing about you, Ashley. He never did." Kevin calls after me. "And I'm beginning to think you don't either."

I nod. "You're probably right. He never did."

"When he brought you the tulips on the beach . . ."

My eyes pop open. "How'd you know about that?"

"I told him they were your favorite. I saw you choose some once in San Francisco when we came out of that garage."

I knew Seth didn't have enough sense to bring flowers. "Let's go eat leftovers from Kay." I take his hand. "We don't have to decide about our future here and now. We've got all the time in the world." Oh my goodness, I sound like Seth. "Then, we can go rescue your parents from mine. Or vice versa."

"Let's go home to your mom's. I mean your parents and my parents. Who knows what ugly secrets they're sharing. There will be leftovers there."

"And lots of relatives, and my brother especially. Let's just go eat quickly at Kay's. Do you mind? Just give me one Thanksgiving where I don't need Tums to settle my angst."

Without another word, Kevin opens my door and we drive home to my place. I see Rhett bounding down the street at the corner as we're driving, but the dog recognizes the car and heads home.

"That dog is going to be the death of me."

Kevin shakes his head. "That dog loves you."

"I like him, too."

Out of the car, Rhett jumps on my Juicy sweatpants, and the autumn-colored yellow, actually called Daisy, now looks like a giraffe print, covered in brown paw prints.

"Rhett!" I bend down and snuggle up with my puppy. "You've been a good doggy, home all day. Come on, let's go get you some doggy treats."

I bound up the walkway after Rhett and open the door. Kay is watching *Terms of Endearment* as we come in. She's sniffling with a Kleenex in her hand, her red-rimmed eyes meeting mine. "What are you doing home?"

"Kevin and I thought we'd grab a bite, if that's okay with you."

Kay flips off the television and starts for the kitchen.

"Sit down, Kay. We can help ourselves."

"No, no. Please let me. It will be good for me to help someone who appreciates it."

"We haven't eaten all day long, Kay. We'll appreciate it like a hardworking cowboy appreciates the wagon train," Kevin says while patting his stomach.

I look at Kevin with my eyebrows scrunched together. "What are you, Clint Eastwood all of a sudden?"

He points at me. "Go ahead. Make my day." He comes close to

me and envelops me in a hug while Kay merrily hums her way into her domain. "So you'll cook for me someday?" He says into my hair.

"I said I wanted to cook for you. I didn't say I could actually do it." I look up. "But I'll try."

"I think it's hot that you want to cook for me," he growls.

Breathe in. Breathe out. "Then, culinary academy, here I come!"

He bends down and kisses me with firm and determined lips. My stomach swirls like a northeastern wind, but I shake it off. Something is not right here. P. T. Barnum said a sucker is born every minute. I feel like I'm standing here with my last nickel, ready to give it away.

29

I don't know what to expect at my parents', and I'm leery of walking in the house. It sounds quiet. Eerily quiet. I mean, these are the people who named me after Ashley Wilkes, and while there's a heartwarming story behind that, no one really knows that. They just think we're a little off-kilter. And they'd be right.

I look back at Kevin. "There's no yelling. That can't be good."

"Maybe they're having dessert. Open the door," Kevin says, like a movie extra waiting to enter the haunted house. Just as we open the door, his beeper goes off again.

I put a forefinger in his chest accusingly. "You've got that thing timed!"

He holds up two fingers and shakes his head. "Scout's honor."

I open the door, and there's my family quietly sitting at the dining room table playing Scrabble. With the Mensa people. Wonders never cease.

"Hi," I say quietly. *Don't want to ruin anyone's triple word score or anything.* I didn't even know my parents owned a board game.

Mei Ling, my sister-in-law, brings herself to her feet and waddles over. There's nothing worse than feeling large next to a pregnant woman. Mei Ling embraces me and whispers in my ear. "Get them out of here."

"Dr. and Mrs. Novak!" I clap my hands together, like I'm

announcing circle time at the local preschool. "I'm so glad you were able to come."

"Oh, Ashley, we had the best time. Did you know your mother used to be Scrabble champion at her high school?"

I look at my mother. I have never seen her play Scrabble. I haven't even seen her do a crossword puzzle. My mom's smile indicates that her teeth are grinding against each other, and I have a feeling the Novaks are not her first pick for a set of in-laws.

Kevin gets his parents to the door by putting on their coats as they rise. I look at him and catch his smile. I guess it's the universal mind to be embarrassed about one's parents. They stand up, he ushers them toward the door, and then moves close to me and I feel his warm breath on my hair. *Seth who?*

Kevin speaks into my cheek. "Whatever you do, do not hold me responsible for my parents' behavior. Remember, they live across the country. You will only see them twice a year."

I nod, but I've already seen them twice this year. And I'm not even officially seeing their son.

"I've got to run to the hospital," Kevin says aloud. "Mother, Father, I'll drop you at my place on the way."

"We're having a fabulous time, Son. Why don't you come back for us?" Elaine says with a smile, but I can tell by the weary eyes of my family members that they're ready for a quiet, familiar evening of *Jeopardy* and *Wheel of Fortune.* They've had enough of entertaining the brain trust.

Dr. Novak Sr. stretches. He flexes his biceps and parades in front of my father. "Look at that, Hank. That's what working out will do for you. I could still take my son in a wrestling match, and I'm sixty-eight."

"Yes, well, Dad, let's get you back home and you can work off some of Mrs. Stockingdale's fabulous dinner. It still smells wonderful in here."

They're out the door and the collective sigh of relief sounds like a rushing train.

"Ash, where did you find those people?" Dave asks.

"Makes me glad my mother is in China," Mei Ling giggles.

My father gets up and heads for the TV. He points at me as he goes by. "You gonna marry that guy?"

"Not necessarily. Mom, what happened?"

"Nothing, Ashley. Kevin is a darling boy. Don't concern yourself with his parents. I married your father, after all."

My father smirks at my mom.

"I'm not getting married. I've just met the man. What happened?"

"Never mind, Ashley. It's not important." My mother picks up the pie plate from the center of the table. "Help me clean up."

Again with the cleaning! "Will you drive me home when I'm done, Dave?"

"You know, I could take Seth droning on about *The Matrix* for a lifetime before I go through that again." He points at the door. "Those people need help, Ashley. Finish up. I'll take you home."

"Come on, no one's going to tell me what happened?"

"I'll tell you," Mei Ling offers, but Dave looks at her threateningly.

"Don't you say a word, Mei Ling. That garbage doesn't need repeating."

I know Mei Ling will tell me later, but apparently I'm going to have to wait.

Three days later I march into the Reasons Sunday school meeting like I'm marching into negotiations in Taiwan. Just try and mess with me. The room is typically Reason. Unlike every other classroom, there's no coffee. There are no donuts. This is simply because no one can be bothered to pick them up at the front of the church where all the Sunday mothers have put together a platter for each and every class. These people are lucky I'm not the violent sort. They're all sitting around laughing, completely ignoring my entrance. And I'm wearing DKNY and looking good, so that's just not right.

I approach Pastor Max and his lovely wife Kelly and they smile at me sympathetically. As in, *poor Ashley can't find a man to save her life*. I hear the murmur as my presence becomes known, and Seth's absence gets talked about. I know what they're all thinking. *Poor, dumped Ashley, can't even land an* Average Joe *reject*.

"Ashley, did you have a nice Thanksgiving?" Kelly asks.

"I did. I'd like to make an announcement before class if that's okay."

Max looks a little unnerved, and Kelly looks uneasy. "Pertaining to?"

"Pertaining to the Christmas party. It's for Kay. I want to make an announcement for her."

They smile their perfect Osmond grins at one another. "Oh sure. Feel free. We'll lead with that!"

I walk up to the board, and I write down the following:

Kay Harding, MSEE
14056 Channing Way
Palo Alto, CA 94301

Ashley Stockingdale, Esq.
14056 Channing Way
Palo Alto, CA 94301

Pastor Max coughs and begins the class. "Well, I hope everyone had a fabulous Thanksgiving. I know Kelly and I did. I trust you all had a wonderful time with whatever plans you had. We're going to start today with announcements, and we have one from Ashley about our upcoming Christmas party."

I clear my throat. "First, I have an announcement about Thanksgiving." I smile broadly and I look at all the blank stares. I am the epitome of Spokesmodel. I could be on *Star Search*, unquestionably.

The complete litany of Reasons lies before me: bald men who think they're Keanu Reeves and Johnny Depp. I shake my thoughts. I am in a house of God.

"Many of you were lucky enough to have a Thanksgiving feast prepared by our own Kay Harding."

"Yeah, Kay!" Greg shouts as a light round of applause starts. Presently, no one has noticed she isn't here.

"I've put her name and address on the board because that's where you can send your thank-you notes. She's at home this morning, crying because no one appreciated her days of effort for dinner. And you *should* appreciate what she did because I know none of you would intentionally hurt a Christian sister."

Kelly starts to edge towards me, as though she's going to wrestle the podium away from me, but I grab the sides of it. "I also put my own name up there. That's where you can send your thank-you notes to me for clearing your plates and throwing away your aluminum cans."

Kelly comes closer and I look at her like *don't mess with me, sweetheart. I've got some righteous anger going on, and I'm not stopping.* "I'd like to read a verse to you all. This is from James 3:13. 'Who is wise and understanding among you? Let him show it by his good life, by deeds done in the humility that comes from wisdom.'"

Their eyes are wide like saucers, and I know I'm about to be gonged, so I go as fast as possible. "Kay does all of these things for you because she loves the Lord. She wants to be useful to Him. Every Wednesday night she hosts a Bible study where King Solomon himself would be happy to dine. On Thanksgiving, she slaved over that stove for two days and brought out the fine china so that you all would feel like you had a place to call home. She doesn't want accolades and attention, but could you all find it in your hearts to say that what she does matters?"

Okay, tearing up a bit.

"That would be really appreciated by me. I love Kay, and I hate to see her hurt. I know you all do too."

Pastor Max nods his head as if to say that wasn't so bad.

As I'm walking out I hear the murmurs, "Boyfriend just left her."

"Can you blame him? That's one angry chick."

"She's out of control."

Just a few things that make them feel better. I turn on my heel and offer one final comment. "The Christmas announcement is . . ." Pause for effect. Little lawyer trick. "That you're planning your own Christmas party. Kay has quite a bit of stress with our remodel, and that's taking precedence."

I walk out of the class with my head held high. Once outside, I bump straight into Arin, who's wearing a violet Indian sari with gold accessories and a bindi dot on her forehead. First thought is *Did Seth bring me the scarf and her the rest of the outfit?*

"Hi, Ashley."

"Arin." *Is it Halloween?* "Are you taking up Hinduism?"

She smiles. "Of course not. I'm going to India. That's what I wanted to talk to you about last week when you raced out of here to be with Brea."

"Right. I heard about it from Seth. Well, best of luck with that." I try to walk away and she grabs my arm.

"I hope you're not angry with me, Ashley. This is really something I feel in my heart that I'm called to do."

"Ministry at all costs. I understand perfectly."

"You're mad about Seth and me."

Just hearing "Seth and me" makes me realize I'm not as over Seth as I'd like to be. But then, I guess no one ever appreciates it when their ex moves on. Especially when it's before your actual breakup. "I don't know what 'Seth and me' means, I suppose." I look straight into her bright blue eyes, and they darken for just a split second. "But whatever. Just be happy."

"There's nothing between us, if that's what you're implying."

"I'm not implying anything, Arin."

She stands, stunned at my reaction, and I must admit, it's a little terse. I think I drank too much coffee this morning.

"I hope your ministry in India goes as well as the one in Costa Rica."

"What's that supposed to mean?"

"Nothing." And it isn't. "Didn't things go well in Costa Rica?"

"Things went fine. Why don't you like me, Ashley?"

Um . . . do we really have that kind of time? "You know, I actually really respect you. If you can get Seth to part with any money, you're a better woman than me."

"There's nothing going on in that way with us."

"There's nothing going on with you, Arin. Did you ever see that show *Average Joe*?" I give Arin a slight hug. "Good luck to you. Go and be safe. I will be praying for you, and that's the truth."

Arin walks away, tinkling from all her golden baubles as she walks. If that's what Seth wants, I was a square peg in a round hole the entire time. And just like that time I tried to shove myself through the doggy door at home when I forgot my key? It doesn't work, and it's not pretty.

30

I race my TT down the street to Gainnet. It's really the only surge I get in the morning because of the traffic, which snarls and snakes at a despicable pace. I've stopped for a double mocha. I'm sure I'll be paying for that this week on the scale, but it was Thanksgiving, after all, and I didn't exactly chow down in typical holiday fashion. I deserve it.

My puppy has a thing for whipped cream, so I have had to forgo the topping on my coffees, which I'm sure my hips are thankful for. Rhett is wagging everywhere—he's so excited to go to work. And I must say, I finally have a use for that passenger seat. I pet Rhett's face, and he plops his head in my lap. It can't be comfortable over the middle console, but I'm thankful for the affection.

When I walk into the office, the security guards are standing around. *Uh oh, someone's getting fired. And right after the holiday? Now that is a bummer.* Tracy meets me outside my office where all the cubicles are lined up.

"The board of directors is in the meeting room. They want to see you."

"The board of directors? Where's Hans?"

She shrugs. "I don't know, Ashley."

I hand Rhett's leash to Tracy. "Can you take him on the porch?"

"Sure," she says.

Luckily, the office crowd is still sparse, but all eyes there do follow me as I enter my office. I drop my briefcase on my desk and look at the darkened brows around me.

"Good morning, gentlemen," I say, with as much courage as I can muster.

"Good morning, Ashley." The chairman, Aubrey Williams, stands up. "We've been made aware of some disturbing information."

I shake my head. "Where's Hans?"

"Hans is gone, Ashley." Mr. Whiting looks at me. "He won't be back."

I shake my head. "What do you mean?"

"This must remain strictly confidential, naturally." Mr. Whiting shuts the door with a slam. "We believe that some embezzlement has taken place." The chairman opens up his briefcase and holds up a packet of papers. "When you went to Taiwan, there were kickbacks written into the contract."

I shake my head. "No, Hans wouldn't do that."

"There was an extra $200,000 written into this contract, Ashley. Can you account for it?" Then he asks me to sit and puts the contract in front of me. "Is this your signature?"

My heart is in my throat. *I only signed it as a witness.* Which is a really weak excuse for a general counsel, and I know better than to say it aloud. I'm not a humble patent attorney anymore. *Fifth Amendment. Fifth Amendment.*

Oh Lord, I have been so busy searching for this promotion that it never dawned on my arrogant mind that I might not be ready for it. Oh Lord in heaven, help me.

"There's also the matter of the jewelry on the company credit card."

I pull my ring finger under the desk. My mother was right. Shopping finally did get me into trouble. "There's a simple explanation for that. I didn't know how to haggle, and Hans taught me. The very next day I went into the same store and bought something for his girlfriend on my account. A ruby ring. I can show you the statement when it comes."

"And Hans's girlfriend is?" Mr. Whiting stands ready with a mechanical pencil.

"Sophia. But she's gone. She left for Italy."

The chairman nods his head slowly. "Can I see the jewelry we purchased, please?"

I pull the ring off my finger and place it in the center of my table. It doesn't look beautiful to me anymore. It looks frightening and evil. I am Lord of the Ring. "I'll pay back every penny. You have to understand I thought I *had* paid for it."

"Miss Stockingdale, you do understand that all of this remains in this room. We don't want our stockholders getting wind of this situation."

"The contract can be voided. They haven't started production, and if we can prove there's an illegal charge padded into the assembly, we'll be all right on international grounds." *That's it, good Ashley. Talk lawyerspeak. They don't just pay you to look good.* But of course, I'm trembling. They may not be paying me at all.

"There's been some talk, Miss Stockingdale," another member of the board speaks up, "about your being in close contact with Hans frequently." I don't even know who this guy is.

"My relationship has been strictly professional. With the exception of that trip to the jewelry store, and a dinner my boyfriend and I had at his place."

"Your boyfriend is?"

"In India."

"My, you two do have the international relations, don't you?"
Actually, they've both just escaped from us internationally. Funny story.
"Silicon Valley is an international place."

The chairman has my personnel file in front of him. "Is there anyone in the office who can confirm what you're telling us?"

I shrug and drop my head into my palm. "I have no idea."

My mocha is congealing in my stomach. Making me wish I'd gone straight for the espresso and not messed with the sugar and dairy for the day. Getting accused of international embezzlement really makes a few extra calories seem insignificant in the scheme of things, but who knows if I could stand it without the insulin rush?

Just then Tracy walks in, her trademark figure poured into a pair of low-rise cords and a tight-fitting faux silk top. "May I get any of you gentlemen coffee?"

The chairman looks at her and starts to answer when he forms a different question. "Do you know the nature of Miss Stockingdale's relationship with Hans?" he inquires.

Tracy looks at me and crosses her arms over her chest. "Hans had a tighter relationship with alcohol and, I think maybe, drugs. Once I saw him drop a bag of powder, and he often came out of his office sniffing." Tracy looks away from me.

Ack! I thought that was because he was allergic to my dog. I'm such a putz. *Oh Lord, I have absolutely no discernment. None. I would have gone to the grave saying Hans was innocent. Yet if I look at all the pebbles along the pathway, I have seen the signs: the wild mood swings, the constant sniffling, the nervous ticks . . .*

"Miss Stockingdale, did you ever see such signs?"

"I'm afraid I wouldn't know what to look for. I saw him drink a lot of wine, but none of my friends drink anything, so I wouldn't know if that was out of the ordinary or not."

"We'll be bringing in outside counsel, Miss Stockingdale. You do understand that?"

I nod. Laid off again. This time with no severance package. Maybe I should have gone to India. "I understand. I'll clean out my office."

"No, we don't want you to leave, Miss Stockingdale. You're a VP now, and we can't be uprooting our entire foundation for fear the stockholders will run. It's bad enough that we're letting the CEO go with no warning."

But can I really stay here? I mean, the entire office thinks I've got something going on with the boss, who has something going on with a crystal white powder. Meanwhile, the board of directors thinks that I'm charging jewelry on the company account, and keeping the former CEO protected legally.

"Mr. Whiting," Tracy suddenly speaks up. "I can tell you that we on the administration staff are knowledgeable about the office atmosphere. I'd lay my life down saying Ashley was innocent. She doesn't deserve a phantom job, if that's your plan."

There it is again. Completely lack of discernment. I would have never figured on Tracy standing up for me.

"If you don't mind," I look around at all the unhappy faces, "I need some time to think. Please take the money for the jewelry out of my paycheck." I stand up, leaving the ring on the table, and grab my briefcase. I make it to the front door when my cell phone rings. There's no caller ID available.

"Ashley Stockingdale."

"Ashley, it's Hans. I need you to get me something out of my office."

I hang up the phone. The last thing I need to add to my repertoire is drug runner.

The phone rings again. "I mean it, Hans. Leave me alone!"

"Ashley?" It's Seth.

"It's not a very good time for me." I stop midstep. "I forgot the dog."

"Ashley, it's midnight here. Please talk to me before I go to sleep."

"Call me back in ten minutes." I hang up the phone and grab Rhett from the back porch and head for my car. The security guards check my briefcase, and I withstand the indignity quite well, all things considered. I get into my Audi and snuggle up against Rhett. "Thank God for you, Rhett. I don't know what I'd do without you." I'm rewarded with a wet, sloppy kiss.

The phone rings again and Rhett groans. "Yeah, I don't want to talk to him either. Hello."

"Ashley," Seth exhales. "It's so good to hear your voice."

My heart doesn't get all warm and fuzzy, and I don't feel giggly like I usually do. This is progress. For the first time in years, I think I'm actually out from under his spell. *I'm free!* But I can be civil. "How are things in India?"

"I don't think it would be for you, Ashley."

"Clearly. Where's the nearest Nordstrom?"

"You don't have to play that shallow image with me, Ash."

Shallow? Now I'm shallow? He has no idea. "Turns out my shopping has incited some international intrigue, actually. I'm deeper than you know."

"Listen, I never really got a chance to explain about Arin. And I want to."

I roll my eyes. "You know, Seth, it really doesn't matter to me. And I don't mean that lightly or even callously. I mean, it *really* doesn't matter to me. If you up and marry Arin tomorrow, I'll send you a nice wedding gift."

"So you're just over me? Like that?"

Like this is so shocking. "Yes. Yes, I am actually." I rub my hand along Rhett's snout. "Look, Seth, when you left for India, that sent me a pretty clear message. I may be the loyal sort, even a bit naive, but I'm also not stupid. There are Christian men out there who want to be with me. Someday, I'll find the right one. Or I'll continue to live in a gorgeous Palo Alto bungalow. Soon to have granite countertops. Not a bad life, actually."

"I'm not with Arin. I just need you to know that."

"Thanks. I appreciate that."

I'm thankful he's found what he wanted in India. Seth wants everything that goes with marriage. He wants the comfort of me by his side, my support for all his actions, and yet he wants to offer me nothing in return. Nothing but this mutt, and it's the best part of himself he ever gave me.

"Look, I'm in a little trouble with the law at the moment. I need to go."

"Maybe we should talk more. You know, later."

"Yeah, maybe," I say.

"I heard you turned the tables over at church yesterday over Kay's thank-you notes." Seth laughs.

Christians sure can gossip. Now I'm fodder around the world, which gives me an odd sense of satisfaction. Short-lived, as I realize that my job promotion is now part of a drug/embezzling investigation.

31

Rhett and I come home to find Kay on the rooftop, fastening strings of Christmas lights together. She's wrestling with the wires, and when I let Rhett out of the car, he whines at my feet. "I know exactly what you mean, Rhett."

I live with Clark Griswold. Kay snaps a plug set together. She smiles and waves at me.

"What are you doing up there?" I slam the car door. "Get down."

"I just thought I'd get started on Christmas decorations." Her eyes light up like a child getting her first look at Santa. "We're going to have the best house on the block. You know, we live on Candy Cane Lane, right?"

Do I even want to ask? "Candy Cane Lane?"

She spreads her hands out. "Everyone on the block decorates their house, and we have this steady stream of cars every night. You'll have to take your turn handing out candy canes to the kids."

I must say, this inspires a bit of fear. Every holiday from Valentine's Day to Admission Day (California flags everywhere), Kay has decorated for the occasion. It should have dawned on me that my house at *The* holiday is going to be something of an event, you know? But the fact that the whole neighborhood gets into it makes me wonder how I got here. I think about the torn-up inside of our house, and life without a toilet, but it's all good.

"What are you doing home, anyway?" I ask her suspiciously. *Lord help us if we're both out of work and have to support this month's festive electric bill.*

"I'm working from home today. I have a couple of phone meetings tonight from Taiwan, so I'm taking the morning off." She approaches the ladder and starts to descend. "Why are you two home?"

"I'm just really contemplating the whole job thing. Maybe I didn't take long enough to decide if Gainnet was the proper place for me."

"Ashley," she says like a disappointed mother. "Did you lose another job?"

Pause here. "I'm not sure exactly." I fiddle with my hair and check my split ends. Time for a haircut. "They're going to let me know more after the investigation." I shake my head. "No, no. I have a job, but I just want to make sure it isn't simply for show, you know?"

Kay rolls her eyes. "There's a bouquet of flowers in the house for you."

"They're not black, are they?"

She looks at me twice. "What? No, I think they're from Kevin. But Seth called here, so who knows?"

Ooh! Flowers. Enough of this conversation. I rush into the house and see a huge array of orange and red sunflowers mixed together in a vase with a big red bow around it. There's a card and I rip it open like it's Christmas morning.

> Dear Ashley,
>   Roses are red, Violets are blue.
>   Some guy ruined tulips
>   So these sunflowers are for you.
>   Kevin

Another poet! I'm thinking we could be the next great love story, like Elizabeth Barrett and Robert Browning. Ack! Doorbell. I shove the card back in the envelope, and Rhett starts barking. I pull myself up off the floor where I've just been having romantic fantasies about the out-of-my-league doctor.

I open the door expecting to see Kay strung in Christmas bulbs, but it's my boss, Hans. Well, my former boss. I look around outside, and yank him into the house. "What are you doing here?"

"I wanted to explain things a bit." He sniffs, and suddenly that habit has a whole new meaning for me.

"You know," I hold up a palm. "Don't tell me anything. I don't want to be an accessory to the crime." I walk into the center of the living room and point to the sofa. "Go ahead and sit down. Do you want anything?"

He shakes his head. I look at his handsome face, and I'm just struck that he would do anything like he's been accused of. I knew what he represented, what his life's works added up to, but I still didn't believe him capable of criminal acts, and really, doesn't the Bible say to look at a person's fruit? Well, Hans was a rotten apple in everything that mattered: as a father, a husband, even a beau. I wanted so badly to believe something different. To be utterly charmed by his brighter side.

"Why would you do all that?" I ask him.

"Listen, Ashley, it's standard practice to pad a contract so things don't look so bad to the stockholders. I didn't do anything dishonest." He doesn't sit. He's still pacing the floor frantically, like a dog at the pound.

"It's standard procedure to pad a budget, Hans, not a contract. Do you think I'm a complete moron? Is that why you hired me? All your talk about my genius patents! I should have known better."

"On the contrary. I hired you because you were the intellectual I needed in that position. Remember, I'm the one who knows about patents being key to a company's success. Ashley, you've got to trust me, I didn't lie to you. Stand behind me, and we'll both have our jobs back tomorrow."

"I didn't do anything wrong! I'll have my job back if I just bide my time." I say this with more confidence than I feel. "Anyway, you did lie. You lied to every shareholder in that company."

"Don't let them lie to you, Ashley. You're done at Gainnet without me. There's no reason they wouldn't replace you if there's a question about your integrity."

What is it about me that attracts trouble like a toddler in a china shop? I'm just trying to live my life. I tried to do a good deed here, to tell Hans and Sophia about God, and look where it's gotten me. The office admins think I'm a loose woman, the board of directors think I'm a thief, and my own steady roommate thinks I'm as unstable as the Russian ruble.

Oh Lord, tell me where to go. Give me words, Lord, because I don't know what to think. What to feel . . . I don't even finish the silent prayer when this overwhelming distaste for Hans overcomes me. It's like all his ugliness has been laid bare before me and he's standing in front of me like some hideous creature. Lost behind the gorgeous European suits, and the elegant façade, is a heart that's hard as a diamond. I blink a few times, but it doesn't go away.

"I'll find another job, Hans." I head to the door and open it.

"Of course you will, but I can make it easier on you."

My reference list is a little sparse at the moment, what with Selectech accepting my resignation when I refused to harm Purvi, my boss, in their takeover bid. It would be so easy to weaken, since I've paid the price once for being honest, but something props me up and holds me steady. Rhett barks, reminding me that I'm not alone. God is here, too, and doing the right thing is always better than doing the easy thing. God says that He'll always provide you a way out. I either believe His Word or I don't.

"You'd better leave," I say quietly. Rhett barks again. I'm scared. Don't let my strong response fool you. This is a desperate man, who most likely has a drug habit to support. He's alone now because he actually took my advice and sent his girlfriend back home to Italy. My heart is pounding in my throat as I wait to see what he'll do. I'm so grateful for Rhett and Kay being home at the moment, I want to lie prostrate at their feet.

"I'll tell them you charged that ring to the company." Hans makes a final threat. He looks to my finger, and sees the ring is conspicuously missing. Yep, let that be a lesson to me: impulse buys are never a good idea.

"I gave the ring back this morning. I knew what they'd think, and I should have known better. It's my own fault. I've been naive, but no more of that."

He scoffs at me. "I have a lot of respect in Silicon Valley. These charges won't stick. You've got what? A degree from a so-so school and a few years' experience?"

"I beg your pardon, but Santa Clara University is not a so-so school." My employment experience? Another story altogether. "I can't help you, Hans. You knew I was a Christian when I started this job, and while you may have expected that to make me completely naive, you never counted on the fact that God has the power to make things right for me."

"Oh please, don't talk about your fantasy heavenly realms. My stomach is shaky as it is." He jumps off the porch without a stair and jogs to his car.

The righteous will live by faith, I say to myself as Hans slams the door to his Jaguar.

Hans won't go to jail. No matter how many millions he's managed to scrape off the top of some poor schmuck's 401k plan, he won't go to jail, because to convict him will only make matters worse for shareholders. He'll find another start-up and he'll begin his game all over again.

Kay brushes herself off on the front porch. "What was that about?"

"That was my boss."

She pauses. "What was he doing here?" Then her eyes widen and she brushes her frizzy tendrils off her face. "Your boss? Or your former boss?"

I exhale a sigh. "My former boss."

"Why can't you just go to work like normal people? Life is not a Greek tragedy." She nods to the flowers as she comes in the house. "Who were they from?"

"Kevin." I start to tell her about his poetry, but decide against it.

"So he seems pretty interested, huh?"

"Either that, or he's apologizing for his parents. Mei Ling called last night. Apparently, his mother pointed out some 'work' my mother might have done at the plastic surgeon's office. Then gave her a card, and invited her to stay with them in Atlanta."

"I can't see that riling your mother, Ashley. She wouldn't even consider such a thing."

"No, but then Dr. Novak suggested my brother come to Atlanta, and said he could make as much being a caddy as a bus driver."

"Still, it's Dave. Why would he care what Dr. Novak said?"

"Because apparently, he offered Mei Ling a free gift of blepharoplasty."

"In English?"

"An eyelid lift to rid her of Asian heritage."

Kay chokes on her bottled water. "Oh, Ashley, I'm so sorry. Did he see Mei Ling? Did he happen to notice how gorgeous she was?"

"He's a bigot, Kay, so I doubt it. He thinks everyone should look like Elaine Novak, with that constantly surprised look of hers."

"Does Kevin know?"

I shake my head. "I don't think so, and I don't know what to tell him."

"You've got to tell him. They can't be coming into the international melting pot of Silicon Valley and offering plastic surgery to various ethnic groups so they can look like white folks. What, does he think we all want to be Michael Jackson or something?"

I shrug. "I'll tell him. Right after I mention my unemployment epidemic."

"Maybe you should get the flu shot this year, Ash. You've had some bad luck."

"Couldn't hurt."

Kay's over any annoyance about my job status already. "Do you want me to make something for lunch?"

"No, but thanks." Maybe I can find some grunt job in the basement where I never have to meet face-to-face with anyone. Nah, nix that idea. Who would ever see my fabulous clothes?

It must be me. I'm the common denominator in all these situations. Maybe I put too much pressure, too many conditions on being employed. And loved. Seth wouldn't commit, and it's hard to overcome that one. Hans has a love affair with cocaine, and he's definitely not dealing with all eight cylinders there. And Kevin has white supremacists for parents. I let my head fall into my hands. If I'm a Reason, my dating repertoire consists of a Who's Who list of Losers 'R Us. It's definitely not me. Right? I'm only a victim of circumstance.

32

So, it's Tuesday, and I have a six-day weekend to explore. Actually, I have an infinite weekend now, but I'm looking at the bright side of life. So yea! Six days. I've been avoiding Kevin's phone calls. I'm just not sure how to tell him that I'm underemployed. Again. Or that his parents have a race issue. I mean, how does one start that conversation exactly? *Oh, Kevin, nice to hear from you. Did you know your parents are . . . segregationists? Would you like me to quote the Civil Rights act of '64 for them?*

The Novaks' love of self and plastic surgery reminds me of that really old *Twilight Zone*, where the woman has several operations and cries at the end because she's a gorgeous woman, not a "beautiful" ape like the rest of the planet. There's something so mystifying about people who think they are the be-all to end-all—the yardstick, if you will, for all others. It makes you want to steal their mirrors and see what you're missing.

I wish I had a magic mirror, don't you? I want to believe that my body is Uma Thurman's. Just think if a mirror could solve this problem—how many "Extreme Makeovers" could be avoided? You just go into Home Depot, and there they are: *This mirror is the fat thigh model—makes you look like Britney Spears when you turn around. Flat chest? That would be the Jessica Simpson model.* I get up and look in my own mirror over my dresser. *Clearly, I have too much time on my hands.*

I sink to my knees and start my day in prayer, thanking God that I've excelled at another job for a month. I'm hopeful that He has a bigger, better opportunity somewhere else. Maybe there's a little wishful thinking in my prayers this morning, but God's bigger than my issues.

Kay raps at my door, and I open my eyes from prayer. "Come in!"

"Hey there. Did you do something at church on Sunday?"

"Why?"

"The mail came bright and early and there's all these thank-you notes for Thanksgiving."

"Cool." I nod my head.

"Ashley?"

"What?" I ask in an overly innocent tone while I straighten out my sheets.

"Are you going to be here this morning? The contractor is supposedly starting."

"I'll wait for him."

"Kevin called again early this morning. He hopes he didn't wake you up."

"He didn't."

"Are you going to call him?"

"I haven't decided yet."

"At least talk to Brea about it before you do anything. At least you listen to her." Kay starts to shut the door, and then sticks her head back in. "Whatever you did on Sunday, thank you for that." She waves the cards at me.

"You're welcome." I plop back on my bed, not quite sure what to do with my overly calm lifestyle of late. I need a little excitement, so I call Brea. She's finally home.

"Hello, Ashley," she breathes into the phone.

"Brea, how's life with your mom around 24/7?" As if I couldn't tell by her tone.

"Am I a complete putz? Because I know I'm not exactly book

246

smart, but I did manage to score myself a pretty good man, a pretty good life here, did I not?"

"Yes, you did."

"Is my child not the most gorgeous little Baby Gap man you've ever seen? Do I understand the concept of dressing him without Garanimals?"

"Things going that well, huh?" I crinkle my nose.

"Come get this baby and take him out for a while, Ashley. He's being nitpicked to death, and I worry we're about to have a shower scene from *Psycho*."

"You know, I really resent being called the drama queen here. Your mother thinks I'm the drama queen because you'll go and be all nice to her and then unleash on me. And you know what? She's going to rip my head off for trying to take baby Miles out of the house."

"But I'm your best friend, and you're coming anyway," Brea states.

"I have two words for you: Dan Hollings. I had a date with Dan Hollings for you."

"That was nearly a year ago, and he wasn't that bad. Quit your whining. It made Seth jealous."

"Could we not mention his name, please?" Now Rhett is whining. "I have to take the dog out and wait for the contractor. I'll be there in a couple hours."

"You better come, or I'm calling Seth in India and telling him you miss him and want to bear his children."

We both start cracking up. "You are such a terrible liar."

"Bring me an espresso on your way, will you? Decaf, of course."

The doorbell rings. "I think the contractor is here. Gotta run." I open the door and my mouth pops open like one of Kay's Christmas choir statues. The contractor has light brown hair (the color of a golden leaf in fall), honey brown eyes, and a chiseled build that probably has a twelve-pack hiding within. I'm so pathetically shallow. But I feel like it's a sign. When the hotties come in on *Average Joe*, does the gal not react? It's a sign. It's perfectly acceptable that I'm attracted to Dr. Kevin Novak.

The left side of his mouth curls slowly and reveals the most perfect set of teeth I've ever laid eyes upon. Clearly, his parents spent some money at the orthodontist. He's packing a tool belt, and it pulls at his Levi's dangerously.

"Hi, I'm Colin. Colin Law." He wipes his hands on his jeans and thrusts one toward me.

"Ashley Stockingdale. Nice to meet you." I open the door a bit wider. "Come on in, I'll tell you where to get started."

I start to walk down the hallway, and I'm realizing this guy is behind me. With all his muscles and rigid cuts on his stomach, what can he be thinking? *When was her last time at the gym? 1980?* "It's just right in there." I point.

"You look very familiar," he says.

"Do I?" I giggle. Yes, I giggled and I can't take it back now.

He's pointing at me trying to place the face. "I can't remember her name. She was in *Pirates of the Caribbean*. You look like her."

More giggling. Just shoot me now and put me out of my misery. I point at the round metal hole in the middle of what used to be the bathroom. "We really need a toilet."

"I've got to get the floor in first." He apologizes with a shrug.

"Well, Colin, you've got two women here trying to get ready. *If* we both have a date." See there, just let him know we're not together. So very subtle. This is why I am a lawyer. "Well, if we both have a date, it's just misery."

He looks at me. "Did you want to get that?"

"Get what?"

"The phone. It's ringing," Colin says.

"Right. The phone. Getting the phone." I back up toward my room, lest he get another view of the full moon. "I'll just be on the telephone if you need anything." I reach for the phone just as it stops ringing. And no ID either. Sigh. I let the answering machine get it.

I clamber into some Halogen jeans (only brand that makes the legs long enough for me), and don a Gap T-shirt under my Juicy sweatshirt. Brushing some powdered foundation over my face and dabbing lip gloss, I figure this is as good as it's going to get without appearing high maintenance. I grab Rhett's leash, and we head up the hallway. Rhett whimpers at the sight of Colin. "I know, huh?" I say to the dog.

"Leaving me?" Colin asks.

"Um, yeah. Gotta babysit today and I'm—"

"Are you a nanny?" he asks.

"No, I'm a lawyer. A patent attorney." You know, a contract geek. He nods at me, as though he has no idea what I do.

"I write patents."

He starts to laugh. "It's okay, I understand. I'm an engineer by training."

"An engineer?"

"Mechanical engineer. But I found I didn't get to work with my hands enough. So here I am, designing bathrooms and kitchens, and doing what I love." He grabs the hammer with gusto. He's looking at me with those wide brown eyes, and I've just forgotten where I am. Good thing Rhett is here to lead me like a guide dog.

"The telephone!" I say, realizing it's ringing again.

He nods like I've got a screw loose upstairs, and you have to wonder.

"Hello?"

"Ashley? It's Kevin."

I think I let out a groan here. "Kev . . ."

"I've been trying to get a hold of you for days. Are you avoiding me?"

I'm silent. Just the sound of his baritone makes me feel guilty. My stomach tingles at the sound of his voice, and I realize Colin in there is just another way for me to avoid what's at hand. My heart is galloping toward Kevin, and I'm grabbing the reins hard trying to halt it.

"Ashley, you there?"

"Uh-huh. I'm here." *Your parents are bigots. Your parents are bigots. Just spit it out.*

"Is there something going on?"

"Yes, actually there is." I am breathing hard here.

Colin asks me for a drink of water.

"Is there someone there, Ashley?"

I look at Colin, who I've pointed to the kitchen. "Just the contractor. I think it's something we should discuss in person, Kevin. There is something I need to tell you."

"There's something I need to tell you, too, Ashley. Are you busy this afternoon? Could we meet on your lunch hour?"

"I have no lunch hour. I'm not working at Gainnet any longer."

He says nothing about the job. "Good, then can we meet at ten thirty at Evvia?"

"How about one o'clock at Fresh Choice? I promised to take baby Miles out for a few hours to give Brea a break from her mom."

"One at Fresh Choice. I'll be there." He pauses for a minute. "Oh, and Ashley, since you're not working, you're going to be wearing jeans, right?" He makes a clicking noise.

Now I wonder. Should I change so I don't look like I was trying to impress him?

Gulp. I come out of the hallway and see Colin swallowing water like he's a camel. He lets out a belch, and then sees me. "Sorry about that. I thought you were on the phone."

"Can I leave the dog here? Will he bother you?" I ask the hottie pseudoengineer with bodily function issues.

Colin takes a gander at Rhett, and then at me. "Suit yourself. Your house."

Perhaps that's what Seth felt for Arin. Just a momentary rush that makes you question everything you know to be true. Kevin is true, but not necessarily for me.

33

Ashley basks in the warm Hawaiian sunlight, the gentle lull of the ukulele's strings bringing her in and out of a restful sleep. She inhales deeply and slowly turns over to allow the rays to reach the bottoms of her feet and the backs of her legs.

"This is the life," Ashley coos.

"Would you like something more to drink?"

Ashley shoots up from her reclining position. "Kevin?" The elegant doctor is clad in Hawaiian shorts, carrying a slushy strawberry drink with a tiny umbrella in it.

"I'd love something to drink." She reaches up for him and Kevin takes her hand.

"Wouldn't you rather have a plain iced tea?" Seth appears, also clad in Hawaiian shorts, and Ashley turns away to avoid the flash of white in her eyes. He removes her hand from Kevin's and takes it into his own, but Ashley is concerned.

"Seth? You better get some sunscreen on."

Seth ignores her warning. "I'd go to the desert for you, Ashley. You don't want that sugary-sweet thing. Simple is what it's all about, Ashley. Simple is what you prefer." She takes the proffered iced tea, and Seth squeezes a lemon into the drink, careful not to splash any on his black socks. She then places the drink on the table beside her without touching it.

"She needs something stronger. A good margarita with a touch of salt *at the brim." Colin, the very brawny contractor, appears out of nowhere, flexing his double six-pack stomach and strong legs in flip-flops, clad in black shorts with a purple shark.*

"What she needs is a touch of the European. A wine spritzer, perhaps?" Hans, dressed to perfection in his Armani suit, holds out a glass of bubbly wine on a silver tray. The crush of ice is heard as he holds the bottle out to fill Ashley's drink to the brim.

Ashley shakes her head. "No, I want water. Pure, filtered water." Ashley looks to her suitors. "Over crushed ice." All of the men stare at one another, unsure of where to get the simple offering. Then, in a flash of light, everyone looks skyward and shields their faces from the sun. "Never mind." Ashley pushes through the men. "None of you has what I want."

"Ashley, get out of your dream world and come in and get Miles. Brea's waiting." Mrs. Browning is tapping her toes, as I sit behind the wheel of my convertible, lost in a better world than this one.

My mind is far away from Mrs. Browning's moving mouth. *I mean, I wish I really looked that good in a swimsuit. I have one of those special mirrors in my dreams. That's a nice place to be.*

"You didn't bring that mutt with you, good."

And then my dream is magically gone. Lost in Mrs. Browning's angular face. Brea's mother has the pointiest nose you ever saw. You almost expect it to start growing as she speaks, like Pinocchio. Not that she lies. It would almost be a blessing if she did because what she really thinks is so much worse than something she might temper with a kind white lie.

"It's nice to see you too, Mrs. Browning," I remark, grabbing my bag and getting out of the car. I'm not in the mood for falsehood this morning, and if Mrs. Browning can't be bothered, neither can I.

"Don't get smart. I've been waiting around all morning, and I'd like to get to the club and work on the Christmas party. Brea said you were coming, and I count on you. Not that I shouldn't know better."

Something in me snaps here. "You know, Mrs. Browning, every parent I have ever met loves me. Even boyfriends who dumped me in high school, I still get Christmas cards from their parents. What on earth makes you hate me so?"

Her lips purse together like an angry bird in a Hitchcock film. "I don't hate anyone. I'm a Christian. And as such, I feel there are certain standards to be upheld. Ashley Stockingdale, do you have any idea what time it is?"

I'm scratching my head here. Not only do I know what time it is here, I also happen to know what time it is in Taiwan, India, and England.

"I'm not late, Mrs. Browning. I'm actually early. I told Brea I'd be over when the contractor arrived." I shut the car door.

"Hmmph." She starts for her Infiniti and looks back at me.

"Your own husband loved me," I remind her.

"I love you too, Ashley. I just don't appreciate you at times. You're self-absorbed."

I nod. "I'll give you that one, but then again, who isn't?" I mean, the country club Christmas craft fair? I hike up the steps to Brea's house, and she meets me at the door. "What are you doing up? Get back in bed."

She lets out a deep sigh. "I'm supposed to move a bit to keep the blood flowing. Poor Miles, he is bored to death. He wants to go see the pretty Christmas lights and maybe Santa."

"Santa?" I ask incredulously. "Santa is definitely something he should do with his Mama."

"It's his first Christmas, Ashley. He needs his photo with Santa and I can't go. Unless you want to push me in the wheelchair and Miles in his stroller—and my mom will take him to a cheap strip mall Santa."

I enter through the screen door and see Miles on the floor gumming a teething ring and looking at his feet. "All right. What's he wearing?"

Brea shows me a little green and red plaid velvet suit. "Heartstrings," she says, spouting a brand I never heard of.

"Darling."

"So you'll take him to the mall?" Brea says like a question, but it's really more of a command. "Stanford. They have the best Santa."

"I have to meet Kevin for lunch at one. Lucky for you, that's where we're meeting."

"You better get moving then. I'm going to keep him in his sleeper, and you dress him there so he doesn't get dirty, okay?"

"Okay, Brea."

Her face relaxes and a peace overcomes her. "His diaper bag is filled with everything you'll need. He needs to eat about eleven."

"Check," I say as Brea hands me the baby bag that would house half the free world. I place Miles in his little carry bucket seat. "Brea, you shouldn't lift this bag. My goodness, what do you have in here?"

"Make sure you comb his hair before the picture. Use the diaper in there to wipe up any spittle before the picture, and Ashley . . ."

"Yes, Brea."

"Thank you. I know John wouldn't comb his hair, and when he got to the mall and saw the traffic, he'd just turn around."

I'd do anything for Brea. She knows that. She'd do anything for me. It's a mutual fan club. "No problem. If there's one skill I have accomplished in life, it's maneuvering the mall. Keeping a job? Not really my thing, apparently."

"If you marry rich, maybe you'll only need to know the mall." Brea winks at me.

"Yeah, well, don't hold your breath. I have yet to meet the man who can keep up with my spending habit."

We both laugh, and Brea gets all serious. "I used to say that I cared about money, and then I met John. I tell you, I'd live in a hovel to be with him."

I hold up my hand. "Don't even go there with me. Seth had money. They say marrying rich, you'll earn every penny. And I believe them."

"Kevin doesn't live like that."

"Kevin's just a friend," I say, forcing myself to avoid the obvious. The last thing I need is to be falling for a guy at this point.

"You'll figure it out. I know you will." Brea smiles knowingly.

I'm not sure I believe that, but sometimes it's nice just to live in a little fantasy world. One where I look like a bachelorette in a swimsuit, minus the sleaze factor, and the qualified men are four-to-one.

The mall is frenzied, since it's the week after Thanksgiving. Stanford is always busy, but when there's an actual reason to shop, other than being well-dressed and/or metrosexual, then it's ridiculously overcrowded.

After circling for an eternity for a parking spot, I pull Miles out of the car in his baby seat and plug it into a stroller contraption. Takes me thirty minutes to figure this out, and I'm a patent attorney, quite accustomed to schematics and all that. Miles just gurgles during my incompetence, and I swear if I could find a man this calm, I'd marry him in a second.

We make our way across the parking lot with our gear, packed as though we could survive a surprise winter storm, though it hasn't snowed here since *I* was a baby. We get to the Santa display and the line forms in a zigzag direction that makes Lombard Street in San Francisco look like an easy downhill hike. I look down at Miles and realize he still needs his little plaid outfit.

"Let's go find the bathroom," I soothe.

He gives me a small squeal as a reward. We enter the bathroom, and I see I'm not the only one with this brilliant idea. There is a line for the diaper changing table. As though the ladies' rooms of America aren't busy enough, now we have to share them with infants and strollers and diaper bags swelled with designer baby items.

Our turn finally arrives. Now, changing a baby sounded easy to me, because the last time I changed Miles, he was ill and didn't struggle against the plan. Today, however, he is like a little bag of moving bones kicking at the indignity of being changed on a plastic table. I have put down his Gymboree blanket, so he'll have no idea where we actually are, but babies are like mountain lions, they understand their environment well.

After what I like to call "the plaid fiasco," we get in the line of screaming infants, tantrum-throwing toddlers, and particular mothers, most with nannies in tow. Santa is currently on his break and the long line isn't even moving. I mutter to myself, "Brea so owes me. She owes me big."

"Ashley!" I hear my name and turn around to see Arin heading toward me without her bindi dot and sari. She actually looks quite cute in a black sweater over a big white collared shirt. Very professional for the likes of Arin.

"Hi, I thought you were in India." I say this as nicely as possible so as not to imply, *I thought you were in India taking off the finishing touches of Seth and his overwhelming fear of commitment.*

"No, not yet. I'm staying through Christmas. My parents are coming out from Boston, and they wanted to spend some time with me first."

I grin dumbly. So Seth is alone for Christmas. When I think of poor lonely Seth in the big country of India . . . okay, I can't help my smile, truthfully. Revenge, while I know it's the Lord's to dole out, really does feel good sometimes. We're sinful creatures. But then my heart gets the better of me, and I feel sorry for him all by himself. No job is worth being away from the life as you know it, unless you're an adventurer. Which I'm not. And neither is Seth, really.

The line starts to move, and I inch away from Arin, but she just follows behind me.

"Is this Miles?"

I nod.

"He just gets cuter and cuter. How's Brea feeling?"

"I think she's getting a bit tired of the bed rest, but she'll need it when she's got two babies to care for. She's still not keeping food down, so they have her on fluids. I can't believe how much work one of these little guys is." As we're talking, I take out Miles's baby brush and start to comb his auburn locks. This baby is idyllically cute.

Arin clears her throat. "I think Seth is coming home from India."

My world just collapsed. "What do you mean, for Christmas?"

"I mean, he doesn't like it there. He's coming back home. He said he tried to tell you over the phone, but you didn't seem all that interested."

"I'm glad for him if that's his choice." Who wants to hear you have to avoid your ex at church again?

"From the sound of it, you're not interested in Kevin either, so what does interest you, Ashley?"

"Why do you say that? That I'm not interested in Kevin?"

"Are you?"

Very good question. He's to-die-for good-looking, chivalrous to a fault, and our chemistry is overwhelmingly magnificent. So I'm at least a little interested. But I have to say, my history with Seth has me questioning the whole need for male companionship in my life. And Kevin's racist parents seem to be the Tupperware lid of closure on the deal.

"Time will tell, I suppose."

Arin nods. "And Seth? Where does he stand?"

"Somewhere in the state of Punjab, I imagine."

Arin seems awfully interested in my love life, and considering how pathetic and paltry it is, I wonder what she finds so fascinating.

"He loves you, Ashley."

"Who loves me?"

She gets this look on her face, like she's going to spill her guts, and I brace myself.

"Seth does. I thought he and I had the same dynamic for ministry. I misread God's guidance. Actually, I think I didn't listen to it. Seth and I are wrong for each other."

"Didn't you stand in front of me and tell me this same thing about Kevin? That he loved me? You know, if a guy loves me? I'm just going to have to figure it out on my own." I switch hips with Miles, "By the way, here's a surefire clue that it's not God's will. When you have to arrange everything to your will? That's whose will it is."

She shakes her head. "I didn't think you two were really in love."

Can't help my smile here. "No one knows what an engineer in love looks like, I imagine."

She nods her head, smiling at me. "I'm sorry. I toyed with Kevin's heart, and then yours. And here I stand, alone and getting sent to a foreign country to serve. I wanted to know I had a place to fall."

One can't help but feel for Arin, with her brilliant blue eyes and Ivy League education. She's been so used to having her way in life, it just never occurred to her that God would change her course. I'm with her. I hate that too. Is there anything worse than discovering you can't really control anything? That you just have to dive into God's current, and enjoy the ride?

Miles starts to cry, and I switch him to the other hip and wrap his blanket about him as I face him toward the colorful, glittering Santa display.

"I'm apologizing, Ashley. Not too well, but I got in between you and Seth. On purpose."

"If Seth truly loved me, nothing could have kept us apart . . . if that had been God's will. It wasn't. I assure you with all I know to be true, Seth had to go searching. He had to cut bait."

"What?"

We get to the front of the line, and Miles spots Santa. He watches the red suit and scary white beard and starts to whimper as if to say, I'm not going up there. Don't you make me go up there. He looks up at me with his eyes wide and his nose red, as if saying *NOOOO!* like Luke discovering Darth Vader is his real father.

"I thought you should know," Arin finally says. "It's you Seth loves, not me."

I laugh. "Seth loves himself, Arin. He'll do whatever he has do to protect himself from the likes of me and real emotions. Learn this lesson young, Arin. If a man doesn't want you? Move on, because God has something much better planned for you."

"You're so mature, Ashley. I hope I'm like you when I grow up."

"I wouldn't wish that on my worst enemy."

"Which package would you prefer, A, B, or C?" an overly enthusiastic elf asks me, and Miles starts to scream at the sight of her.

"C," I say, not even glancing at the package. It's the most expensive, and from my experience with Brea and baby photographs, she wants the most possible.

I hand Miles to Arin for a moment. She shows him the blocks and he starts to simmer down, being an equitable distance from the man in red. Grabbing him back, I smile at Arin. "Thanks for telling me all that. I appreciate your honesty." But my mind is with the elf.

"I'll see you Sunday, Ashley."

I take Miles back and lift him up to the Santa platform, and he starts to scream like a horrified victim. I try to calm him down, but his face gets redder. "Can I just walk him a bit?" I say to the sprightly elf.

The elf looks at the crowd. "You gotta be kidding me."

"It's for my best friend, and she'll kill me if he's screaming. Let the next person go. Please."

I walk Miles up and down the walkway and he's like an on/off button. Every time we move away from Santa he calms, and every time we get close he starts to bawl.

"I'll be back," I say with all the confidence of Arnold Schwarzenegger. I walk Miles until he falls asleep in my arms. I take him back to Santa and we take the picture with Miles sleeping peacefully in the Christmas icon's lap.

I feel like I've just climbed Everest. In every way. My muscles hurt from heaving the healthy baby Miles around the shopping center and my feet ache, even in my Kate Spade flats. But really, I'm thinking about Seth, and his coming back. What if he really does love me? Can I ever forget that he dumped me with a simple phone call and left me with sole custody of our puppy? I'm thinking no.

34

When I arrive for lunch at Fresh Choice, I'm lacking the lady-of-leisure look I was hoping for. Frankly, the look a currently un-employed woman *should* have. My hair is flying in inexplicable waves with no time for a comb, as it took me another half an hour to figure out how to secure the car seat. And simply because sparring with an elf about Santa photos takes something out of you. My lipstick has long since faded into oblivion and I don't even want to look for my compact. I've dug through the diaper bag forty times, and I just don't have the energy to tackle my handbag too.

In my mood, this date is more like a sentence than a date. Miles is not in particularly good spirits either. But I cart him into the loud restaurant with a prayer that he'll stay asleep during our meal. The Santa tantrum took a lot out of him, so I'm hopeful.

Kevin greets us with his warm smile and I must admit I melt a bit. Just mop me up off the floor—he has the ability to bring light into a room. Like the sun coming out, Kevin's smile makes you feel warm inside. As I continue to remind myself, I'm usually immune to the woefully gorgeous types, but not Kevin. Could it be I'm suddenly immune to bald men? Like, Seth was the vaccine? You get a little in your system, and then your body rejects it.

I must remember my complete lack of discernment in the last year. Then there's the racism issue we have to discuss, so I admit that this is not the dream date I might have been hoping for. On a happy note, I read this morning that the number of single people between the ages of thirty and thirty-five had tripled since 1970, so at least I'm in good company if this turns out to be my last date ever.

Kevin takes Miles's heavy baby seat from me and half-embraces me, kissing me on the cheek. "I'm glad you made it."

"Me too. I wasn't sure with the Santa line. Those mothers are vicious."

"And you weren't with Miles?"

"That's not the point here," I laugh.

"You sure you want to eat here? It's awfully loud."

I ponder the idea. This is the very same restaurant where Seth met me when he dumped me, while hoping for a shot with the petite Arin. He brought a coupon for the occasion. But if I'm ever to reclaim my life from Seth, I have to reclaim the restaurants we attended together.

"I don't mind the noise and I admit, I'm a sucker for Christmas music—even bad Christmas music. Hopefully, it will be a sweet melody in Miles's ear and he'll sleep."

"I have something I want to talk about." He looks around the restaurant. "This doesn't seem like the place, but you know, Ashley, your life is crazy. If my life is chaotic, yours is in hyperdrive. If I don't just blurt it out, I'll probably never get the chance."

I laugh nervously. Does anyone ever want to hear they "need" to be talked to about something? I mean, is that ever a good thing? I pray he's not going to tell me that he's going back to Arin. I could take a lot, but right now, that just isn't on my radar. Being dumped twice for the same woman is more than sad, it's kind of up there in proportion with Biblical plagues.

"My life is chaos. That's a bad thing?" I say.

We get in line for our salads, while Kevin picks up the baby's seat as we move. It's amazing to me how Kevin thinks of things. As sure as we stand here, I know it would never occur to Seth to pick up the baby seat or take the diaper bag from me. I'd be schlepping everything and the baby too. It's not that I'm trying to compare the men, just trying to point out to myself that maybe Seth was not the norm.

Kevin doesn't get lettuce. He gets spinach. (Like Popeye. He's strong to the finish.) If Brea was here, she'd be telling him that spinach causes constipation. Luckily, she's not, but she is in my mind and I'm immaturely giggling at the sight of a plate full of it.

"What's so funny?" Kevin asks.

"Nothing. Just thought of something that Brea told me once." Or a hundred times.

When we finish in the line, I have a bevy of toppings on my salad, Kevin has spinach with a few sunflower seeds and cherry tomatoes. Kevin prays over our meals, then meets my gaze. "So. Tell me why you're avoiding me."

"I'm not avoiding you." Mostly.

"Are you planning to tell me what my parents did?"

His forthrightness shocks me. "How do you know your parents did something?"

"Because I know it wasn't me. I'm charm personified. My parents, however, have no friends, other than at the club, where *none* of them have any friends, only associates. They all hang out together and compare face lifts, so they don't actually know they have no friends." He plows in a forkful of spinach. "So I look at the timing and I figure they did something offensive. I also figure you know what that was."

He's made it easy on me. So I just blurt it out, "Your parents are, um, a bit racist." Can someone be a bit racist? I mean, you are or you aren't, right?

He nods his head in agreement. "I know. How'd you figure that out? Thought I'd be safe."

"Mei Ling,"

And he winces like I've hit him. "Mei Ling, of course."

"So you know they're, um, a bit racist?"

"Do you think I grew up in a bubble, Ashley? I grew up in

Atlanta. Trust me, if my parents were racist, there wasn't much hiding it in Atlanta. Did you ever think there's a reason I live in California and they live in Atlanta?"

"You seemed to get along really well with them. I mean, that time up in San Francisco when we met them. You seemed to want to impress your father."

"Name me a son who doesn't. I want him to know that working at a children's hospital is not less than a respectable a job, even though he sees it otherwise. I'm proud of my job, and I've done fine without his name." Kevin stabs another spinach leaf. "He thought I wouldn't be able to do it without him. But here I am."

I take his hand. It seems appropriate for the moment.

"You're a great doctor. Brea says the nurses go on and on about you at the hospital."

"I'm not racist, Ashley. Do you believe that? Because I need you to believe that."

I nod my head. I do believe that. I've seen him with the kids at the family shelter, and there isn't a racist bone in his body. When he plays horsey with the preschoolers, he never makes a distinction in any child. He seems to love them all. And hey, if we're going to start taking on our parents' sins, I couldn't dress for the life of me. Certainly, we can tell by my shoes alone that I've moved past the fashion glitches of my mother.

"Anyway, I'm sorry they said something. I assume they offered free plastic surgery advice?"

I nod gently. "Eyelid lift."

He shrugs. "Look on the bright side: you must all be under his appropriate weight level or he would have told you which kind of liposuction to go for: ultrasonic or power."

I drop his hand. "So? Are you going to tell me? You can't just leave info like that dangling."

He pretends to look at my bum and raises a single eyebrow. Oh how I love how he does that. "No, I don't mess with perfection."

Beet red now.

"I'm sorry I embarrassed you, but that's my professional opinion." He's still smiling.

"Cut that out!" I slap his hand.

"Ashley?" I look up and see my boss Hans standing over me. If unemployment has been hard on him, you can't tell. He looks as gorgeous as ever. And as well dressed. Granted, it's not like it's been ages since he was fired, but still.

"Hans, what are you doing here?"

"Christmas shopping. Listen, I wanted to tell you I was sorry. I'd had too much to drink that day."

"Hans, meet Kevin."

Hans purses his lips together in thought. "Much better." He winks at me. "Kevin, nice to meet you. Hans Kerchner."

The two men shake hands.

"Pleasure," Kevin says.

"There's my date. I'll see you a bit later." Hans walks away, and I see Sophia come into view. Well, I'll be. She never left for Italy. I guess the black roses were domestic.

I turn my attention back to Kevin and brace myself for the impending doom. Miles awakens and starts at the sights and sounds of Fresh Choice. "Let me get him a bottle." I go hunting for warm water, mix up the vile powdered drink, and head back to the table where Kevin is holding the baby.

"You're a natural," I say.

"I'm a professional." He looks at Miles. "See, Miles can tell."

I feel myself relax for the first time in ages. "I can tell, too."

Kevin takes the bottle from me and starts to feed the baby. "Now, I'm going to get this out before one more interruption. Eat your lunch."

I finish up my salad and get too long of a piece of lettuce; it's hanging out of my mouth like a rat in a snake. I take my fingers, and shred the offending leaf, but it leaves ranch dressing on my upper lip.

I'm looking for my napkin when I see that Kevin has it under the baby. "Excuse me," I say as I go hunting for a napkin. I come back to the table. "Okay, I'm ready."

He clears his throat. "When I saw you on that plane to Taiwan, it was all the confirmation I needed. The sign."

I think back to that time, when I thought Kevin was the most gorgeous man I'd ever seen, and my very overly enthusiastic fantasy life. How I wanted everything to be perfect and left his side on the plane to wait for the magical "Fabulous Friday" when I could meet him as Deborah Kerr herself at the Top of the Mark. The whole thing is just embarrassing. A "ready" Ashley, is after all, still Ashley.

"I wanted to tell you," he shouts over the busboy who's clearing our plates. The clinks of dishes are overwhelming, and Miles starts to sputter.

"I think he needs to stop for a burp," I mention.

Kevin breathes in deeply and puts the baby over his shoulder. Miles proceeds to spit up the entire contents of what Kevin just fed him, right down the back of a crisp white dress shirt.

Kevin stands quickly, and I take a diaper out of the bag and soak up what I can when Kevin turns around and his face is next to mine.

"I had hoped for wine and roses, but I'll have to settle for iced tea and wilted lettuce because otherwise I will never get your attention." He takes the diaper from me and puts Miles facing outward, the baby's innocent pucker hard to ignore. I force my eyes to Kevin.

"Brea says I wasn't cut out for romance, that I'd squash a romantic like a bug, so don't take it personally."

"When I heard you sing, that first day in church." He looks at me making sure he has my attention.

"Uh-huh?"

"Before I was ever a Christian, I felt drawn to you like the moth to the proverbial flame." He laughs a bit here. "I know that sounds cheesy. Forgive me."

Bring on the brie. My entire body is quivering, and I'm no longer sitting in an obnoxiously loud chain restaurant without waitresses. I am on a tropical island, floating on a raft, basking in the soft warmth of such unreal words.

"Why?" I say suddenly.

"Who do you see in the mirror, Ashley?"

I shrug. *Average-looking girl masked by some really great clothes.* "I don't know. A good dresser."

"It's not who the rest of us see," Kevin says, holding on to Miles's balled-up fist.

My eyes widen and I shift uncomfortably. "What do you mean? You don't think I have great clothes? Have you seen my shoe collection? And boots are back. I love boots."

"Ashley, focus here a minute, will you?"

I nod.

"I want us to know each other better."

And here it comes. He wants us to move in together or "try things out" in the bedroom or to see if we're compatible, yada, yada, yada. My invisible wall begins building itself and I feel my jaw tightening.

"If I don't get on your calendar, I don't know how I'll ever become a priority. And Ashley, I want to be a priority. So if you don't object, I want your Palm Pilot." He holds out a hand, balancing Miles on his knee.

I'm no fool. I fumble through my purse and come up with my PDA. "It's a Blackberry. Cute, huh?"

Kevin hands me Miles and begins to tap away on my minute keyboard. I'm completely out of control, and for once in my life, I don't care.

35

When I get home, I realize that Kevin has a point. It's been a long time since I prioritized my life. I slide down the side of the bed, onto the hardwood floor, and Rhett rests his face in my lap.

"I coulda been somebody, Rhett. I coulda been a contender," I say in my best Marlon Brando. Rhett just looks at me questioningly. It's probably not a good thing when you confuse your dog.

I used to make lists all the time so I would accomplish my goals. Somewhere along the line, I just started letting life happen to me instead. I reach under my bed, while Rhett sticks his nose as far as it will go. I rummage through my old journal with a few of my many lists from back then. Oddly, the first one I come across is one I made on the plane with Kevin—about who I would date.

I will not be attracted to guys who:

1. Play video games.
2. Watch science fiction movies more than once.
3. Confuse Jesus with Frodo.
4. View dutch treat as an acceptable first-date option.
5. Take me for a meal with a coupon in hand. (They should value me!)

As I look over this old scribbled list, I realize that Seth meets every one of those criteria. I've blamed him for everything, but I see now that I knew better all along. Seth is a fabulous person, but he is who he is, and that was completely wrong for me. Why did I waste a year of my life figuring out what I already knew? From the looks of this list, I knew long before I started seeing him. I rip out the list and stuff it in my pocket.

I look up at the ceiling, and I realize that God did probably tell me a few times, but I thought Seth coming to Las Vegas to sweep me off my feet at my brother's wedding was the sign I was looking for—a clear and vibrant sign that what I wanted was God's will for my life. But how could it have been? It took me away from my singing with the band. Away from my evenings out with my church group, and away from my regular stint at the family shelter. When something is God's will, it should take you toward Him, shouldn't it?

"Well, couldn't You have told me that in the first place?" I say out loud to God. But I can almost hear Him laughing at me and my theories. *Fish or cut bait.* It was my turn all the time to cut bait. I had the power all along and never took it.

If I'm ever truly going to be in control of my life, I have to let God be in control of it. I take out my Blackberry, determined to start a *new* list. A list that I actually look at once in a while and take seriously. I turn on the PDA and my calendar comes up and I just start to laugh.

At the start of every day, Kevin has written the following:

Wake up. Pray!
Notice how gorgeous I am.
Call Kevin!

How on earth did he do that so fast? I scroll through my calendar, and it's written on each and every day as though a standing appointment. But I've learned my lesson. There's no sign here. I need to think, so I'm heading to the beach. Whenever I feel that I can't get close to God, or that the shouting is overwhelming His voice, I head toward the mighty waves where I can think clearly.

My phone trills and the calendar-boy contractor is pounding away on the bathroom next door. Is it any wonder I can't concentrate? "Hello," I answer the phone with a bit of attitude. No caller ID. Sigh.

"Ashley Stockingdale, please."

"Who's calling, please?"

"Ashley, it's me, Tracy. From work."

"Tracy, I'm sorry. How are things going? Did you find everything you needed for the board? I hope you're not having any trouble because of me."

"On the contrary. They saw your draft for that new product, and Ashley, they went crazy! They want to know if you can come back in today. They'll end your probation period and promise not to put any of this Hans business on your permanent record."

Act. Don't react.

"Tracy, can you put them off for the day? I just need a little time to gather my thoughts."

"No problem, Ashley. I'll just say I didn't get a hold of you. I'm so happy I'll have you back. These men are rotten bosses!"

"Tracy?"

"Yeah."

"Thank you. For believing me about Hans and fighting for me when I didn't deserve it."

"Us girls gotta stick together. It's a dog's world out there."

"Amen to that." We laugh, and I hang up the phone with more confidence. I pick up Rhett's leash and grab my cell phone when the oddest thought occurs to me. Without really contemplating, I call up Kevin's pager and punch my number in.

"Come on, Rhett. Let's go play fetch on the beach." I grab my journal and a jacket. I don't feel good enough to slap on makeup, so I go au naturel. I dig through the kitchen and find some brie and crackers left over from this week's Bible study. I grab that and a Diet Coke and a banana and put them all in a basket, with a bowl and some bottled waters for Rhett.

As I'm exiting the house, I dial Kevin.

"Hi, Kevin, I'm not really sure why I called, actually."

"Because it's in your Blackberry. I know you're a slave to the PDA, so I've made your PDA my slave."

"Yes, that was quite ingenious of you to figure out the standing appointment feature. I see where the Mensa membership comes into play."

"You're never going to let me live that down, are you?"

"Um, no." Rhett is pulling on his leash, so I head to the car and start it, allowing the convertible's top to lower. "Rhett and I are going to the beach," I say, somewhat hopefully.

"I wish I weren't on call," Kevin says.

I shrug. "I understand. It's not all of us who can live a life of leisure and unemployment continuously."

"You'll have your job back soon, Ashley."

I nod, even though he can't see me through the phone. "I start back today. But I still need a time to gather my thoughts. I've been going full-steam ahead in the wrong direction. I found a list of qualities I didn't want in a man. Today, I'm going to make a list of qualities I do want."

"Well, that's simple. You want what every girl wants: a good Christian pediatric surgeon, who loves children and would go to the ends of the earth for you."

I feel my face flame. But I have to say, his list makes a good deal of sense.

"And would buy me a two-carat princess-cut diamond," I add facetiously.

"Ooh, thank you for playing our game, but that is our parting gift. I was hoping you were more the antique chip-diamond sort of girl."

I start to giggle. "No, I'm really sorry to let you down, but actually, I am the two-carat sort. Remember that old African tale about the seven-cow wife, and how a husband paid seven cows for his wife when the going rate was only one cow?"

"I'm not familiar with that story. But I have a feeling you're going to enlighten me?"

"The husband paid seven cows because he wanted a seven-cow wife. I, however, prefer to think of myself in carats. I'm a two-carat wife."

"I prefer to think in terms of rubies, and you're worth far above them," he says, reciting Proverbs 31. Our joking banter dies in his words. I got myself in trouble once before by not stopping and hearing the voice of God. I can't do it again.

"I need to get to the beach. Rhett's getting anxious and there's nothing more lovely than a beach in winter."

"Be careful," Kevin warns.

"I intend to." I hang up the phone, wrap my hound's-tooth scarf around my hair, and place my DKNY sunglasses on my face. Grabbing the steering wheel, I look to my copilot. "Ready, Rhett?"

He whimpers, and I start up the car with a roar. We don't get out of the driveway when my phone trills again. "Hello, Ashley Stockingdale," I say professionally as I remove the scarf from my ear.

"It's Seth."

My reaction is not registering. I don't know what I feel at the sound of his name. Really, I guess I feel nothing, and that's a good thing.

"Hi, Seth, how's India?"

"The software engineers aren't getting it, and they can't make the telecommunications transformers work. We're coming back to America. This was a lesson in futility."

"You'll have to be sure and see Rhett when you come back. He's gotten so big, Seth." I rev my engine again and squeal out of the driveway as I put the cordless feature into my ear.

"*I'm* back now, Ashley. The company is moving back within the month."

Think of your list, Ashley. His presence means nothing to you. You are a woman in control of her destiny. Because God is in control.

"Maybe I'll see you around then. I need to get going. I have a date this afternoon." I look at Rhett and pat his head while I push the "end call" button.

I don't enjoy the drive to the ocean, like I usually do. Although the sun is out and the air is crisp among the great redwoods, my heart is in utter turmoil. Life used to be so easy when it was about my theories and the way life should be. But life isn't that way. It doesn't follow the road I've mapped out, but it's more fun than I planned for.

I drive into the beach parking lot, and my eyes fall to the page where my Bible is opened. There's only one verse highlighted on the page, and it reads, "The mind of sinful man is death, but the mind controlled by the Spirit is life." And it dawns on me, like the sun breaking over San Francisco Bay, that I am controlled by my whims.

Life is a decision. Every day I wake up and decide who I'm going to be. Brea decided to be a mother. I decided to be a woman whose life was controlled by utter chaos. Well, no more. From this day forward I make the decision to live life to the fullest. And I know exactly what that means.

36

Back at home, I'm still thinking about life. I'm thinking that living out loud means living truthfully. Not just in my faith and deeds, but in my emotions. We live in a world where it's safer to protect your heart from disaster. I've done that by staying pure, but you know what? The Bible also says to live free of fear, that fear doesn't come from the Lord. I look it up in 1 John, just to make sure, and there it is: "There is no fear in love. But perfect love drives out fear . . . the one who fears is not made perfect in love."

And, you know? I've had such a full-frontal view of that fear: Seth. He's afraid to commit to a church, to a job, to a person . . . and eerily, I think a little got passed on to me, because hello? Kevin is fabulous and interested—and interesting. It's better to walk the path and find out if something might happen than to protect my heart with Kevlar and never know for certain! Right?

Doorbell.

I open the door and Rhett rushes toward Kevin, who looks heavenly in his leather bomber jacket and brown dress pants. He's woefully out of style, but looks so hot, I could really care less.

"Hi!" He takes Rhett's snout in his hands. "How ya doing, boy?" *If he notices my new dress, I am so in love.* "Hi."

"Wow, beautiful dress. Is that new?" He's in.

"Yes. I went shopping for our date." Okay, this is honesty at its barest. A woman generally never admits that she's shopped to look good for a person, until you're practically engaged. This is for Kevin, and I'm telling him. *No fear. No fear.*

"Well, you did well."

I did. Fifty percent off at Ann Taylor. Great scoop-necked blouse in black and a red pencil skirt with black embroidery and best yet? My Stuart Weitzman pumps in red. Now, you might think red pumps are just a bad investment, but I have had these for years, and every time I wear them? I feel like queen of the runway. So worth every outrageous penny. While I haven't trained Rhett out of his hosiery fetish, I have found that opaque hose do not run as easily. See? Nearly every problem is fashion-solved.

"I have play tickets for *Les Miserables* in the city." He holds up two tickets and I reach for them.

"No way! It's my very favorite!" I break into song. "Without him, the world around me changes . . ."

"Ah, an Eponine fan, but you shall never know unrequited love if I have anything to say about it."

Kevin models life without fear, does he not?

"Marius has nothing on you, Kevin. You wouldn't fall for the simpering Cosette."

"True. I like my women with a little bite to them." He wiggles his eyebrows. *Okay, yum.* "Will Kay be all right with Rhett all night? The play is long."

Kay walks into the room, and I've got that pleading grin on my face. "What now?" she asks.

"Kevin has play tickets in the city."

"And this affects me how? As if I didn't know." She looks down at Rhett, who lifts his head.

"Go," she says. "The singles group is coming over to watch a movie. Well, those of us without dates."

Hmm. Been there, and it's fun actually.

You know, living with Kay and being truly single has been the best part of my life. Because I realize now that it isn't so bad. I had so much fear about living alone, without a boyfriend and having a woman roommate. How pathetic I thought that looked. But you know? We have so much fun! We can go out to eat when we feel like it. We can shop. We can take Rhett running at Rancho San Antonio. We can hang out with the singles group when they're doing something fun. We can go out to a movie after a long day at work . . .

It's just a good life, and I think that's what got me over the fear thing. The worst thing that can happen if Kevin dumps me—or hey, if I dump him—is that I'll go back to the life I live. And that's just not as bad as living in constant hope of the phone ringing, and the beggarly state I lived in with Seth. Life with good friends is so much more vivid than life with a mediocre boyfriend.

"What are you watching tonight?" Kevin asks.

"We knew Ashley was going out, so no chick flicks. I imagine it will be science fiction of some sort."

"Kay, you like my chick flicks. Admit it, I've expanded your world."

She crosses her arms. "I am an engineering director, and I could have lived my entire life without knowing *How to Lose a Guy in Ten Days*."

I look at Kevin, and the corner of his mouth lifts. "What are you grinning at?"

"I'm just thinking of some of those ways: get a really big dog that has attention deficit disorder, question your allegiance to a bald engineer, call a guy on his parents' racism issue . . . I could go on."

"So could I." I cross my arms in front of my chest. "*Possess* racist parents, tell a woman she's with the wrong man, work horrendous hours, and keep a beeper with you to go off at inappropriate moments."

Kevin comes toward me and wraps me in his arms. "You win, you win."

I snuggle my face into his chest and breathe in deeply. He smells divine. *I do win.*

Dinner is one of the most elegant places I've ever been. A little hole in the wall in San Francisco. There are appetizers of raspberry-pecan salad, and then a luscious cream of mushroom soup, followed by a main course of artichoke chicken over wild rice.

"Dessert?" Kevin asks me.

I clutch my stomach. "I'm so full."

"But we're going to be walking to the theater. And everyone knows dessert fills a different part of the stomach."

"Is that a medical opinion?"

"Absolutely."

He orders a single plate of chocolate mousse and proceeds to hold the spoon before me. I shake my head and he stuffs the spoon in my clamped mouth. "Oh, it's to die for!"

He drops the spoon on the table and leans over our intimate table. "I love you, Ashley."

Then he kisses me on the cheek with his hand placed perfectly behind my neck. *I love you, too.* I try to force the words out, but fear overtakes me and I can't say it. I mean, it could be the chocolate talking. A woman should never admit to love after mousse.

"We'd better get to the play," I say, after glancing at my watch.

He smiles gently and nods his head. "Waiter? Can we get our bill. We've got a show to catch."

I'll regret this moment for a lifetime. I just know it. *Perfect love casts out fear.* We exit the restaurant, and Kevin's demeanor hasn't changed at all. He grabs my hand and points out a dress in a shop window. "That would look gorgeous on you. I wish they were open."

"I love you, too, Kevin."

He stops on the sidewalk and envelops my face in his masculine, skilled hands. We gaze into each other's eyes for what feels like an eternity, and my stomach just does its share of somersaults and I feel ridiculous for ever having fear. Jumping off the cliff is how you feel the hand of God underneath you.

37

New Year's Eve, it's the time of resolutions and another upcoming birthday. I will turn thirty-two. I am still not married like I'd planned to be, but I guess I've met my resolutions, because it doesn't concern me. The Reasons are having their annual New Years' gala at San Francisco's Gift Center, courtesy of Kay's administrative skills (I know, I know, she fell off the wagon), and I have another date with my Prince Charming: Dr. Kevin Novak.

By the way, he gave his parents the what-for on the eye-lift controversy and they were asked to not show up unexpectedly, but plan twice-a-year visits when he could get time off to spend with them. I'm telling you, he did wonders for my own boundary issues because he just out-and-out said it! He didn't gossip, he didn't vilify his parents, he didn't obsess compulsively, but he *did* apologize profusely with a big bouquet of roses to Mei Ling, and a dinner certificate for her and Dave at Black Angus (she's craving prime rib).

I've grown to really love how Kevin handles life. He's so confident in his decisions, and if he does make a mistake, he shrugs it off like that's life. "It's not surgery," he says, jokingly, as he wouldn't dare make a mistake there. He understands what is really important in life. Rhett has kind of adopted him. I guess Kevin is the better parent because he gives Rhett access to kids at the hospital. (Rhett loves children.)

Hans, on the other hand, is still handling his life with the same cliff-diving excitement. He's now employed by our competition, doing business with the same company he padded the contract for at Gainnet.

I've heard through the grapevine that Seth is officially back in town and will be at the New Years' party. But you know what they say, the greatest revenge is looking good. And I do. I've been to Bloomingdale's and shopped for one of those special occasion dresses I've never seen a need for—until now.

Actually, I didn't really buy the gown at Bloomingdale's, even though I did shop there. I bought it on eBay. It's a gorgeous black velvet Shelli Segal Laundry gown with sheer mesh shoulders enhanced by rows of intricate black beading. Its fabric was cut on the bias, so it clings to me like I paid a mint for it. I got it for about one-quarter the price, and Rhett will live to eat another day.

Doorbell.

I open the door to Kevin wearing a black tuxedo with a gray wool collar. "You look incredible."

"So do you." And he does. He holds out his trademark flowers. Tonight, it's stargazer lilies. "You're spoiling me, you know that?"

"Someday, you'll truly let me spoil you, Ashley."

"I have no idea what you're talking about. I was born to be spoiled."

"Uh-huh. My Christmas present?"

Ruby earrings. "Too extravagant."

"The Christmas dinner I had planned?"

Evvia by candlelight. "I had steaks I needed to use in the fridge, and I told you I wanted to learn to cook for you."

"But you did accept the twenty-pound bag of dog food."

"I'm not insane. You even brought it into the garage. That's half the battle right there."

"But it was *dog food*, Ash. It's not exactly the whisper of moonlight, you know?"

"You in that tux is the whisper of moonlight," I say softly, grabbing his lapels and pulling him toward me. He presses a kiss to my lips.

"That kiss is a whisper in the moonlight. The rest is insignificant."

"I've waited a lifetime to spoil someone, Ashley." My heart is pounding in my throat. Kevin is like this. He's always talking in the extremes: lifetimes and moonlight. It's enough to scare a poor obsessive like me to death, even after I've made the resolution to live without fear. The fact is, the closer you get to someone, the deeper you know you're in. And the harder the actual fall can be.

My entire adult life has been spent whining about commitment-phobe men, and every time Kevin takes a step toward me, I want to retreat. Lest I get hurt again. A certain bald engineer keeps me from trusting anyone but Jesus for the time being.

"Let me get my bag." Oh my bag! It's a vintage-looking Max Azria beaded clutch that matches my dress divinely. Also on eBay, can you stand it?

After the long drive up to the city, we enter the Gift Center in San Francisco and it's drenched in a cacophony of Christmas lights and pounding music. *Wow, the Reasons are moving up in the world.*

As we enter the building, Brea and John greet us, holding their new bundle of joy. "What are you doing here? It's way past your bedtime!"

"We were invited, and Jonathan wanted to get out." She passes the baby to me, and I cuddle him close. He's like a little heat ball, and his precious sleeping face is enough to send my biological clock raging. "Miles is with Grandma."

I watch the baby breathe, and it's with his entire being. *In. Out. In. Out.* He's got yoga mastered. "Who would have ever guessed this heavenly creature could have caused his mother so much trouble?"

"He was worth it," Brea says. "Every single day of bad television in the hospital."

Kevin looks at the baby and then at me. "Can I take him for a minute?"

Kevin loves babies. It's the oddest thing. Usually, guys run the other way when a baby becomes the topic of conversation, but Kevin is fascinated by them, which I guess makes sense as he is a *pediatric* surgeon. He's a natural. He takes a squawking baby and calms it like Jesus calming the raging sea. I watch him as he eyes the baby with such a mixture of love and yearning. There's a gentle side of Kevin that doesn't belong in Silicon Valley. An aversion to the harsh reality that is life in high tech.

Kay approaches us, and she looks fabulous in a suit she picked out at Coldwater Creek. It actually has little sprinkles of beads on the jacket and screams *festive*. "Hi, Kay. Everything looks great."

"Oh, I hope so. What do you think of the band?"

"They sound wonderful."

"What?" she screams. I make the okay sign over the noise, and then I see him: Seth Greenwood. He looks good. Rested and dressed in a pair of pressed navy slacks and a crisp white shirt under a sport coat. He changed churches, apparently, for my sake. Kay looks back at him and then to me. "I came to warn you," she whisper-shouts in my ear.

"I can handle it," I smile, squaring my shoulders as I say it.

Seth comes toward me, and I feel my stomach react. I'm nervous, much more so than I thought I would be. I haven't seen him in months, and when you see someone after such a long time—someone you loved—your mind becomes a jumbled mass of memories and lost dreams until it reaches the same conclusion that once took nearly a year.

"Hi," I say to him.

"You look beautiful."

Yes, I do. Thanks for noticing. "Thank you."

"Did you hear I was back?"

I nod. "You're going to a different church?"

"Yeah, Sam and I decided it was time for a change."

Can't commit to a church either. I nod again. "So . . ."

"You and Kevin still seeing each other?"

I look at Kevin cuddling the baby and my heart races. "We are."

His cheek flinches, and I must say I have a little gut reaction of joy here. *Bad Ashley.*

"Have you talked to Arin?"

He nods. "I got an e-mail from her. She's still in India. Says she loves it, and the people. I don't imagine she'll be back anytime soon."

"That's great." *And you can have a full-on relationship with someone who isn't here to marry. How convenient is that?*

"I just wanted to say hi," he says.

"Sure. Nice to see you."

He waves, not bothering to greet Kevin or Brea and John, and waltzes off to the group of guys in a circle. No doubt they're discussing the orcs' great battle.

Kevin walks up to me and hands me Jonathan. "Was that okay?" he asks, looking toward Seth.

"It was better than okay. It was life-affirming." I start to giggle.

"Hmm. Life-affirming. Was it Kevin-affirming?"

I look down at the baby and back to those lustrous green eyes. "It was."

And then he kneels down in front of me. Brea comes and takes the baby, and a circle of my friends gather. I look at all of them in confusion, and then back down at Kevin.

"What's going on?" I ask.

Kevin clears his throat and takes my hand. "I knew from the moment I laid eyes on you—"

My eyes start to sting with tears. "No," I say in disbelief. My friends gather closer, and I feel Brea and Kay at my sides.

"I knew from that moment there would never be another woman for me."

I look at Brea, and she just smiles for reassurance.

"Your crazy theories make me laugh, your sparkle brings me joy every day, your inability to parent a dog has me completely scared, and your messy closet—and don't think I haven't noticed it—frightens me to no end. But Ashley, the way you always try to help others, no matter at what cost to yourself, the way you're just out there being Ashley and bringing fun with you . . . well, I just knew there would never be anyone better for me."

I shake my head. "My theories aren't all crazy. Women live ten years less if married unhappily."

"And longer if they marry happily. Yes, you've told me. Ashley Wilkes Stockingdale, will you be my wife?"

Then he holds up a ring. It's a vintage platinum number in Art-Deco style. My heart is in my throat. "This was my grandmother's ring. It's just a stand-in until you pick the one you want. Two carats, I think you said."

"Three." I giggle.

"You're not answering my question."

"Kevin." I look around at my friends. "Everyone. This man, I cannot understand why he would want to share his life with crazy me. But Kevin . . ." I look into those green eyes and I know in all certainty. "Nothing would make me happier than to be your wife. Even if it costs me ten years off my life."

"I'm hoping to extend it. If I could, I'd do it, I'd give you eternity."

I look up at the ceiling. "I'm taken care of for eternity. I just need an extra decade from you."

"Done." My friends erupt into applause.

He slips the ring on my finger, and I can barely breathe. I've never seen anything more beautiful. "I don't want another ring. This one means everything to me."

I look at Kevin, and then to my friends. And I know, even with the many ways I blow it, God is so looking out for me. He is always in control, and you know what? He's so much better at it than I am.

See the *She's Out of Control* movie trailer
at www.westbowpress.com